Science and Society in Modern India

The book delineates the role and place of the Western scientific discourse that occupied an important place in the colonization of India. During the colonial period, science became one of the foundations of Indian modernity and the nation state. Gradually, educated Indians sought to locate modern scientific ideas and principles within Indian culture and adopted those for the economic regeneration of the country.

The discursive terrain of the history of science, especially in the context of a society with a very long and complex past, is bound to be replete with numerous debates on its nature and evolution, its changing contours, its complex civilizational journey, and, finally, the enormous impact it has on our own lives and times. The book offers a useful introduction to science, society, and government interface in the Indian context.

Deepak Kumar is Honorary Professor, Department of History, Maulana Azad National Urdu University, Hyderabad. He has taught at several universities within India and abroad and retired as Professor of History of Science and Education from Jawaharlal Nehru University in 2017. He has recently published *Aatam Khabar: Sanskriti, Samaj aur Hum* (2022) and *'Culture' of Science and the Making of India* (2022). For more than four decades, he has tried to popularize the history of science, technology, environment, and medicine (HISTEM). He has also authored *Science and the Raj* (2nd ed., 2006) and *The Trishanku Nation: Memory, Self and Society in Contemporary India* (2016).

T0384702

Science and Society in Modern India

Deepak Kumar

CAMBRIDGE
UNIVERSITY PRESS

CAMBRIDGE
UNIVERSITY PRESS

Shaftesbury Road, Cambridge CB2 8EA, United Kingdom

One Liberty Plaza, 20th Floor, New York, NY 10006, USA

477 Williamstown Road, Port Melbourne, vic 3207, Australia

314–321, 3rd Floor, Plot 3, Splendor Forum, Jasola District Centre, New Delhi – 110025, India

103 Penang Road, #05–06/07, Visioncrest Commercial, Singapore 238467

Cambridge University Press is part of Cambridge University Press & Assessment, a department of the University of Cambridge.

We share the University's mission to contribute to society through the pursuit of education, learning and research at the highest international levels of excellence.

www.cambridge.org
Information on this title: www.cambridge.org/9781009350655

First published 2023

Printed in India by Nutech Print Services, New Delhi 110020

A catalogue record for this publication is available from the British Library

Library of Congress Cataloging-in-Publication Data

Names: Kumar, Deepak, 1952- author.
Title: Science and society in modern India / Deepak Kumar.
Description: Cambridge, United Kingdom ; New York, NY : Cambridge
   University Press, 2023. | Includes bibliographical references and index.
Identifiers: LCCN 2023002895 (print) | LCCN 2023002896 (ebook) | ISBN
   9781009350655 (hardback) | ISBN 9781009350648 (paperback) | ISBN
   9781009350617 (ebook)
Subjects: LCSH: Science--Social aspects--India--History. |
   India--History--British occupation,--1765-1947.
Classification: LCC Q175.52.I4 K86 2023 (print) | LCC Q175.52.I4 (ebook)
   | DDC 306.45/0954--dc23/eng/20230120
LC record available at https://lccn.loc.gov/2023002895
LC ebook record available at https://lccn.loc.gov/2023002896

ISBN 978-1-009-35065-5 Hardback

ISBN 978-1-009-35064-8 Paperback

For
Vedika, Ayan, Ayushman,
my grandkids, my future

Contents

Preface

South Asian society has always nurtured a thinking civilization. It has never lived an isolated existence and never displayed xenophobic tendencies. The techno-scientific tradition in South Asia has largely been synthetic, continuously evolving because of each politico-cultural interaction with the outside world and social change within the region. In pre-modern times, South Asia was known for its contributions to astronomy, medicine, and mathematics. Scientific and technological activity, throughout the medieval period, as is evident from the number of contemporary manuscripts, was both continuous and vigorous.

Western scientific discourse occupied an extremely important place in the colonization of India. The study of plants, animals, minerals, and so on, known as natural history in the early colonial days, was introduced in India in the late-18th century by European surgeons, botanists, army engineers, and missionaries. Over the next 200 years, science became one of the foundations of Indian modernity and the nation state. Colonialism also facilitated the introduction of technologies such as the railways, and later electricity. Gradually, educated Indians sought to locate modern scientific ideas and principles within Indian culture, and, by the end of the 19th century, to adopt these for the economic regeneration of the country.

Approaches to the study of the history of science have undergone critical changes in the last three decades. Historians have explained science and colonialism in India broadly in two different ways. Some have seen science as a 'Western' or colonial construct imposed on India and used by the British to exploit her natural resources. Others have advanced a more nuanced articulation and assimilation of modern science within Indian society and culture. The discursive terrain of the history of science is replete with numerous debates on its nature and evolution, its changing contours, its complex civilizational journey, and, finally, the enormous impact it has had on our own life and time.

Young students and scholars from different disciplines may find in this short volume (of about 60,000 words) a useful introduction to our inheritance, and the interface of science, society, and government in the Indian context until the end of the 20th century. The 21st is too close to my eyes! I am grateful to my student Suvobrata Sarkar for help in preparing the text and a select reading list.

Acknowledgements

During an almost five-decade-long academic journey, one learns from so many people and gathers so much debt that it becomes almost impossible to acknowledge them individually. I received institutional support from the National Institute of Science, Technology and Development Studies (New Delhi), Jawaharlal Nehru University (New Delhi), St. John's College (Cambridge), Hebrew University (Jerusalem), Universiteit Leiden, and the Smithsonian Institution (Washington DC). Primary data were sourced from the National Archive of India (New Delhi), National Library (Kolkata), West Bengal State Archive (Kolkata), Maharashtra State Archive (Mumbai), the British Library (London), Library of the Wellcome Trust (London), Library of the Royal Botanic Garden (Kew), the National Archives of Scotland (Edinburgh), Hebrew University Archive (Jerusalem), and the Rockefeller Archive Center (North Tarrytown). My gratitude to all of them. I remain grateful to the referees and editors of the Press for a meticulous reading and suggestions. This work is dedicated to my grandchildren in the hope that their generation may also find it useful.

Abbreviations

AICTE	All India Council for Technical Education
AIIHPH	All India Institute of Hygiene and Public Health
AIIMS	All India Institute of Medical Sciences
AMD	Army Medical Department
BCPW	Bengal Chemical and Pharmaceutical Works
C-DoT	Centre for Development of Telematics
CSAS	Centre for South Asian Studies
CSIR	Council of Scientific and Industrial Research
DAE	Department of Atomic Energy
DPI	Director of Public Instruction
DRDO	Defence Research and Development Organisation
FA	First Arts
GSI	Geological Survey of India
GSLV	Geosynchronous Satellite Launch Vehicle
IACS	Indian Association for the Cultivation of Science
ICAR	Indian Council of Agricultural Research
ICMR	Indian Council of Medical Research
IIT	Indian Institute of Technology
IMS	Indian Medical Service
IOR	India Office Records
ISCA	Indian Science Congress Association
ISRO	Indian Space Research Organisation
MIT	Massachusetts Institute of Technology
NAI	National Archives of India
NCEPC	National Committee on Environmental Planning and Coordination
NNR	Native Newspaper Reports
NPC	National Planning Committee
PWD	Public Works Department
RAC	Rockefeller Archive Center
USSR	Union of Soviet Socialist Republics

1

The Inheritance

Among all nations India was known as the mine of wisdom and the fountain-head of justice. Although their colour belongs to the first grade of blackness, yet God the Exalted has kept them immune from evil character, base conduct and low nature. He [God] has thus exalted them [Indians] over many brown and white peoples ... They also obtained profound and abundant knowledge of the movements of the stars, the secrets of the celestial sphere and all other branches of mathematical sciences. Moreover, of all the peoples they are the most learned in the science of medicine and well-informed about the properties of drugs and the nature of composite elements.

—Qadi Said al-Andalusi (1029–1070)[1]

Wrote thus the author of probably the first work on the history of science in any language, in his *Ṭabaqāt al-Umam*. And he was right in his estimation. Indian society, from a deep distant past, has nurtured a thinking civilization. It has never lived an isolated existence, remained largely plural, and seldom displayed xenophobic tendencies. In his *Brihat Samhita*, the astronomer Varahmihir (6th century AD) declared the *mulechchha* (unclean) Yavanas (Ionians or Greeks) to be as honourable as Hindu *rishi*s (sages) because the science of astronomy was firmly established among them. Even in the most ancient Vedic times when knowledge was expressed through *mantra*s and *sutra*s (incantations and aphorisms), one can find not only a high philosophical tradition but also some practical geometrical knowledge. *Sulba-sutra*s, for example, provided a range of geometrical knowledge required for the Vedic altar-builder in a systematic form. One who was well-versed in that science was called *samkhyajna* (expert in numbers), *parimanajna* (expert in measuring), and *sulba-vid* (expert of the *sulba*).[2]

From numerous historical examples, one can safely surmise that the techno-scientific tradition in India has largely been a synthetic one, continuously evolving as a result of each politico-cultural interaction with the outside world and social change within the region. In pre-modern times, India was known for its contribution to astronomy, medicine, and mathematics. In terms of techniques and technologies, metallurgy, textile, and structural engineering stand as examples of India's competence and innovativeness. It is true that India could not expand its knowledge base like post-Renaissance Europe did. But it definitely had a foundation which can be called 'proto-science and technology' and this is exactly what one finds in 18th-century India on the threshold of impending colonization.[3] This 'proto' phase probably had the possibilities and potentiality of flowering on its own had colonization not intervened.

Premium on Knowledge

The distant past always fascinates and often tends to border on romanticism. Yet its reconstruction must be exceptionally difficult—the paucity of sources, knowledge of classical or almost extinct languages, problems in textual interpretation, and the necessity for contextualization, all these make it a formidable exercise. How does one place scientific and technological developments in our civilizational growth? What constitutes science in the context of our ancient past? How much of it is metaphysics or religion? Unlike the Greeks who looked at knowledge in material terms, ancient Indians treated knowledge as a tool for liberation, and looked for knowledge that liberates (*sa vidya ya vimuktaye*). But liberation from what? Was it from hunger, disease, ignorance, or from worldly problems? No, it was taken as liberation of the soul, and a huge philosophical tradition developed around this. Knowledge came to be divided between *para* and *apara* or *deen* and *duniya* (other-worldly and this-worldly). This looks like a neat division but in reality, it is not. Thinkers and educators moved from one to the other with great elan and ease, but education was caught in the middle of the muddle. One thing is, however, certain; the significance of knowledge was always recognized. Unfortunately, it was limited to too few people. The priestly class derived their power from this control. Knowledge did advance but slowly and incrementally. A type of knowledge once accepted and canonized could not be challenged. So, every generation wrote commentaries which did allow some addition and some subtraction but little fundamental change. Paradigm shifts were difficult and almost impossible but knowledge did advance through the writing of commentaries. For example, once the *Charak Samhita* (1st century BC) became a canonized text, every successive generation wrote commentaries and *nighantus* with due respect but without substantial differences. Knowledge was thus created, discussed, and disseminated in a limited way and within certain boundaries. Caste was one such insurmountable boundary. Lower castes and women had no opportunity at all. Education was imparted at *tols*, *chatuspatis*, and *agraharas*, or near temples, which were basically privately run local schools. Muslim rule brought *maktabs* and *madrasas*, but here also the emphasis was more on *deen* than *duniya*. They were used more for theological training than anything else. Yet despite the obvious limitations, Indian society built up a significant knowledge corpus in terms of philosophy, linguistics, astronomy, medicine, and other areas.

In ancient texts, however, one finds numerous references to *yukti* (reason), *tarka vidya* (science of reasoning), *anvikshki* (investigation), *anumana* (intelligent inference), *pramana* (proof), and *hetusastra* (dialectics). The celebrated *Charaka Samhita* talks of *yukti bheshaj* (rational medicine). It says, 'any success attained without reasoning (*tarka*) is as good as sheer accidental success'.[4] Though Indian traditions did accommodate certain rational explanations, yet taken as a whole, more reliance was placed on *anubhuti* (experience) than on anything else. Premium was put on experiential knowledge. The great philosopher Sankara preferred *anubhuti*, not *suska tarka* (dry reason). This 'experience' along with creative imagination and some rationale was codified into sacred texts which gradually acquired canonical status. To question or challenge a canonical text or knowledge (*sastra-sammat jnan*) has never been easy in any society. Many perished in the process and a vast majority had to compromise. Brahmagupta (the author of the *Brahmasphuta Siddhanta*, 628 AD) knew the real reason for eclipses but since the *puranas* had claimed that it happened because of the demon Rahu, he preferred to save his skin by endorsing the *pauranic* claim. He took one step forward and then two steps backward. The power of tradition and the weight of canonical knowledge were so formidable that even great minds had to succumb.

But this was not always the case; sparks of reason and change continued to emerge. Aryabhatta (476–550 AD) is an immortal name. He was probably the first astronomer to talk of the rotation of the earth on its axis, and also provided the correct explanation for eclipses. He was followed by Varahmihira (c. 505–587 AD), Bhaskara I (c. 600–680 AD), and Brahmagupta (598–668 AD). Varahmihira's *Brihat Samhita* is basically an encyclopaedia dealing with astronomy, architecture, agronomy, and even psychology. Bhaskara I was the first to write numbers within a decimal system with a circle for the zero! His contemporary Brahmagupta was a great mathematician and his works were translated by the Arabs, which started a new trend of mathematics-based astronomy. Another landmark appeared in the 12th century in the works of Bhaskara II (c. 1114–1185 AD). His *Siddhanta Shiromani* still retains a pre-eminent position among astronomers. He dealt with arithmetic, algebra (*bijaganita*), the knowledge of spherics (*goladhyaya*), and astronomical instruments (*yantradhyaya*). Scholars agree that despite its scriptural orientation and being couched in religious terms, the astro-mathematical knowledge of ancient India represents a thinking society.[5]

The tradition continued. In Kerala, for example, from the 14th to the 16th century flourished a school of astronomy and mathematics that produced pioneering mathematical research such as on infinite series, much before the development of the theory of modern calculus in Europe. They also provided a logical geometrical explanation of planetary motion at which Tycho Brahe (1546–1601 AD) and Johannes Kepler (1571–1630 AD), too, arrived without knowing the other tradition.[6] One of its protagonists, Neelakantha (1444–1545 AD), had calculated the different velocities of planets and argued that 'one should first try the method of demonstration, for logical reasoning is limited, endless and sometimes inconclusive'.[7] He even decreed *etat sarvam yukti-mulam, eva na tva agama-mulam* (All this is rooted in reason, not in dogmas). Despite the wide prevalence and dominance of *aastha* (faith), *yukti* (reason) was never abandoned.

This tension was seen in Islam as well. Al-Kindi (801–873 AD) was given 50 lashes for his rational views and for upholding that truth is universal and supreme. Al-Razi (865–925 AD) spoke openly of the superiority of reason over revelation. He was accused of blasphemy and blinded. Ibn Sina (980–1037 AD), the great author of *al-Qanun*, survived persecution attempts several times. Finally, by the end of the 11th century, the orthodox, led by al-Ghazali, had routed the rationalists. Abu Hamid al-Ghazali (d. 1111), perhaps the most celebrated theologian in Islamic history, wrote and warned against those

> whose god (*ilah*) is their undisciplined passions (*hawa*), whose object of worship (*mabud*) is their leaders, whose direction of prayer (*qibla*) is the dinar, whose religious law is their own frivolity, whose will (*irada*) is the promotion of reputation and carnal pleasures …[8]

He repudiated all attributions to physical laws and re-established God as the sole cause of everything in the world. For example, on the question what burns cotton, fire or God, Ghazali would say God. This is exactly what medieval India had inherited. There was little scope for *falsafa* (reasoning/philosophy) now. What to say of orthodox Islam, in *Sufism* also there was little room for reason or science.[9]

Knowledge in the Islamic framework was divided between *ilm-al-Adyan* and *ilm-al Dunya* (other-worldly and this-worldly). Accordingly, Muslim scholars were divided into those who relied on *manqul* (traditional knowledge) and those who favoured the touchstone of reason (*maqul*). The former, greater in number and more powerful, opposed Sultan Muhammad bin Tughlaq (1325–1351) when he tried to patronize *ilm-i-maqulat*. However, Mughal India was somewhat eclectic, and because there was no consolidated, systematic, and detailed curriculum, channels of learning were not at all closed to *maqul* ideas. Rather, in the eastern regions of Awadh and Bihar, subjects bearing on *maqulat* were compulsory. Northwest India was more orthodox, and here these subjects were optional. Along with the debates within the Islamic framework, there were several attempts at cross-cultural fertilization. In the late 14th century, Mahendra Suri (an astronomer at the Court of Firoz Shah Tughlaq [1309–1388 AD] and author of *Yantraraja*) had tried to introduce Arab and Persian astronomy into the Sanskrit *siddhanta* tradition. This flow of astronomical ideas, as well as instruments, continued into the 17th century, providing the basic materials for those training in the Ptolemaic system.[10] Similarly, in 1337, a compendium of general medicine (*Majma'ah-i-Diya'i*) was compiled at the order of Sultan Muhammad bin Tughlaq on the basis of numerous Arabic, Zoroastrian, Persian, Buddhist, and Hindu works. Later, in 1512, Mian Bhuwah prepared a manual of medicine (*Ma'din al-shifa-i-Sikandar-Shahi*) based on the Ayurvedic and Yunani traditions.[11] However, no real synthesis could emerge. The Sanskrit *tols* and Islamic *madrasas* continued to cling to their own distinct astronomical and medical systems. These schools did influence each other and occasionally came together under an enlightened ruler, only to fall apart once again.

It seems that during the late-medieval period, no comprehensive attempt was made to explore India's scientific heritage, much less to keep abreast of developments then taking place in the Western hemisphere. Unlike al-Biruni's *Kitab-ul-Hind* (11th century AD), Abul Fazl's *A'in-i-Akbari* (a classic on Mughal times, 16th century AD) barely touches science. Al-Biruni could cite numerous Greek texts; Abul Fazl refers only to Aristotle and Ptolemy. It appears that scientific curiosity was in decline, and Abul Fazl admits it.[12] But he shows great interest in technology, especially the smelting process and liquor distillation. Abul Fazl appreciated the importance of technological improvements for the state economy; socially he enunciated Sulh-i-Kul which emphasized tolerance and coexistence; and intellectually he was not at all dogmatic. Yet he was unable to move beyond classical theoreticians. The only Mughal noble who took a little more interest in modern astronomy, geography, and anatomy was Danishmand Khan. He employed the French physician Francois Bernier (1659–1666 AD), who translated for him the works of Pierre

Gassendi (1592–1655 AD) and Rene Descartes (1596–1650 AD). Bernier even dissected a sheep to explain William Harvey's (1578–1667 AD) discovery of the circulation of blood. But the Indian followers of Galen (practitioners of Yunani Tibb) remained unimpressed. Similarly clocks and watches did not impress the Mughals, who, unlike the Ottomans and Manchus, refused these marvels a closer look. But items of military concern such as artillery and ship-building, were favourably looked upon. Other items, such as mirrors, window panes, pumps, and pistols aroused interest, but no attempt was made to learn the techniques behind them.[13] So, the scenario remains complex, with several grey areas. In the absence of a deeper understanding of the texts written in classical languages, and sometimes in the absence of an authentic source itself, it is difficult to say with precision why certain new scientific ideas did not germinate or find favour, or why a new technique was ignored. A theory of decline does not explain everything. One thing, however, appears certain; Indians were not xenophobes. They accepted those that suited their economic and cultural requirements

Medical Heritage

As mentioned earlier, medicine has always been a significant part of Indian heritage. Flourishing around 2000 BC, the architectural design of Harappa does point to a conscious concern for public health and sanitation. Does the fabled Great Bath of Mohenjo-daro (like the Roman bath) point to hydropathy as a therapeutic measure? An Indus seal portrays a figure seated in a yogic posture with a horned head-dress, which could be a proto-Siva or a shaman (a medicine man). Unfortunately, very little is known of the Indus people. The *Atharvaveda* is probably the first repository of ancient Indian medical lore, which was later transmitted through *Brahmana* texts. It was magico-religious in nature and incantations (*mantras*) were frequently resorted to.

The theoretical framework of Ayurveda may not be Vedic, but its *materia medica* did evolve from Vedic literature and could even be pre-Vedic![14] Ayurveda as 'the science of (living to a ripe) age', sans *mantras*, emerged around Buddha's time. Buddha appears as a dissenter and gives medical men a place of honour. Later he was himself hailed as a healer *par excellence*, much like Jesus, but without miracle or magic at his command.

The concept of humours or *dosas* which has been central in Ayurveda is nowhere seen in Vedic literature. Nor does it reflect Hippocratic or Galenic thinking. Ayurveda's emphasis on humoral 'balance', moderation, and so on, seems rather closer to Buddha's 'Middle Path'.[15] Disease causation in

Ayurveda is not only because of humoral 'imbalance' (*vaisamya*) but for a variety of reasons like weather, food, emotional agitations, sins from past life, and even 'sins against wisdom'. Its protagonists might have been inaccurate in their knowledge of human physiology but they were extremely good at plant morphology, and its medical functions and therapeutics. Both Charaka and Susruta emphasized direct observation. They are the two stalwarts of our medical tradition; one, a physician, the other a surgeon, both separated probably by two or three centuries. Buddhist sources mention Charaka as a contemporary of Kanishka, the Kushan ruler (1st century BC). Interestingly, the *Charaka Samhita* begins by paying respect to Brahmins and the cow, thus insulating itself from any social trouble; and then goes on to prescribe all kinds of meat for different diseases. This *samhita* excels in diagnosis, prognosis, therapy, and pharmacy. It puts emphasis on moral values and righteous conduct; it even argues that corrupt rulers bring about epidemics.[16] Epidemics are referred to as *janapadodhvamsa* (devastation of a country), and not much could be done about them. These deadly visitations come because of the vitiation of *vayu* (air), *udaka* (water), *desa* (locale), and *kala* (season) on account of our own *karma* (doings). But Charaka does not promote fatalism and provides a positive prognosis. By and large, the emphasis remains on *prakriti* (nature), *swabhav* (characteristics), and *prabhav* (impact).[17]

Unlike Charaka who gives brief descriptions of surgical techniques, Susruta goes much deeper in describing how a surgeon should be trained, and how surgery could be performed using knives and other instruments. He advocates dissection of dead bodies, a practice that unfortunately fell into disuse for religious and cultural reasons. In the *Susruta Samhita*, there is also a reference to Viskanya (the Venomous Virgin), a symbol of seduction used for political assassinations. Around 600 AD comes another medical text *par excellence* called the *Ashtanghridaya* (Heart of Medicine) by Vagbhatta. It encapsulates the entire ayurvedic tradition and knowledge and is a guiding star for *vaidyas* even now. Vagbhatta puts great emphasis on the environment and the concept of hot (*usna*) and cold (*sitala*). To him the whole world is a combination of *agni* (heat) and *soma* (substance that cools).

Alchemical experiments were widely prevalent. Buddhist *tantrics* and Saivsiddhas were adept in experiments with mercury. With its due *shodhan* (purification), they could claim supernatural powers.[18] Nagarjuna, Matsyendranath, and Gorakhnath were some renowned Siddha preceptors, and a very strong tradition of *rasasastra* (alchemy) had emerged.[19] These developments have been mostly internal but the possibilities of external influences from other cultures cannot be ruled out. Fascination with alchemy, for example, most probably arose out of early contact with China where a Taoist speculative alchemical tradition had been developing since the 2nd century AD.[20] The *Anandakanda* (The Root of Bliss, 13th century AD) encompasses almost the entire Hindu alchemical tradition in 6,000 verses. It is the sole attempt to fuse *rasa siddhas* (alchemists) with *nath siddhas* (spiritual *tantrics* or yogis). A 13th-century text by Sarangdhara is probably the first to recommend opium and cannabis for medical as well as sexual purposes. Obsession with sex (*vajikarna*) and the desire for a male child are very obvious in all these texts. Unfortunately, these texts have no anatomical or surgical illustrations. It is difficult to see how such techniques as rhinoplasty could have persisted purely textually. Dissection became a taboo and knowledge became secretive, confined to families or caste networks. *Todarananda* (a 16th-century encyclopaedic work), for example, says that *rasavidya* (alchemy) is to be kept 'as secret as mother's genitals.'[21] Even mineral classification reflected caste divisions. For example, diamonds are described as of four types, Brahmin, Kshatriya, Vaisya, and Sudra; they are also male, female or *napunsaka.*[22] But all these *samhitas* (compendiums) were very clear on their purpose, as an 11th-century commentator, Chakrapanidatta, puts it:

> The recommendations of medicine are not intended to help someone achieve virtue (*dharma*). What are they for, then? They are aimed at achieving health.[23]

But a physician must conform to his own profession-specific *dharma*; he should never lie (*nanrtam bruyat*), remain honest, and show compassion always. Charaka warns that those who practice only for money, 'selling medical treatment as a trade, are devoted to a heap of dust, having abandoned gold'.[24] Susruta complains of the difficulty in treating Brahmins and rajas, for they would not listen to their physician, and physicians are powerless in enforcing the required medical regimen on them. Moreover, such patients tend to overeat! Charaka repeatedly warns against overeating. He also says that the poor could be left out of the medical purview because they would be unable to afford long-term treatment which was bound to be expensive. *Vaidyas* thus faced social and moral dilemmas and they had to deal with them the best they could.

The scenario became even more interesting when Islamic medical men introduced the Galenic tradition to India. When during the 13th and 14th centuries, Chengiz Khan and Timur razed the mosques and *khanqaz* of Central Asia and Iran, many proficient in *deen, tibb,* and *falsafa* left the cities of Shiraz, Isfahan, and Gilan, and migrated to Agra, Lucknow, and the Deccan.

Caravans of men and streams of thought constantly moved and flowed between India, Iran, and Central Asia, resulting in intimate cultural relations. The Mughal court patronized notable hakims. Hakim Abul Baqa and al-Harawi served Babur. Hakim Shams-al-din-Gilani, who attended Akbar, was not only an expert physician, but a theologian and jurist as well. Orthodox as he was, he did not like Akbar's eclecticism. Hakim Gilani authored the famous commentary (four volumes) in Arabic on Ibn Sina's *al-Qanun* called *Sharh-i-Gilani*. Another great *hakim* in Akbar's court was Fathullah Shirazi, who was also a remarkable technologist and innovator.[25]Abul Qasim under Jehangir (1605–1627 AD), Mir Muhammad Hashim during Aurangzeb's period (1658–1707 AD), and Mir Muhammad Jafar under Muhammad Shah (1719–1748 AD) were other noted *hakims*. Many more *hakims* continued to arrive at the Mughal and other courts.[26] They brought the *materia medica* of *Tibb-i-Unani* as epitomized in Ibn Sina's *al-Qanun*. This book, like the *Charaka Samhita*, held sway until the end of the 18th century, and is still revered by Yunani physicians.

There gradually appeared a hybrid Muslim–Hindu system known as the Tibb. While they differed in theory, in practice both traditions seem to have interacted and borrowed from each other. A fine example of this interaction is the *Ma'din al-shifa-i-Sikandar-shahi* (1512 AD), which was authored by Miyan Bhuwah. He leaned heavily on Sanskrit sources and even thought that the Greek system was not suitable for the Indian constitution and climate. From the Islamic side, the concept of *arka* (distilled fluid) entered Ayurveda. Several Sanskrit medical texts were translated into Arabic and Persian, but instances of Islamic works being translated into Sanskrit are rare. The 18th century is significant because of the appearance of two Sanskrit texts, *Hikmatprakasa* and *Hikmatparadipa*, which refer to the Islamic system and use numerous Arabic and Persian medical terms. Earlier the concept of individual case studies and hospitals (*bimaristans*) had also come from Yunani practitioners. In 1595, Quli Shah built a huge Dar-us-Shifa (house of cures) in Hyderabad. During the reign of Muhammad Shah (1719–1748 AD), a large hospital was constructed in Delhi. Numerous medical texts, mostly commentaries, were written during this century; for example, Akbar Arzani's *Tibb-i-Akbari* (1700 AD), Jafar Yar Khan's *Talim-i-Ilaj* (1719–1725 AD), Madhava's *Ayurveda Prakasha* (1734 AD), and the *Bhaisajya Ratnavali* of Govind Das. A Christian Mughal noble, Dominic Gregory, wrote the *Tuhafat-ul-Masiha* (1749 AD), which, along with descriptions of diseases, anatomy, and surgery, contains important notes in Persian and Portuguese on alchemy and the properties of various plants, along with drawings of instruments, and interestingly, a horoscope.

An outstanding physician of this century, Mirza Alavi Khan, wrote seven texts of which *Jami-ul-Jawami* is a masterpiece embodying all the branches of medicine then known in India. Another great physician during the period of Shah Alam II (1759–1806 AD) was Hakim Sharif Khan who wrote 10 important texts, and enriched Yunani medicines with indigenous Ayurvedic herbs. Some works were unique and ahead of their time. For example, Nurul Haq's *Ain-ul-Hayat* (1691 AD) is a rare Persian text on the plague, and Pandit Mahadeva's *Rajsimhasudhasindhu* (1787 AD) refers to cowpox and inoculation.[27]

A number of European physicians visited Mughal India. Francois Bernier, Nicolo Manucci, Garcia d'Orta, John Ovington, and many others (c. 1550–1750 AD) wrote extensively on Indian medical practices. The Western medical episteme was not radically different from that of Indian physicians; both were humoral, but their practices differed greatly. Neither of them was able to develop a comprehensive theory of disease causation, but there seems to be a general agreement that Indian diseases were environmentally determined and should be treated by Indian methods. Europeans, however, continued to look at Indian practices with curiosity and disdain. They preferred bloodletting whereas *vaidya*s prescribed urine analysis and urine therapy. But in the use of drugs, Europeans and Indians learned from each other, as the works of van Rheede, Sassetti, and d'Orta would testify.[28] The Europeans introduced new plants in India that were gradually incorporated into the Indian pharmacopoeia. They had brought venereal diseases with them such as syphilis which was noticed as early as the 16th century by Bhava Misra, a noted *vaidya* in Benaras, who called it Firangi *roga* (disease of the Europeans). Indian diseases received graphic description in Ovington's travelogue. The best account of smallpox and the Indian method of variolation was given by J. Z. Holwell in 1767. To him, this method although quasi-religious, still appeared 'rational enough and well-founded'.[29] The travellers depicted Indian medical practices more as a craft and one that was governed by caste rules and wrapped in superstition. Yet they could not help admiring the wonder called rhinoplasty (on which modern plastic surgery is founded), nor could they deny the efficacy of Indian drugs. Indians for their part did not completely insulate themselves from 'other' practices. As the interaction grew in the 18th century, *vaidya*s even took to bleeding in a large number of cases. Yet while European medical men were gradually moving, thanks to the works of Andreas Vesalius (1514–1564) and William Harvey, from a humoral to a chemical or mechanical view of the body, Indians remained faithful to their texts.

Medieval Astronomy

Perhaps the best example of 'proto-science' in Mughal India can be found in the realm of astronomy, especially in the construction and use of astrolabes and celestial globes. The astrolabe was probably introduced in India by al-Biruni in the 11th century, and between 1567 and 1683, a number of these instruments were produced by the family of Allahdad at Lahore. Of this family, Diya al-Din Muhammad was most prolific and versatile; he produced about 32 astrolabes and 16 celestial globes with innovative designs.[30] These instruments figure in several Mughal miniatures and testify to royal patronage. This patronage, however, was motivated more by astrological than other considerations. Unfortunately, Hindu astronomers did not make much use of these instruments even though many of them took notice of their worth. Padmanabha (about 1400 AD) and Ramchandra Vajpeyin (1428 AD) discussed astrolabes extensively. Later, a Jaina monk, Megharatna, used several Arabic and Persian technical terms. In 1621, Narsimha from Benaras referred to the celestial globe as *bhagola* but added, 'The stars known to the Muslims do not serve our purpose. Observation of unfamiliar stars would lead to misfortune'. Hindu astronomers were interested in the coordinates of a very limited number of stars and not in all the 1,018 stars marked on the Islamic globe. In Akbar's time, serious attempts were made to bring the two close to each other. Several Sanskrit works were translated into Persian, and Ulugh Beg's (1394–1449 AD) astronomical tables were translated into Sanskrit. Yet there remained a cultural gap. It was only at the beginning of the 18th century that there appeared a scholar–prince who tried to assimilate and synthesize the astronomical knowledge then available to him. He was Sawai Jai Singh (1688–1743 AD) of Amber.[31]

Jai Singh ascended the throne of Amber in 1699, and later emerged as a trusted lieutenant of the Mughal king Muhammad Shah, who was besieged by numerous rebellions and attacks. The Mughal empire was crumbling, and it was a period of uncertainty and unrest. At the same time, the European presence in India had increased, and some members of the Indian nobility had evinced interest in certain aspects of European ideas and artefacts. In the midst of such politico-cultural turmoils, Jai Singh tried to do something different. He wanted to explore why the times of different celestial phenomena, especially the eclipses of the sun and the moon, differed according to *siddhantic* and Greco-Arabic astronomy and why they did not often tally with actual occurrences. He consulted a large number of almanacs, traditional scholars, and European travellers. He was not satisfied with calculations done through astrolabes (brass instruments) and thought that stone observatories, larger and fixed in one place, would give more-accurate results. So, he constructed large masonry observatories (Jantar Mantar) in Delhi, Jaipur, Mathura, Ujjain, and Varanasi. He was also presented with a telescope by a French Jesuit.

Jai Singh is also credited with evolving a systematic scientific method. He sent his scholars to Central and West Asia and invited European scholars to his court; the results of his efforts were compiled in the *Zij-i-Muhammad Shahi* (1728 AD), which is considered to be the most important astronomical work of medieval India. Several commentaries were later written on it. That same year he sent a delegation to Lisbon led by a Jesuit priest, Emmanuel de Figuerado, who in 1730 brought de la Hire's *Tabulae Astronomicae*. Although Jai Singh was convinced of the reliability of his own data, he borrowed from de la Hire's tables some refraction, corrections, and geographical coordinates. Later, in 1734, Jai Singh invited two French Jesuits—Claude Boudier (1686–1757 AD) and Francis Pons (1698–1752 AD)—who confirmed the defects in de la Hire's tables. Jai Singh planned to send another scientific delegation to Europe, but death intervened in 1743. Critics argue that his choice of Lisbon was not appropriate; he should have contacted astronomers in Paris and London. Again, his obsession with masonry instruments (which was not the European tradition), accuracy, the calendar, and so on, is usually taken to mean that Jai Singh's outlook was medieval and limited to the Ptolemaic concept of the universe. In all probability, he remained ignorant of the contents of the De *Revolutionibus Orbium Coelestium* (1543 AD) and the *Philosophiæ Naturalis Principia Mathematica* (1687 AD) till the very end of his days. Some scholars, however, believe that though Jai Singh does not acknowledge Copernicus and Kepler explicitly, he may have known their theories.

Well, Jai Singh was no theoretician and he adhered to the old Ptolemaic concept, yet there is no doubt that he at least thought that brass astrolabes were not accurate, and he was brilliant enough to devise new ways of measurement. But his obsession with finding the exact moment of eclipses with accuracy calls for some explanation. Was it motivated by astrological concern? Obsession with the exactness of time (for example, the time of *yagna* or marriage) has been an important feature of Indian social life, and Jai Singh was naturally part of it. Moreover, he was an intensely religious and ritual-minded person and had performed difficult Vedic *yagnas* (sacrifices) such as the Vajpeya and Asvamedha. Was his *Zij* intended only as a means to compute accurate time and not as a treatise to show off his acumen or document his new findings? The telescope had come to India even before Jai Singh's birth. He was definitely aware of it, but it is doubtful that he made full use of it.

In the absence of a chronometer, one could see distant objects through a telescope but not measure them. So, despite his enthusiasm and efforts, Jai Singh may appear as a sort of historical anachronism who belonged intellectually to the medieval tradition (of *Zij* astronomy) but lived chronologically in the modern age of astronomy.

This, however, is not to minimize Jai Singh's efforts. With a little more foresight and courage, he could have transcended his cultural limits. It was not as if the Ptolemaic system was always blindly followed in India. Earlier, during Shah Jahan's time, Mulla Mahmud Jaunpuri had ventured to raise doubts about the system in his *Shams-e-Bazegha*. Jai Singh and his associates may not have known new astronomy, but they did not adopt the old one blindly. Their parameters, eclipse tables, and a number of subsidiary planetary tables differ from those of Ulugh Beg. They determined new parameters and new tables for the planets, the obliquity of the ecliptic, and the geographical coordinates of a number of localities in India. They did not, however, attempt to change Ulugh Beg's basic planetary models (based on Ptolemy) despite their contact with Europeans.

A significant aspect of Jai Singh's reign is that he brought together a number of astronomers and scribes from different parts of the country and established a virtual colony of astronomers. Notable among them were Jagannath Samrat, Vidyadhar, Kevalverma, Nayansukha, and Harilal. Jagannath had learned both Arabic and Persian. In 1727, he translated al-Tusi's Arabic version of Euclid's *Elements* and called it *Rekhaganita*. In 1732, he wrote *Samrat Siddhanta* based on the Arabic recension of Ptolemy's *Almagest*. Similarly, Nayansukha did not simply render an Arabic text into Sanskrit literally but instead expanded those passages that he found particularly difficult. Kevalverma was rigid in following the *Surya Siddhanta*, and even ignored the new parameters being worked out by Jagannath and Jai Singh. Although Jagannath himself respected observation as *pramana* (proof), he would finally succumb to the *siddhanta*s (canons) as 'divine' authority. Jai Singh and his pundits just could not transcend these barriers.

But the tradition continued even after the arrival of British rule. In 1841–1842, Ghulam Hussain Jaunpuri (1790–1862 AD) composed the *Zij-i-Bahadurkhani* but he incorporated European advances. Jaunpuri was probably the first Indian traditional astronomer on record to systematically make modern astronomical observations, namely those of a bright comet in 1825 with a sextant, and of Uranus, Ceres, and Pallas in 1826 with a telescope.[32] An almost astonishing achievement in the *siddhantic* tradition came from a poor amateur astronomer from Odisha, Samanta

Chandra Sekhara (1835–1904 AD). Without the use of any optical instrument, he noticed that the *siddhantas* had gathered errors in the course of time and needed to be rectified. His ancient predecessors had placed the sun at a distance of not more than 14 times that of the moon from the earth. Samanta hiked this ratio by more than 10 times to 154 which is much closer to the modern value of 390. Thanks to this, the accuracy of his predictions on solar and lunar eclipses improved dramatically, and the method is still being followed at the Jagannath Temple in Puri.[33] Like Neelkanth and Tycho Brahe, Samanta also believed that the five planets go around the sun and the sun with his companions goes around the earth. He was honoured with the title Mahamahopadhyay and in 1899 the famous journal *Nature* hailed his labours as greater than that of Brahe![34]

Science in Islamic Education

Several *madrasas* and *maktabs* in India had adopted the *Silsilai Nizamiya* (a curriculum taught at the Firangi Mahal, Lucknow) in conformity with educational practices throughout the Islamic world. The main subjects taught according to this system were grammar, rhetoric, philosophy, mathematics, theology, and law. Philosophy included physics and metaphysics (based on Aristotelian principles), and mathematics meant Ptolemaic astronomy, algebra, geometry, and arithmetic. The main feature of this general curriculum was the balance between scientific and humanistic studies, but in practice theological knowledge (*manqul*) seems to have received greater attention than the rational (*maqul*).[35] Akbar wanted the syllabi to include mathematics, medicine, agriculture, geography, and even some Sanskrit texts such as Patanjali to balance the orthodox emphasis on Islamic studies. Even a deeply religious monarch such as Aurangzeb is said to have reproached his teachers for not teaching geography and other subjects useful for administration, and having wasted his youth 'in the dry, unprofitable, and never-ending task of learning words'!

The 18th century saw two great educationists in North India: Shah Waliullah, who taught at the Madrasa Rahimiya in Delhi until his death in 1762, and Mulla Nizamuddin Sahalwi, who taught at Firangi Mahal, Lucknow, until his death in 1748. The former was scholastic and orthodox. The topics of his writings range from the deep nuances of Quranic words to how the sun in reality revolves around the earth! In contrast, Mulla Nizamuddin developed a curriculum called the *Dars-i Nizami*, which of course included the *hadiths* and *tafsirs* (traditional studies) but put more emphasis on *mantiq* (logic) and *hikmat* (metaphysics).[36] The result was that the eastern regions had a little more exposure to *maqulat* (reason) than the northwestern regions. But 'new' (modern) knowledge was yet to enter. At best, prevalent approaches tried to bring together secular and theological education in the Greco-Arab tradition. This was in conformity with Safavid and Mughal practices, and in contrast to the Ottomans, who patronized *manqul* more.[37] As greater numbers of Iranians settled in India under the Mughals, Iranian skills in the rational sciences came to the fertile grounds of the country. Here they were not seriously attacked by 'purists', who later did so when faced with 'new threats' from an expanding Europe.

Apart from *madrasas*, private tuition was also in vogue and was popular with the upper classes. A *riyazi* (mathematics) scholar could earn good money by producing horoscopes, calendars, or revenue estimates. Similarly, physicians were always valued by the nobility. Astronomers as well as physicians remained tradition-bound. They virtually ended where they began, always invoking the authority of Aristotle or Charak, Ibn Sina or Bhaskara. Numerous commentaries were written; they were not mere repetition, but none was trail-breaking. Pre-British India had no scientific society and no network of communications between experts. Individual brilliance operated under severe sociocultural limitations.[38] A parasitic nobility encouraged parasitic intellect. It took the surplus from the land but did nothing to introduce new tools or methods in craft or agricultural production. Of course, some new texts were written about fruit trees and cash crops, but their influence remained rather limited. The lack of vernacular prose literature as a vehicle for the expression of knowledge prevented craftsmen from transmitting their experiences and problems. They were unable to obtain any theoretical knowledge that could help them professionally. Yet, at least in name, useful knowledge and crafts were honoured. In the 18th century, a Bangash prince, Qaim Khan, is known to have excelled in grafting, leather shoes, and casting cannons. Another Pathan, Muhammad Hayat Khan, became an authority on arithmetic, algebra, and astronomy, including the *siddhantas*. Medieval India had sparks of individual brilliance but this was not enough to galvanize society.

Tools and Technologies

India being a predominantly agricultural country, there is no doubt that agricultural tools, irrigation methods, and certain crafts were 'appropriate' and in tune with existing capabilities and requirements. The variety of agricultural implements, the drill plough, the system of rice transplantation, the rotation of crops, and experiments in fruit crops speak of the rich experience of Indian peasants.[39] Similarly, local conditions determined irrigation methods, which involved community management of water resources. These systems were the outcome of the experiences and collective wisdom of 'practical' peasants. For example, Arghatta operated with a human-energy-rim around which buckets were attached while Saqiya, a Persian wheel with a bucket-chain and pin-drum gear, was moved by bullocks. These techniques met the then existing requirements in the Indian context. In medieval Europe, social conflicts were inherent in the very process of production and this transformed the production system by restructuring and redistributing the means of production. In medieval India, this was not the case; here the social conflict pertained to the distribution and redistribution of the peasant's surplus produce.[40] Innovation was missing. Similarly, in sharp contrast to 18th-century Japan, where row cultivation was introduced, the number of plant varieties was increased using deliberate seed selection, and irrigation by treadmills and Dutch pumps was improved and extended, Indian cultivators were satisfied with whatever they could produce for themselves.

Was there anything like a science of botany in pre-colonial India? Probably not; there are of course, references to Krishitantra, Vrikshayurveda, and Bhesajvidya in the works of Kasyapa, Parasar, Saraswata, and Kautilya but this knowledge was definitely made subservient to philosophy, the science of medicine, or techniques of agriculture. The Mughals are known for their keen interest in plants and gardens. A 17th-century text, *Dar Fann-i-Falahat*, describes the various methods of grafting, preparation of soil, harvesting techniques, water and manure requirements, and so on. Interestingly, it also refers to male and female plants!

After agriculture, the most important sectors were textiles and steel manufacture. Textiles involved the labour-intensive processes of starching, bleaching, dyeing, winding, warping, and weaving.[41] Europeans tried to imitate Indian dyeing techniques, without much success. But their growing commercial interest in Indian textiles led to the introduction of the filature system, drum warping, and the fly shuttle technique. These tools were used for mercantilist 'penetration' or 'intervention' by European companies, and Indian weavers gradually suffered impoverishment and virtual elimination. Later, a similar fate awaited Indian steel producers, but in the 18th century, this industry was considered a success story. Historians of metallurgy believe that Indian iron smelters had acquired an advanced and precise knowledge about the technology for the production of iron and steel—their thermo-mechanical behaviour, heat treatment, and so on.[42] The result was a high-carbon ingot (*wootz*) that commanded respect in international markets. The Dutch carried a large amount of *wootz* from Masulipatnam to Batavia and Persia. So *wootz* was neither 'handicraft' nor a 'primitive traditional' production, yet it remained localized at a time when Europe was fast moving toward mass production. The Indian smiths could not obtain high temperatures or opt for large furnaces because they did not know how to generate power except through the use of draft animals or charcoal. Except in one or two places, water power remained unthought-of and untapped. This resulted in a high cost of production, and so naturally, Indian peasants kept the use of iron to a bare minimum.

Similarly, mining itself was done on a small scale. It involved barely more than scratching the surface of the earth using crowbars and spades. Mining below water level and haulage were simply out of the question. Curiously, although gunpowder was used for armament, it was never used for mining purposes. But there did exist a flourishing metallurgical industry, which was run almost like a cottage industry.[43] Slags of iron and steel and metals such as copper, zinc, lead, and, to a smaller extent, silver and cobalt, in parts of Rajasthan, Bihar, and the Deccan bear testimony to this. Zinc production in India preceded that in Europe.

In the realm of armaments, the finest example of Indian ingenuity lay in the use of 'Bana' rockets by Hyder Ali and Tipu Sultan, who ruled Mysore during the last quarter of the 18th century and fought several wars against the British. These Mysore rockets were much more advanced than any the British had seen or known; the propellent was contained in tough iron tubes, which gave higher bursting pressures in the combustion chamber and hence higher thrust and longer range for the missile. The rockets consisted of a tube (about 60 millimetres in diameter and 200 millimetres in length) fastened to a 3-metre bamboo pole, with a range of 1–2 kilometres. In the battle of Pellilur (1780), the British were defeated because their ammunition tumbrils were blasted by the Mysore rockets. In the last Anglo-Mysore war, Wellesley (later the hero of Waterloo) himself was shocked by the 'rocket fire'. Several rocket cases were sent to Britain for analysis, and these led to a great interest in rocketry in Europe.

There is no doubt that in war-weapons, rulers in late-medieval India were willing to learn, adapt, and adopt the European system, and their guns, and so on. Fathullah Shirazi could make a multi-barrel gun, probably a precursor of the modern machine-gun. But other mechanical toys like clocks did not excite the Indian nobility. They patronized only those which had an aristocratic flavour (for example, Noor Jahan ka Bhapka, also known as *itr-i-Jahangiri*). The individual artisan, however competent, had no money to invest in tool-improvement. Enough merchant capital was available but its owners would not invest in tools. They were making large profits through trade and commerce; so why invest in manufacturing or innovation?[44] Possible avenues of proto-industrialization (that is, when an economy moves from commercialization to invest in tools, raw materials, and labour) were generally discounted. The Mughal government promoted *karkhana*s (factories), but these catered exclusively to royalty and the army.[45] In any case, the Mughal money economy did not lead to a machine economy. As a result, medieval India, which was hardly behind medieval Europe, definitely fell 'behind' modern Europe.

Similarly, another point to ponder is that, unlike the West, pre-modern India did not witness any intense debate on issues of reason, science, or religion. Indians remained obsessed with spiritual and social matters. Instead of scientific thinkers or innovative technologists, India produced social reformers in large numbers. They, in turn, produced an unprecedented stream of *bhakti* (devotion). Numerous *sufi*s, *auliya*s, *sant*s, *mahatmas*, and the like contributed to philosophy, literature, and above all, to social peace. The ruling class, in contrast, was busy building forts, palaces, mausoleums, and tombs. In terms of ideas, age-old concepts and practices were repeated with very little variation. Theological considerations retained their predominance and grip over society.

Tools remained simple and stagnant for centuries, yet craftsmanship was superb. The remarkable feats of structural engineering can be seen from the Brihadeshwara temple (10th century AD) to the celebrated Taj Mahal (17th century AD). The rust-free iron pillar in Delhi (6th century AD) remains an unusual example of metallurgical skills. Society excelled in making use of stone, marble, and iron. It also knew how to make glass. Bangles were made for several millennia. But unfortunately, it could not move beyond bangles! Renaissance Europe was grinding glass which led to the development of such powerful tools as the telescope and microscope. But Indo-Islamic society remained obsessed with marble and tiles and ignored glass. In a sunny country, the need was to keep light out by the use of stone and marble while the colder Europe needed to tap sunlight through glass. The result was that our *garbhgriha* (sanctum sanctorum), metaphorically speaking, remained dark. This was probably also because the people who worked with their hands and tools (like potters, carpenters, blacksmiths, and other artisans) were denied entry there. A society which continued to play with mere stone and marble had to pay the price in terms of cutting-edge knowledge, material development, and even sovereignty.

Another important aspect that needs to be taken into account is the caste system, which has always been a unique feature of Indian society. P. C. Ray was the first historian of science who saw in the caste structure 'something that made science a prey to creeping paralysis'.[46] Caste led to the ruinous separation of theory from practice—of mental work from manual work. Ray wrote as follows:

> The intellectual portion of the community being thus withdrawn from active participation in the arts—the how and why of phenomena—the co-ordination of cause and effect—were lost sight of—the spirit of enquiry gradually died out. Her (India's) soil was rendered morally unfit for the birth of a Boyle, a Descartes, or a Newton.[47]

During the post-Renaissance epoch (that of Descartes and Newton), Europe began to outdistance all other culture-areas. The major differences may not be in the state of knowledge, but in the state of organization and activity. In Europe we begin to see the emergence of a different tradition, through the establishment of scientific societies, establishment of universities and academics, and printing, making possible the cumulative growth of knowledge and continuity of effort. Sadly, this was missing in India. In the 18th century, this distance became virtually unbridgeable. For India, this century proved unique in the sense that it saw the decline of pre-colonial systems as well as the inauguration of systematic colonization. During this period, the rise of modern science itself coincided with the rise of merchant capitalism and colonial expansion. Probably they grew in tandem, feeding each other. The result was that not only Mughal India but the Safavids in Iran, the Manchus in China, and the mighty Ottomans had also begun to show signs of cracking. Some resurgent nations like the Portuguese, the Dutch, the French, and the English, now ruling the waves, came in and through their trading companies captured large areas. Their sails, their guns, their training were substantially different. They had 'new' knowledge behind them.

Notes

1. M. S. Khan, 'Qadi Said-al-Andalusi's Account of Ancient Indian Sciences and Culture', *Journal of the Pakistan Historical Society*, 45 (1997): 1–31.
2. For details, see Bibhutibhusan Datta, *The Science of the Sulba: A Study in Early Hindu Geometry* (Calcutta: University of Calcutta, 1932).

3. R. A. L. H. Gunawardana, 'Proto-Science and Technology in Pre-colonial South Asia', in *Cultural Interaction in South Asia in Historical Perspective*, ed. S. A. I. Tirmizi (New Delhi: Hamdard Institute of Historical Research, 1993), pp. 178–208. See also Deepak Kumar, 'India', in *Science in Eighteenth Century*, ed. Roy Porter (Cambridge, MA: Cambridge University Press, 2003), pp. 669–687.

4. D. P. Chattaopadhyay, *Science and Society in Ancient India* (Calcutta: Research India Publication, 1979), pp. 7, 13.

5. For details, see S. N. Sen and K. S. Shukla, *History of Astronomy in India* (New Delhi: Indian National Science Academy, 1985).

6. It is said that the works of Ibn al-Haytham (1000 AD) were later studied at the Ponnani *madrasa* near Kannur. During the 17th century, Jesuit visitors were aware of works like the *Tantrasangraha* and *Yuktibhasa*. G. G. Joseph, *The Crest of the Peacock: Non-European Roots of Mathematics*, 3rd edn (Princeton: Princeton University Press, 2011), pp. XIX, 311–444.

7. For details, see M. S. Sriram, K. Ramasubramanian, and M. D. Srinivas (eds.), *500 Years of Tantrasangrah: A Landmark in the History of Astronomy* (Shimla: IIAS, 2002).

8. S. A. Jackson, *On the Boundaries of Theological Tolerance in Islam* (Karachi: Oxford University Press, 2002), pp. 44–45.

9. Irfan Habib, 'Reason and Science in Medieval India', in *Society and Ideology in India: Essays in Honour of Professor R.S. Sharma*, ed. D. N. Jha (Delhi: Manohar, 1996), pp. 163–174.

10. S. R. Sarma, 'From Yavani to Sanskritam: Sanskrit Writings Inspired by Persian Works', *Studies in History of Indian Thought* no. 14 (2002): 71–88.

11. C. A. Storey, *Persian Literature: A Bio-bibliographical Survey*, Vol. II, Part 2 (London: Luzac & Co.,1971), p. 321.

12. Irfan Habib, 'Capacity of Technological Change in Mughal India', in *Technology in Ancient and Medieval India*, eds A. Roy and S. K. Bagchi (Delhi: Sundeep Prakashan, 1986), pp. 12–13.

13. See A. J. Qaisar, *The Indian Response to European Technology and Culture 1498–1707* (New Delhi: Oxford University Press, 1982).

14. For details, see K. G. Zysk, *Medicine in the Veda: Religious Healing in the Veda* (Delhi: Motilal Banarsidass, 1996).

15. The medical knowledge of the Buddhist shamans (wandering physicians) was gradually assimilated and processed by the Brahmins 'to fit into an orthodox Weltanschauung'. See also K. G. Zysk, *Asceticism and Healing in Ancient India: Medicine in the Buddhist Monastery* (New York: Oxford University Press, 1991).

16. How true and contemporary! The idea that disease is a consequence of greed and evil conduct is to be found in all through history and in all cultures. Theology treats it as divine punishment.
17. For the *Charak Samhita*, see J. G. Meulenbeld, *A History of Indian Medical Literature*, Vol. 1A (Groningen: Egbert Forsten, 1999), pp. 9–104.
18. Some even claimed to fly with the help of mercury pills! N. V. K. Varier, *History of Ayurveda* (Kottakkal: Arya Vaidya Sala, 2005), p. 195.
19. For medical commentaries (*nighantus*) from 600 to 1600 AD, see J. G. Meulenbeld, *A History of Indian Medical Literature*, Vol II B (Groningen: Egbert Forsten, 2000), pp. 131–180.
20. A. Gordon White, *The Alchemical Body* (New Delhi: Munshiram Manoharlal, 2004), p. 53.
21. Meulenbeld, *A History of Indian Medical Literature*, vol. II A, p. 278.
22. Ibid., p. 286.
23. Dominik Wujastyk, *The Roots of Ayurveda: Selections from Sanskrit Medical Writings* (New Delhi: Penguin, 1998), p. 8.
24. A medieval text, *Suktiratnahara*, refers to a physician's greed in verse:

> He can't extend the life you have led
> Though for that he'll charge his fees:
> His skill's in running from the dead
> And in performing moneyectomies!

Cited in Dagmar Wujastyk, *Well-mannered Medicine: Medical Ethics and Etiquette in Classical Ayurveda* (New York: Oxford University Press, 2012), pp. 50, 152.
25. Through his own teaching Fathullah Shirazi encouraged the widespread study of rational subjects and their incorporation into the curriculum. Shirazi's work was sustained and later developed by Mulla Mahmud Jaunpuri (d. 1652), author of the *Shams al-Bazegha*.
26. Hakim Abdul Hameed, *Exchanges Between India and Central Asia in the Field of Medicine* (New Delhi: Institute of History of Medicine and Medical Research, 1986), pp. 5–27. For more details, see Seema Alavi, *Islam and Healing: Loss and Recovery of an Indo-Muslim Medical Tradition, 1600–1900* (Raniket: Permanent Black, 2007).
27. A. Rahman (ed.), *Science and Technology in Medieval India: A Bibliography of Source Materials in Sanskrit, Arabic and Persian* (New Delhi: Indian National Science Academy, 1982), pp. 129, 165.
28. John M. de Figueredo, 'Ayurvedic Medicine in Goa According to European Sources in the Sixteenth and Seventeenth Centuries', *Bulletin of the History of Medicine* 58, no. 2 (1984): 225–235.

29. Harish Naraindas, 'Of Therapeutics and Prophylactics: The Exegesis of an Eighteenth-Century Tract on Smallpox', in *Disease and Medicine in India*, ed. Deepak Kumar (New Delhi: Tulika Publications, 2001), pp. 94–119.

30. S. R. Sarma, 'The Lahore Family of Astrolabists and Their Ouvrage', *Studies in History of Medicine and Science* 13, no. 2 (1994): 205–224.

31. Till date the best work on Jai Singh is: V. N. Sharma, *Sawai Jai Singh and His Astronomy* (Delhi: Motilal Banarsidass, 1995).

32. R. C. Kapoor, 'Ghulam Husain Jaunpuri: An Early 19th Century Modern Indian Astronomer', *Current Science* 110, no. 12 (2016): 2309–2314.

33. L. Satpathy, 'Samanta Chandra Sekhara and His Treatise Siddhantdarpana', in *500 Years of Tantrasangraha: A Landmark in the History of Astronomy*, ed. M. S. Sriram, K. Ramasubramanian, and M. D. Srinivas (Shimla: Indian Institute of Advanced Study, 2002), pp. 128–136.

34. *Nature* 59 (1899): 436–437.

35. Francis Robinson, 'Ottomans–Safavids–Mughals: Shared Knowledge and Connective Systems', *Journal of Islamic Studies* 8, no. 2 (1997): 151–184.

36. Muhammad Umar, *Islam in Northern India During the Eighteenth Century* (Delhi: Munshiram Manoharlal, 1989), p. 272.

37. G. M. D. Sufi, *Al-Minhaj: Being the Evolution of Curriculum in the Muslim Educational Institutions of India* (Delhi: Idarah-i-Adabiyat-i-Delli, 1977), pp. 68–75.

38. Surendra Gopal, 'Social Set-up and Science and Technology in India', *Indian Journal of History of Science* 4, nos. 1 and 2 (1969): 52–57.

39. S. Sangwan, 'Level of Agricultural Technology in India 1757–1857', *Indian Journal of History of Science* 26, no. 1 (1991): 79–101.

40. For details, see Harbans Mukhia, 'Agricultural Technology in Medieval North India' in *History of Technology in India*, Vol. II, ed. Harbans Mukhia (New Delhi: Indian National Science Academy, 2012), pp. 37–62; and Irfan Habib, 'Pre-modern Modes of Production and Transmission of Power', in *History of Technology in India*, Vol. II, ed. Harbans Mukhia (New Delhi: Indian National Science Academy, 2012), pp. 248–275.

41. V. Ramaswamy, 'South Indian Textiles: A Case for Proto-industrialization?', in *Science and Empire*, ed. Deepak Kumar (Delhi: Anamika, 1991), pp. 41–63.

42. B. Prakash, 'Metallurgy of Iron and Steel Making and Blacksmithy in Ancient India', *Indian Journal of History of Science* 26, no. 4 (1991): 351–371. See also H. C. Bhardwaj, 'Development of Iron and Steel Technology in India During the Eighteenth and Nineteenth Centuries', *Indian Journal of History of Science* 17, no. 2 (1982): 223–233.

43. A. K. Ghose, 'History of Mining in India 1400–1800 and Technology Status', *Indian Journal of History of Science* 15, no. 1 (1980): 25–29.

44. This dilemma continues to plague present-day India too. Commission-based commerce flourishes, manufacturing remains at a low, and our obsession with defence-related technologies remains at a high.

45. A focused example can be seen in S. H. Khan, *Art and Craft Workshops Under the Mughals: A Study of Jaipur Karkhanas* (Delhi: Primus Books, 2014).

46. Debiprasad Chattopadhyay, *History of Science and Technology in Ancient India: The Beginnings* (Calcutta: South Asia Books, 1986), p. 10.

47. P. C. Ray, *History of Hindu Chemistry*, vol. 2 (London: Williams and Norgate, 1909), p. 195.

2

The Age of Exploration and Consolidation

Our spirit rules the world. Our wisdom enters into the composition of the every-day life of half the globe. Our physical as well as intellectual presence is manifest in every climate under the sun. Our sailing ships and steam-vessels cover the seas and rivers. Wherever we conquer, we civilize and refine. Our arms, our arts, our literature are illustrious among the nations. We are a rich, a powerful, an intelligent and a religious people. No place is too remote for our enterprises or our curiosity. We have an insatiable energy, which is of the utmost value to the work. We have spread ourselves over all regions. We have peopled North America, civilized India, taken possession of Australia and scattered the Anglo-Saxon name and fame, language and literature, religion and laws, ideas and habits, over the fairest portions of the globe.

—*The Illustrated London News*[1]

This was the proud and justified boast of a nation which had helped produce the scientific and industrial revolutions of the 17th and 18th centuries, and had almost simultaneously embarked upon colonizing large parts of the world. Colonial expansion required knowledge of the terrain, its people, its resources, and so on. No domination could be established without this knowledge. And this knowledge could not be obtained without scientific explorations and surveys. Next to the guns and ships, these were the most potent tools in the hands of a colonizing power. Through them it could afford to know unknown people, chart untrodden paths, and estimate local resources. So, surveyors marched by the side of conquering armies. Topographical surveys had military origins and this relationship was maintained throughout (India got its first civilian Surveyor General only in 1991!). Similarly, meteorological observations and data were important for a seafaring colonizer and an agro-based colony. Geological surveys came late. They started as a part of topographical explorations but as British rule stabilized, they acquired their own identity and played a major role in the economic exploitation of the country. But botanical explorations had started much earlier, in the 18th century itself, in some cases, even before. After all, the colonies were called plantations; they traded in plant products, and had a lot to do with botanical knowledge.[2]

This exploratory phase had certain interesting characteristics. First, the explorers always looked for data and materials that would be 'useful', commercially or otherwise. Second, they never lost sight of the knowledge value of their enterprise. They worked under some sort of a dual mandate under which both the commercial and knowledge components had to be taken care of. Third, unlike Victorian Africa where the explorers arrived much before the flag and trade, in India, the three moved in tandem. There was not much planning and coordination but their interests did converge and there did exist a 'method' in the colonial 'madness'. Fourth, they could not only claim conceptual and technological superiority but also dismiss the 'other' or local knowledge, tools, and techniques as useless and antiquated. Under colonial conditions, 'A' could easily claim that he knew 'B' better than 'B' knew himself, and therefore, had to work, legislate, and rule for the latter's welfare. This is precisely what the 'civilizing mission' was. And it had the 'desired' effect. The colonized were suitably impressed. As two Parsees visiting England wrote:

> Oh! Happy England, possessing within yourself this source of employment, of manufacture, and of wealth, old happy England, you are, and long will be the wonder and envy of the world; you possess materials that enable you to work machinery, that allows you to bring cotton from India, thousands of miles, to manufacture it into fine muslin, and to send it back to India and to sell it there much cheaper than it can be made there ... what is there in England that cannot be done by steam? Carriages fly upon iron railroads heated by coal, wood is sawn by steam, iron is hammered into anchors, and rolled into plates, bars, and wire by steam.[3]

The colonial developments cannot be understood solely in terms of politics or trade. There was indeed a strong cultural context to all that was happening on the eve of colonization. These were the formative years wherein one can find the seeds of future transformation. It was an exciting time of transition. Formidable Asiatic empires from the Ottomans to the Manchus had begun to show signs of decline. The old order was crumbling; the new was yet to emerge, and when it did, it came via new routes and with new knowledge. It is not difficult to see fluidity in such a situation. Exchange in terms of both materials and ideas was possible and even visible. There were some who evoked a sympathetic chord but there were many who condemned Indian traditions and practices as most primitive, crude, clumsy, and unscientific.

This condemnation may have well been part of the process of hegemonization. It is also possible that for European observers there may have been some genuine difficulties in understanding an abstruse treatise or in appreciating a simple technical device which would appear 'appropriate' only when viewed against the existing socio-economic context.

The Beginnings

Pre-colonial India had a strong polity and an administrative apparatus, but to think of a science-based administration would be far-fetched. Several instances of scientific and technical knowledge were obviously there but scientific institutions are modern icons. These came to India as part of the colonial baggage, and soon became the carriers of new ideas and in fact symbolized modernity itself. One of the earliest institutions that gradually became the fountainhead of new knowledge was the Asiatic Society established by William Jones, a jurist with a literary flair, in Calcutta in 1784. This society soon became the focal point of all scientific activities in India. This was a unique experiment, probably the first such in Asia. The scope and objects of its enquiries were: 'Man and Nature; whatever is performed by the one, or produced by the other.' What could be colonial in such a magnificent objective! Nothing. The difference lay in practice. Though the criteria for its membership was nothing more than 'a love of knowledge and zeal for the promotion of it', Indians were not taken as members until 1829, and no Indian made any scientific contribution to its journal until the 1880s. Yet this society remained a beacon of knowledge for long. It was the sole organ of research in Asia for more than a century. Whatever was done in geology, meteorology, zoology, and botany was done through the society. Gradually all these branches developed on lines of their own and blossomed into separate departments. The society grew by fission, like the 'philoprogenitive sponge' and gave birth in successive epochs to the Geological Survey, the Indian Museum, the Meteorological Department, the Botanical Survey, and the Linguistic Survey.[4]

The East India Company appreciated the significance of botanical and geographical investigations and encouraged its interested employees to undertake such activities.[5] An early example is of James Anderson who joined the East India Company in 1759. In 1778, he obtained from the Madras Government a large piece of land near Fort. St. George which he developed as a botanical garden where he experimented with the introduction of cochineal insects, silkworms, and plants of commercial value such as sugarcane, coffee, American cotton, and also European apples. In Bengal, another military official,

Robert Kyd, conceived of the idea of supplying the Company's navy with teak timber grown near the port where it could be used in ship-building. In June 1786, he submitted a scheme for the establishment of what be appropriately called a 'Garden of Acclimatisation' near Calcutta which was promptly accepted. It is a treat to read this 'Memorandum on Agriculture Productions, Commerce, Population and Manufactures'. Obviously, Kyd took a long view and worked on a huge canvas. He defines policy which reflects a deep insight and muses on what the government should do. He wrote:

> Policy in its genuine signification being the art of ordering all things for the benefit of the citizens of the state ... is the common sense of Government, or rather common sense as applied to Government; is everywhere requisite serving in some nations to restrain, in others to excite, in all to methodize, and direct the endeavours of a Nation.[6]

This statement coming from an army officer and an amateur botanist stationed in a colonial outpost is significant and quite characteristic of the early explorers who formed an integral part of the colonial process.

Why Survey?

While proposing to survey Mysore in January 1800, John Mackenzie clarified that his object was

> to obtain as soon as possible a clearer and better defined knowledge of the Extent, Properties, Strength and Resources of a Country ... to elucidate many objects of Natural History, connected with commercial views and therefore interesting to the Company, exclusive of the advantage in the improvement of scientific knowledge.[7]

The reference to 'improvement of scientific knowledge' is interesting and sets out the dual mandate which a colonial explorer-cum-scientist had. Here exploration emerges more as a state enterprise. Unlike Victorian Africa where the explorers arrived much before the flag and trade, in India the three had moved together, hand in hand. Notwithstanding some 'internal' conflicts and adjustments, their interests largely converged.

Surveyors were the forerunners of scientific exploration. They came from the military and it is from their ranks that we find early geologists, meteorologists, and astronomers emerging. A seafaring nation intent upon conquering new lands needed to know the vagaries of wind, rain, and other climatic factors, especially the monsoon. Once on the shore, they needed to know the local topography, the flora and fauna, and of course, the people. Another set of early scientists came from a medical background, trained in the universities of Edinburgh, Glasgow, and other parts of north Europe. They became the early botanists and zoologists. They were knowledge-seekers no doubt, but they also knew that their knowledge was crucial for control over alien lands and people. They were a talented and dedicated lot. They were the men on the spot who largely determined what was advantageous to both trade and their country. They also enjoyed a certain amount of flexibility and autonomy. The East India Company for which they worked would be unobtrusive for the most part. As a pioneer surveyor noted, 'Whatever charges may be imputable to the managers of the Company, the neglect of useful science ... is not among the number'.[8] In 1825, John Goldingham, who had set up an observatory in Madras back in 1792, testified that 'the English Company desired to have everything done for the benefit of science'.[9]

There were tremendous difficulties but also enormous opportunities to sight and discover new things. Support from metropolitan scientists added to their confidence. The agenda of the colonial explorers was not entirely derivative, however; they too influenced metropolitan discourses (for example, on the deposition of coal-seams, nature of cholera, and so on). Sometimes the periphery could and did alter the terms at the centre![10] Richard Grove, a fine environmental historian, has shown how the idea of environmental conservation came from the colonies, and colonial planters, botanists, and foresters contributed a great deal to the initiation and maturation of conservation debates in metropolitan circles.[11] During the 18th century, there emerged a network of surgeon-naturalists stationed in Java, Ceylon, Bengal, Malabar, Aden, and elsewhere who corresponded with each other and exchanged relevant specimens. To their metropoles in London or Paris, they used to send 'annually' by homeward-bound ships all kinds of seeds, bulbs, roots, plants, trees, flowers, and so on, for the sake of 'curiosity and also medicine'.[12] But they were no slaves of the metropole nor mere extensions. They were collaborators par excellence. These early European pioneers were studying Asia, its flora, and its knowledge not as 'an extension of its construction in Europe but as a phenomenon in its own right'.[13]

Gradually, a new concept of state scientist emerged in the colonies and in most cases, he remained true to his dual mandate. Thus James Rennell, John Goldingham, R. Lambton, Robert Kyd, William Roxburgh, George Everest, Thomas Oldham, and many others appear as pioneers who faced enormous physical and conceptual problems, yet contributed significantly to both the colonial state and the world of knowledge. All of them had twin purposes; the gratification of enlightened curiosity as well as more 'utility-oriented' general and practical purposes. This duality had created certain practical difficulties; it was not easy to make a clear demarcation between practical economy-oriented works and those of scientific value. As noted geologist T. H. Holland wrote,

> In the preparation of our annual programme, we are not wholly free to follow the line which we think is best for the country in the long run; questions of economic importance sometimes cannot be postponed without immediate loss and inconvenience whilst an un-surveyed area, about which nothing certainly is known, is neglected from one field season to another ... India cannot, perhaps, afford to rank itself beside the more thoroughly developed European countries, where pure science is so richly endowed; and the practical difficulty here is to discover *the profitable mean course* in which scientific research, having a general bearing will, at the same time, solve the local problems of immediate economic value.[14]

Consolidating the Gains

Institutions were needed to house the different kinds of knowledge on the local people, topography, resources, and so on, that were coming from the numerous agents of trade and the state. They were also needed to enlist the support of the local elite and gradually create a subordinate cadre that would help consolidate the colonial state. These institutions were not mere replicas of the metropolitan institutions. The government had, of course, its own motives, but the institutionalization of geological and botanical works proved to be of historic importance—a milestone in both the history of science and the history of imperialism. In many cases, the provincial governments were responsible for the administration of scientific organizations and institutions, and on-the-spot decisions were taken as and when required. But the final authority rested in London, and metropolitan interests, pressures, and pulls weighed heavily on colonial administrators. Excessive administrative control exercised at different levels, in turn, ensured that colonial scientists would always dance to the official tune. This bred dissatisfaction, and often led to demoralization among the scientists. Some found themselves saddled more with administrative responsibilities than research, while others resented their hopeless dependence on the bureaucracy for every minor favour. Sometimes they found their role chafing. Thomas Oldham (a geologist), George Watt (a botanist), and Ronald Ross (a medical scientist) expressed their disappointment on several occasions. But they could never transcend the economic and political considerations on which the Raj itself rested. Colonial pragmatism demanded the complete subjugation of personal viewpoints to economic interests.

It is not that the bureaucracy of the Raj deserves opprobrium all the time. Several district-level officials reported and sometimes published interesting accounts of scientific relevance. In 1878, for example, a magistrate of Monghyr district published a detailed account of the 'natural history' of the area, which was reviewed in the famous journal *Nature*. When such officials graduated to senior positions, they showed respect for 'local knowledge' and tended to favour local talent. The civilian officials naturally felt inclined to study the social ecology of the society they were sent to govern. Local knowledge was vital for them but not for the experts who were products of a 'technical discourse' of science, and who used certain universal parameters to which local variations had either to conform or get rejected. The colonial system in any case excelled in hierarchization and marginalization.

Among the scientific surveys, the Geological Survey appeared to be the most organized. Naturally so, the knowledge of mineral resources gave the British enormous revenue prospects. By the 1890s, mining had gathered momentum. Numerous private prospectors and companies had emerged. But no Geological Survey officer was allowed to work for private firms. In White-settler colonies like Australia and Canada, it was allowed, even encouraged, but not in India. The government thus enjoyed total monopoly on all resources and total control over its scientific cadres. As, in 1894, an Australian mining magnet complained to the then Governor General, Lord Elgin:

> There is an awful deal of circumlocution and sitting at ease in Government Departments in India … Long delays and neglect are fatal to capital and enterprise, and the salvation of India depends now on the unstinted development of the material resources of the country. And I believe, Sir E. Buck, who is the Secretary charged with mineral matters (he is one of the legacies left to India by Lord Lytton!) is a particularly slow man, besides being thoroughly ignorant of the subject.[15]

The mining prospectors' fulminations were natural. But it is equally true that from 1890 onwards, mining and export of ores like iron and manganese picked up fast. This was resented by educated Indians. As a Malayalam weekly, *Bharata Bandhu* wrote,

> There is no capital worth the name available in India and poor India cannot afford to dispense with foreign capital to develop her industries. Foreign capital to prove beneficial should be placed under certain restrictions and should not be allowed to drain the material wealth forever. All big industries like gold mines in Mysore, kerosene mines in Burma, and coal mines in Bengal, etc.

are entirely engrossed by capital of the foreigners and all that the Indians get is the coolie hire out of them.[16]

Though the colonial government was most interested in the economic aspects of geological works, there had never been an attempt to convert the Geological Survey into a mere prospecting or mining department. The Government of India did recognize purely scientific work as an important duty of the Geological Survey of India (GSI) and regarded the advancement of science as a thing to be desired and encouraged on its own account. The result was that many discoveries were made which influenced the course of geological science. For example, for the first time, worldwide recognition was won for the importance of deposits formed on land. It was proved that the Gangetic alluvium, formerly looked upon as a marine deposit, was a land deposit and also that the stones and conglomerates of which the foothills of the Himalayas are composed were formed, not in the sea, but on land. The other achievements were, of course, the preparation of a nearly perfect geological map of India and a very significant study of earthquakes in India.[17]

Under both the Company and Crown rule, the maximum revenue came, not from mining or minerals, but from agricultural and plant resources. After all, the Company was the biggest zamindar in the world and, not without reason, the colonies were called plantations! This had a lot to do with plants and the knowledge of plants. But the Botanical Survey could never acquire the structural homogeneity and cohesiveness which characterized the GSI or Survey of India. It was not that the colonizers were oblivious of its importance; rather they preferred to keep it administratively flexible so that it could be conveniently put to fairly diverse uses. The botanists could not get an imperial cadre. Some of them were attached to the revenue department, some to agriculture, and a few to forestry and medicinal works. The nature of assignments was equally varied. Apart from full-scale transfers, services were also sought on a temporary basis for specific purposes. In 1872, for example, the curator of the Calcutta Botanic Garden, John Scott, was deputed to the poppy districts of Bihar. He was asked to make two sets of reports, one to the Board of Revenue regarding practical points relating to the poppy plant and opium, and the other to the Superintendent of the Botanic Garden regarding scientific points in physiological botany. Such dual reporting, both in administration and research, remained the chief characteristic of the Botanical Survey throughout the century.[18] In contrast, geologists and topographers had the advantage of belonging to distinct administrative units though as investigators they also often had to perform double roles.[19]

An impressive institutionalization alone could have consolidated the gains that accrued from exploration. It may be interesting to observe how and in what form a particular scientific organization at a particular historical juncture worked for the then-existing politico-economic structure. The geological and survey departments, for instance, received the maximum patronage from the government. Next ranked botany. Agriculture remained a Cinderella until the 1890s, though a few private agricultural and horticultural societies did try to give it a commercial drift. To the new rulers, the agricultural potentialities basically meant cash crops and the profits that accrued. After all the British did not come here to fight famines! They wanted Indians to grow cotton, jute, opium, tobacco, indigo, and tea. The Indian cultivator had limited use for these articles of commerce but was forced to work on commercial crops in place of food crops. Moreover, he had practical knowledge and experience but no capital. Hence the colonizers asked British merchants and trading companies to invest in cash-crop-oriented agriculture. But the response remained fairly limited and cautious. The railways got a better response because here the government guaranteed profit.

The half-starved *raiyats*, with their half-starved bullocks, working on half-starved soil were not the men to compete with the millionaire farmers of Europe and America. In Europe, agricultural instruction was given to farm-holders and labourers alike. But in India such education was to be imparted not to the *ryot* but to a new generation of *zamindars* who certainly were not as ignorant as their *ryots*. The economics of their time taught them to behave more as tax-gatherers than as landlords. The British had all along been very particular about not disturbing existing class relations. The upper classes were their natural allies. Through this class-understanding they prevented a cultural clash in the accepted sense of tradition opposing modernity. The average Indian cultivators, however, had their own reservations, and perhaps valid ones. Once a British investor offered seeds of Bourbon cotton to some *ryots* who got quite convinced of its advantages but said that they dared not cultivate any new article. 'Our zamindar would make demands far beyond the profits', was the reason assigned.[20] And how true they were! In the White colonies the farmers had some capital but little experience; in India they had no capital but a wealth of experience.

This was vouched for by J. A. Voelcker, an agricultural chemist, who reported on Indian agriculture in 1892. He had a sympathetic understanding of the needs and capabilities of Indian peasants. He was against the import of foodgrain technology or expertise, and wished for native experts; that too, trained in India, not in England.[21] He found there was no class in India, unlike in England, which could invest in and improve agriculture. Instead, the Permanent Settlement introduced by Cornwallis had produced a rapacious class of *zamindars*. Therefore, he asked for the whole revenue system and land relations to be changed. This was too much for the alien government and the report was promptly shelved.

The Department of Agriculture was dominated largely by commercial and land-revenue concerns, and not by a desire to improve or innovate for the sake of agriculture itself.[22] It was a 'cash raj', collecting rents in cash and forcing cash crops.[23] Later this 'cash raj' gave way to a 'regulated' *laissez faire*, always subservient to the requirements of British capital. Of course, there were certain experimental farms, a few agricultural schools, and some agricultural exhibitions and *mela*s were also organized. But these were like a few drops on a frying pan. Also, as a newspaper argued:

> ... unless the masses are reached, it is a mere waste of money, because in India there are no large farmers or syndicates as in America or England to control agriculture. Education is, indeed, at so low an ebb that if one has to wait till the masses educate themselves so far as to understand the dry, obscure and scientific language of the agricultural ledgers and memoirs, one will have to wait till, say, doomsday![24]

Private scientific bodies were often more vigorous than the government machinery. Among them could be counted the Asiatic Society of Bengal, the Bombay Branch of the Royal Asiatic Society, the Scientific and Literary Society of Madras, and the medical and physical societies in Presidency towns. Changing economic needs, the proliferation of scientific establishments, and the growing concern shown for them by educated Indians made the government think in terms of an apex body to regulate scientific affairs in India. In 1898, at the instance of the Home Government, the Royal Society formed an Indian Advisory Committee, and in 1902 the Government of India established a Board of Scientific Advice.[25] These experiments unfortunately generated more heat than light and ended in a whimper. Still these institutions had brought the government, science, and economic considerations into a close relationship. The economic interest-group wanted research to gain immediate and practical ends. And economic ramifications can well be spotted in the growth of industries fed on applied science, namely, coal, cotton, jute, tea, and so on. One may argue that scientific development in British India should be treated as individual romances with natural history without linking them with the political economy of the time. But where would natural sciences be without industry and commerce? However, the light of science had certainly been dimmed by the smoke of commercialism.

Excessive government control of scientific undertakings often hampered the logical development of modern science in India. The government would always goad the various organizations to work only along economically beneficial lines. Most of them buckled under this pressure. George Watt, a noted botanist, was asked in 1903[26] to prepare an abridged volume of his famous *Dictionary of Economic Products*. But he was not given a free hand in selecting the products. He was asked to include only those which were of commercial value. The result was that instead of a dictionary of economic products, he produced a manual of commercial products.

Why Science or Technical Education?

In the educational scheme, science was never given a high priority. The Charter of 1813 called for the introduction and promotion of the knowledge of science among the inhabitants of British India. But it remained a pious wish. Moreover, the charter gave no indication of which system of science, indigenous or Western, was to be preferred. In 1835, Macaulay not only succeeded in making a foreign language (English) the medium of instruction, his personal distaste for science led to a curriculum which was purely literary. The entry of science was thus delayed. A few medical and engineering schools and colleges were opened but these were meant largely to supply assistant surgeons, hospital assistants, overseers, and so on. The curriculum, the instruments, and the very organization of these colleges were geared to meet the requirements of only subordinate services. The authorities in India looked to Western models but they seldom incorporated their good points, and in the name of adapting these models to local conditions often made a mess of them. For example, accepting the London model, the universities established in 1857 in the Presidency towns were meant only for examinations, but the fact that London University granted science degrees was conveniently ignored. Even Oxford offered honours in mathematics and the natural sciences and Cambridge a tripos in the natural sciences. But the Presidency universities had to remain content with only one paper in science. Later in 1870, Indian universities began to show some inclination towards science education. In 1875, Madras University decided to examine its matriculation candidates in geography and elementary physics in place of British history. Bombay was the first to grant degrees in science; Calcutta University divided its BA into two branches—an 'A' course (that is, literary) and a 'B' course (that is, scientific).

Despite the usefulness of the 'B' course, the 'A' course was far more popular. Science was not taught at the secondary school level nor did it figure in the entrance examination; for first arts (FA), classical language was compulsory. Hence 'the possibilities of studying natural, physical and applied sciences were altogether crowded out by the weight of other subjects'.[27]

Even this slow growth of science education was beset with many problems. First was the very aim and essence of the educational policy, that is, 'character formation'. For this purpose, a liberal–literary education was found more suitable. The British government did not interfere directly in social issues; they were scared of ruffling the feathers of Indian society. There is an interesting example. When Grant Medical College was opened in Bombay in 1845, the government expected a good response. But very few students turned up for admission; the Brahmins refrained probably because the new medical school required them to touch and dissect dead bodies. For several successive years, seats remained vacant, so the principal wrote to the Director of Public Instruction (DPI) of Bombay asking for permission to admit students from the lower classes (castes). The DPI shot back, never do this. 'The lower-class people once they get this new higher education will earn more when they return to the society and will thereafter demand higher social status. This would upset the social balance. We have come here to rule, not to cause social upheavals', the DPI warned and made the forecast, 'the Brahmins would come once they see money in modern medicine'.[28]

A second problem was the shortage and unequal distribution of funds. In 1900, the four colleges of Patna, Cuttack, Hooghly, and Krishnagar cost the government 55,441 rupees while the Presidency College of Calcutta alone claimed 114,702 rupees. For want of funds, the Gujarat College in Ahmedabad had once closed its science classes.[29] Added to this was the attitude of the authorities in India who, as mentioned, looked to Western models but seldom incorporated their advantages. Indian institutions would not offer anything like a higher form of scientific or technical education. What the country got was some sort of a hybrid emerging out of a careless fusion between industrial and technical education. What is more, the adoption of English as the sole medium of instruction in science rather hampered its percolation to the lower classes.

In Bombay, the most important school for science was the Poona College of Science which had arisen out of a school established in 1854 for the purpose of educating subordinates for the Public Works Department (PWD). This college was not an exclusive engineering institution; it held classes on agriculture and forestry also. The result was a hotchpotch of various types of instruction, and that too, without adequate staff. Engineering colleges existed for the PWD and were called 'civil' engineering colleges, the most important being the Thomason Engineering College at Roorkee. In 1886, MacDonnell, the then Home Secretary, on Lord Dufferin's recommendations prepared an elaborate memorandum setting forth the history of technical education in India, the actual conditions, and the lines of future development. Regarding engineering, MacDonnell pointed out that the nature of teaching at Calcutta, Madras, and Roorkee was too theoretical and these colleges were completely isolated. Further suggestions were put forward regarding the teaching of science and drawing at the primary school stage and starting the 'modern side' of high schools and divisional or district technical schools but all this was to remain on paper.[30]

The nature and pattern of engineering education in India differed from that in Britain. Whereas in England it evolved from below and gradually became a part of the university curriculum, in India it was organized from above. Though it was organized from above in France also, the motive and situation differed greatly. In Europe, engineering education was developed in order to facilitate the process of industrialization. In India, there was no such imperative. Every aspect of engineering education was dictated and controlled by the PWD. Imperial consolidations involved enormous construction works like the railways, irrigation, and so on; and as such, civil engineering received all the patronage. Industry-oriented branches, like mechanical, electrical, and metallurgical engineering, came much later, in the third decade of the 20th century, that too, thanks to the post-Great-War circumstances and restive nationalist demands.

Here in India, hopes were pinned not on 'material' but on 'moral' uplift. In fact, the whole aim of colonial education was 'moral development "and" character formation'. The 'native' character was considered defective, immoral, and superstitious. The 'new' education armed with Western rationality was supposed to correct it. But the PWD-oriented education could not have achieved this. Yet, the new openings in education in India and the response of the emerging middle class raised the hopes of Britain's 'civilizing mission'. As a British journal wrote:

> the young native students who present themselves for examination at the Universities established in the three Presidencies show a very hopeful and commendable aptitude for science, perhaps more so than for literature. Is this to be taken as an indication that at no very distant day, there will be in the East a number of ingenious recruits ready to take part in the great work of advancing science?[31]

But until the end of the 19th century, this remained a dream. Responsible or high positions were denied to Indians, however well-trained or even if educated in England itself. To one chief of the Geological Survey, H. Medlicott, Indians appeared utterly incapable of any original work in natural science. He wanted to wait until the 'scientific chord among the natives' was touched and added almost contemptuously, 'if indeed it exists as yet in this variety of the human race ... So let us exercise a little discretion with our weaker brethren, and not expect them to run before they can walk'.[32] W. T. Blanford, another senior geologist, agreed with Medlicott and wrote to the Secretary of State that Indians 'show no aptitude for scientific investigation and do not undertake it, as European students do, without pecuniary inducement'.[33] This they wrote obviously oblivious of the fact that a few enlightened Bengalis had already established an institution, the first of its kind in Asia, that is, the Indian Association for the Cultivation of Science (IACS), at Jadavpur in 1876.

Even agriculture, from which the colonial government and its *zamindars* drew the largest revenue, remained neglected, leading to frequent famines. No doubt, the government had started a few experimental farms and there were certain agriculture and horticulture societies but all these were interested in promoting mostly cash crops which could be exported and earn the government more money. Even the agricultural institute which was established with a grant from one Mr Phipps of the USA (hence the name PUSA) in Bihar experimented more on indigo than on food crops.[34] Commenting on its inauguration by Lord Curzon in 1905, a Tamil daily wrote:

If Lord Curzon were averse to pomp and show, he would begin from the bottom and not from the top, i.e., instead of establishing one research institute in some remote place and spending a large sum on it, he would open small schools and farms in several villages and create some interest in the people. While spending a major portion of the money in the establishment of village schools, he should also open large schools in each province for training the Indian, so that they may be able to impart agriculture education in village schools. The Government of Madras did not accept the proposal of Mr. Chatterton who takes a lively interest in agriculture, to establish 150 model farms at the cost of the state. If this proposal had been accepted by Lord Ampthill, the results could be seen by the *ryots* in a short time. The present arrangements of Lord Curzon are such as to promote the cultivation of the crops raised by Englishmen and to involve a large outlay of money and not to benefit the agriculturists in small villages who will continue to be ever ignorant.[35]

Technological Ramifications

Technology—whether as tool or form of knowledge—is not value-free; it always manifests political qualities. In colonial conditions, it naturally acquired the contours of the colonial power, both commercial and administrative. Technological imperatives and their consequences beg certain questions. For example, what impact did colonization have upon the technological systems and capabilities of the colonizers on the one hand, and the colonized on the other? How did colonialism determine the transfer mechanisms? Did it mean only the geographical relocation of technologies or could it encourage cultural diffusion as well?[36] The latter half of the 19th century was a period of consolidation and institution building. These institutions not only 'imported' knowledge, they imported tools and techniques as well. They also imparted and, to some extent, generated knowledge. But could they diffuse new knowledge? Forging India into a network of irrigational works, railways, telegraphs, mines, and manufacturing, the colonial state introduced and oversaw the introduction of modern technologies. Telegraphs and railways were the high-technology areas in those days.[37] Telegraph operations remained a purely governmental exercise, while the railways, raised on guaranteed profits, depended on wholesale imports from Britain. Even the repair-cum-manufacturing establishments, like the Jamalpur workshop, proved to be islands in themselves. No technological spin-off could emerge, much less galvanize, the neighbourhood of a railway colony. It remained 'enclavist' and functioned more like a 'colony within a Colony'.[38] Mechanical engineering came later and remained a dismal cousin of engineering in the PWD. Irrigation and later hydraulic engineering definitely benefited from the large irrigation works. The Roorkee Engineering College was closely linked to Cautley's Ganges canal. Whether the generation or refinement of irrigation technology at Roorkee or Guindy reduced or increased India's economic dependency is arguable and a matter of several statistical debates. But the social impact of the railways was no doubt phenomenal. The colonized 'natives' were not bystanders in this imposition of an imperial technology from above. Rather they influenced the nature and direction of the impact of an oft-celebrated 'tool of Empire'. This imported 'tool' put the nation on the move, and perhaps it forged a nation![39]

But there were other areas wherein there were no controversies and acceptance was almost universal. For example, electrification in India began in 1883 with the establishment of an electric supply station in Surat, and by the 1930s, several major Indian cities had been electrified.[40] Electricity had a great impact on medical science. Introduction of x-rays, for example would not have been possible without electricity. But these enterprises were basically technology 'projects' with specific aims and purposes, and not technology 'systems' with a wider canvas and, of course, greater results.

It is true that the first engineering college in India was established in 1847, while the Imperial College, London, was founded in 1879. The engineering colleges established in colonial India served as models for replication in England and the colonial encounter contributed to the development of technical education in Britain, no doubt. Moreover, the technical institutions that were established in India helped the emergence of a colonial capitalist state in later years, little distant from the mercantilism of the Company rule. By the end of the 19th century, Indian intellectuals had developed a strong critique of colonial education. Gradually they realized the interdependence between technical education and industrialization.[41]

The introduction of the steam vessel, steam railways, electric telegraph, printing technologies, and later electricity, attracted the attention of the local people like nothing else. The new tools and technologies that the British pushed were soon to be pulled by the Indians themselves. But technology transfer under colonial conditions offered very little scope for the adaptation of these technologies by the Indian people. In fact, almost all the machinery came packed from outside, often along with technicians to handle it. A geographical relocation of technology (as in the case of the railways) was possible and was achieved, but a cultural diffusion of technology is very different and much more complex. The British could always blame the natives for their 'in-built cultural bias against technology'. Technical education was deficient, so technology transfer was impossible, and it was not even on the agenda. The professional colleges were so controlled that they could not induce change at a fast or even perceptible pace.

The medium of instruction was also a factor to be considered. The Japanese had insisted on their own language. The result was that modern knowledge and scientific spirit could percolate down to the masses in Japan. As P. N. Bose, the first Indian geologist, wrote:

> ... that an Oriental nation like the Japanese has, within so short a space of time as a decade or two, risen to scientific eminence, shows that the mere fact of his being an Oriental does not argue an inborn incapacity for scientific research in the Hindu ... We see no reason why with an improved system of scientific education, and with just and sympathetic treatment of the young men trained in science, they will not be able to take a place in the modern scientific world. The reason of the recent success of the Japanese in the field

of science is that their young men, trained under western scientists, instead of being thwarted, discouraged, and set down as incapable, have been aided, encouraged and stimulated by their government to pursue science.[42]

In India, colonial education widened the gulf and accentuated the age-old divide. Even in government institutions, growth was kept under a self-regulatory check. The Massachusetts Institute of Technology (MIT) was established in 1865, and by 1906, it had 306 teachers. In contrast, Roorkee, even after 100 years of existence (that is, in 1947), had only 3 professors, 6 assistant professors, and 12 lecturers. The inference is simple. The natives had to be educated only up to a point. Beyond that, knowledge belonged to the masters. Not only was there government apathy, technology transfer or innovation had to depend on the market forces that the new technology generated or was supposed to generate. The real challenge was 'not merely to meet a demand' but 'to create the demand' for which both technical education and capital were equally necessary.[43] In the wake of the Swadeshi movement, certain chemical industries came up, even flourished for some time, but thanks to the Great War and the subsequent depression, simply collapsed. To the commercial class, it was far easier to export the raw materials than to process them. This is true even after 75 years of independence!

Very often it is argued that Indians have historically lacked technological creativity, innovation, and an experimental tradition, and that such limitations are explicable in terms of Hindu culture and its shibboleths. But such assertions seem demonstrably untrue. Even 'conservative' peasants were not averse to adopting new implements or seeds provided they were economically beneficial and technologically viable. Nor did craft- and skill-based innovation depend upon the acceptance or rejection of external models. As far as specific mechanically driven or steam-based technologies were concerned, the Indian response was neither xenophobic nor 'oriental'; rather it was 'scrupulously selective', depending on convenience and utility as then perceived. If not, how does one explain the quick acceptance of 'small' but crucial technologies like the bicycle, watch, petromax, bioscope, radio, typewriter, and the sewing machine?[44] Gandhi, clad in a loin cloth, always carried a pocket watch. He lauded the Singer sewing machine and called it a 'labour of love' (as it had emerged out of Singer's care and concern for his wife whose fingers were hurt sewing shirts). Later it became more popular than the *charkha*. Big and expensive technologies like the telegraph, canals, and railways had also become popular in no time. Sir Proby Cautley who had built the Ganges canal in the 1840s was hailed as an incarnation of the mythical king Sagar who had brought the Ganges to earth!

One can concede that Indian society at large lacked an entrepreneurial propensity and skills. Yet there were some like Jamshedji Tata, R. N. Mookherjee, Walchand Hirachand, and Laxmanrao Kirloskar who responded to the call of entrepreneurship magnificently. They hired talented engineers who were coming out of the engineering colleges at Sibpur, Jadavpur, Guindy, Poona, and so on. In addition, there were many self-taught local *viswakarmas* who worked and served as 'subaltern technologists'.[45] For example, Shibdas Sil, the proprietor of 'Dey, Sil & Co.—Electricians, Electrometallurgists and Brass Founders', introduced the electric industry in Calcutta way back in the mid-1880s. Apart from arranging for lights at meetings, parties, wedding processions, and so on, they manufactured a wide range of apparatuses: carriage lamps lit by batteries of their own device, sewing machines and table fans worked by electric motors. While electric lamps were introduced in Calcutta by foreign businessmen in the early 20th century, Bengali manufacturers invested in this field in the 1930s. A notable example is the Bengal Electric Lamp Works established in 1932 by three engineer brothers Suren Roy, Kiran Roy, and Hemen Roy.[46] A decade earlier Jogesh Chandra Ray, a science teacher at Ravenshaw College (Cuttack), had patented two of his appliances, one was 'an improved hand mill' and another was 'an improved lift pump for liquids'. One Bepin Behari Das, a self-taught mechanic, was the first builder of a swadeshi motor car. In 1931, it was sold to the Banaras Hindu University and leaders like Pandit Madan Mohan Malviya and Pandit Motilal Nehru used it. The informal sector had many innovators without any formal training but they did help usher in some change in both rural and urban life. Unfortunately, there was no bridge between the 'intellectual technocrats' and the 'subaltern technologists' and the gulf remained wide.

No doubt, the pace of industrialization left much to be desired. For the slow and tardy progress and lack of welfare, the onus was put on the military character of the colonial government. As *Swadeshmitran*, a Tamil daily, wrote:

> Though the revenue of India is far greater than that of any other country, the military expenditure and the salaries of the European officials swallow up almost the whole of it and so our government has not sufficient funds left to help an education conducive to the welfare and improvement of the people. In no country in the world things are as bad as this.[47]

Research in Science

As noted in Chapter 1, pre-British India had *maktabs*, *chatuspatis*, and *agraharas* but no scientific society. There was scientific curiosity, but its institutionalization and professionalization came gradually as part of the colonial baggage. As mentioned earlier, the first such experiment, probably in the whole of Asia, was the establishment of the Asiatic Society in Calcutta in 1784. Within a few decades, several other societies like the Literary and Scientific Society in Madras, the Bombay Branch of the Royal Asiatic Society, and the Agricultural and Horticultural Society, and the Medical and Physical Society in Calcutta were established. Thanks to the spread of the printing press, these societies began to publish their own journals. Research papers were presented, discussed, and then published in these journals. Surprisingly, Presidency towns like Calcutta, Bombay, and Madras, with a relatively small reading public, could support dozens of scientific journals, while today, even with their teeming millions, scientific journals have become scarce.

Colonial researchers often found themselves unable to distinguish between 'basic' research and 'applied' research. This was particularly true of geologists and botanists. Their dilemma was fairly acute. Some of the specialists (especially the botanists) felt slighted. A few received a great deal of attention while others none; for example, large sums were spent on geological explorations and nothing on the examination of agricultural soils. George Watt thought it 'absurd to suppose that the Geology of India requires fourteen European experts, while the Agriculture and the Industries of India must be content with two or three expert investigators'.[48]

A significant feature of this phase is the relative neglect of the medical and zoological sciences, and this is in sharp contrast to larger investments in botanical, geological, and geographical surveys from which the British hoped to get direct and substantial economic and military advantages, while the former did not hold such promise. Western medical classes, for instance, were started in 1822, but it took another 30 years to produce the first exhaustive compilation of information on tropical disease in India. The treatment and study of tropical diseases was undertaken by individuals who were separated both geographically and professionally and so, naturally, a consistent body of knowledge failed to develop. This was true for every branch of knowledge.

Health issues and medical research were of paramount importance for a tropical country like India which was virtually a pathological reservoir of immense proportions. Until the mid-19th century, both the Western and Indian medical systems had almost similar medical epistemologies; both believed in humoral imbalance and miasma. But they were not willing to collaborate and the final rupture came with the emergence of the germ theory of disease. New bacteriological investigations brought a paradigm shift. The aetiology of the disease had to be sought out. The cholera epidemic of

1861 made colonial medical men think in terms of the cause of a disease and then new remedies like vaccines. Health-related laboratories were established in Poona, Agra, Mukteshwar, Kasauli, Coonoor, and later in Madras. Medical commissions like the Cholera Commission, Leprosy Commission, Plague Commission, and Malaria Commission were formed to deal with these terrible diseases at different points of time. They were no doubt honest attempts but their recommendations were mostly shelved by the government as their implementation would involve huge costs. When faced with epidemics, segregation and vaccination were undertaken, but these remained of limited value and could not prevent massive casualties.

Another important feature is the almost total absence of pure or theoretical research. Research activities in sciences like physics and chemistry, which had by then reached 'a professional stage' in Europe, were hardly noticeable in India. Goldingham of the Madras Observatory did certain astronomical and pendulum experiments and also worked on the velocity of sound but this was very exceptional.[49] In the Centenary Review of the Asiatic Society, P. N. Bose apologetically wrote: 'Our chapter of chemistry at the Asiatic Society is near being as brief as the proverbial chapter on Snakes in Ireland.'[50] Until the advent of P. C. Ray, only one chemical paper had appeared—by A. Pedler on the volatility of some of the compounds of mercury. There were chemical analysers in every province but their job was confined only to medico-legal cases and the inspection of government stores.

Some Indians also benefitted from certain new openings. For example, Mohsin Hossain of Arcot could show his skill as an instrument maker; he made a theodolite for survey purposes. Radhanath Sikdar was a mathematician of extraordinary ability. Working at the Calcutta Mint during the 1850s, he is known to have calculated the height of what later came to be known as Mt. Everest. Some Indian astronomers like Keru Laxman were not just engaged in drawing and photographing solar eclipses but also offered theorizations in relation to them. Indian surveyors like Nain Singh and Kishen Singh explored parts of central Asia and Tibet on foot dressed as lamas. Their labour and achievements were simply remarkable.[51] These interlocutors did not inform 'Western' knowledge with 'Indian' knowledge. Their engagement was basically 'experiential'. There was indeed no dovetailing of 'Western' and 'Indian' scientific paradigms. The *siddantas* were now presented as exercises anticipating modern astronomy rather than stressing their inferiority.[52]

On the whole, India was found suitable only for field research. She was in fact used as a 'vast storehouse' with exotic varieties of flora, fauna, and minerals which were to flood European laboratories for many years to come.

The real research was to be done in the metropolis. India could get only ancillary units. And, this happened in a century when England itself was undergoing a phase of transition wherein professional scientists, the government, and industrialists who understood the full potentialities of science were all attempting the very difficult task of integrating science into the English government, industry, and education. But in India this was not to be so. Here the story was different: Scientific explorations brought the government, science, and economic exploitation into a close relationship.

Here an important question which still begs attention and exploration is: Was this process influenced by non-European epistemologies of nature? Was there little or substantial incorporation of local knowledge in mainstream or metropolitan science? Was the network or web of knowledge largely a one-way process? Did a divide exist between the 'indigenous' and the 'other'? Connections were definitely there. How about borrowings? As a well-meaning surgeon wrote:

> The indigenous system of India has been a cause of disappointment to us not because they are successful rivals of modern medicine, but because we have been able to borrow or steal from them so little that is of real value.[53]

In the numerous accounts of colonial interactions during the 18th and 19th centuries, how many Indians are referred to as 'botanists'? One reference is of Murdan Ali, a munshi at Saharanpur who is described as 'a very intelligent and respectable Syyud, the first of his race who addicted himself to Natural History' and in whose honour Dr Royle established the genus Murdannia.[54] He was said to be preparing a vernacular flora of North India using the natural system but the manuscript in Urdu could not be published for want of support and seems lost. Indians appear mostly as artists and illustrators, and even in this regard carried the blame for any 'imperfections'. Local 'help' was always taken. Illustrations and paintings of exotic flora and fauna were mostly made by local 'collaborators'. In Madras, Rungiah and Govindoo painted numerous plants for their botanist master Wight between 1825 and 1845. Even a microscope was used in 1832 to improve the drawings.[55] There are many examples of early colonial medical men collecting medicinal plants from the neighbouring forests and discussing their virtues with the 'locals' and these were even published in the *Philosophical Transactions*.[56] But the locals remained 'unnamed'. This 'mediation' could never flower.

The story of science policy like most other policy areas in India during the 19th century was essentially an effort by the British rulers for the consolidation of their empire, though incidentally it conferred some benefits on the country. At the same time, the individuals who were involved in implementing the policy had contradictory views. One group always looked upon Western models as the ideal and hence wanted them reproduced in India. The opposite view was that India and the West were not the same and that the imported models should be modified in their application to India. Civilian officials were concerned about traditions and customs, and did not wish to unsettle them (for fear of revolt). But technical men like engineers were not enamoured of such considerations. They were less interested in 'local knowledge and practices'. Their technical discourse was universal. Thorough professionals that they were, their real concern was to ensure the most efficient use of nature in the service of the state.

The motto of the Imperial College of Science and Technology, established in London in 1907, was: 'Scientia Imperii Decuset Tutamen'—'Science is the Pride and Shield of Empire.' This encapsulates the relationship between science and colonization. But a colonial enterprise (and science itself) should not be seen in monolithic terms. Its objectives and machinations might have some kind of uniformity but it elicited variegated responses and produced both desired and undesired results. While dealing with the question of scientific researches, one needs to keep in mind that colonialism was not philanthropy and a colonial government would only go up to a point and not beyond. Theoretical research in science at par with the metropole was not possible until a few absolutely determined and brilliant people emerged at the turn of the century. Yet within the limited opportunities, a great deal was achieved as mentioned above, at least when compared with other non-settler colonies in the world.

Notes

1. 13, no. 327, 22 July 1848.
2. For more details, see chapters 2 and 3 of Deepak Kumar, *Science and the Raj*, 2nd edn (New Delhi: Oxford University Press, 2006); Satpal Sangwan, *Science, Technology and Colonisation: An Indian Experience, 1757–1857* (Delhi: Anamika Prakashan, 1991); and for a far more lucid and informed account, see David Arnold, *Science, Technology and Medicine in Colonial India*, The New Cambridge History of India, Vol. 3.5 (Cambridge: Cambridge University Press, 2000).
3. J. Nowrojee and H. Merwanjee, *Journal of a Residence of Two Years and a Half in Great Britain* (London: Murray, 1841), p. 5.

4. H. H. Risley, Presidential Address, Proceedings of the Asiatic Society of Bengal, 6 January 1904, p. 26.

5. For examples and assessment, see Anna Winterbottom, *Hybrid Knowledge in the Early East India Company World* (Basingstoke: Palgrave Macmillan, 2016); Vinita Damodaran, Anna Winterbottom, and Alan Lester (eds), *The East India Company and the Natural World* (Basingstoke: Palgrave Macmillan, 2014).

6. Robert Kyd, 'Memorandum on Agricultural Productions, Commerce, Population and Manufactures', Calcutta, 1786, Home, Public, nos.13–14, 16 June 1786, National Archives of India (NAI).

7. Grenville Papers, Mss. Eur. E. 309, Box 2, India Office Records (IOR), British Library, London.

8. James Rennell, *Memoir of a Map of Hindustan* (London, 1788), p. 15.

9. S. J. Stephen, *A Meeting of the Minds: European and Tamil Encounters in Modern Sciences, 1507–1857* (Delhi: Primus Books, 2016), p. 762.

10. For details, see Pratik Chakrabarti, *Western Science in Modern India: Metropolitan Methods, Colonial Practices* (Ranikhet: Permanent Black, 2004).

11. For unusual insights, see Richard Grove, *Green Imperialism: Colonial Expansion, Tropical Island Edens and the Origins of Environmentalism, 1600–1860* (Cambridge: Cambridge University Press, 1995). See also Richard Drayton, *Nature's Government: Science, Imperial Britain, and the 'Improvement' of the World* (New Haven: Yale University Press, 2000). The title of this book, 'Nature's Government', is significant. But did 'Nature's Government' condition or change the 'Government's nature'? See also Deepak Kumar, Vinita Damodaran, and Rohan D'Souza (eds), *The British Empire and the Natural World: Environmental Encounters in South Asia* (New Delhi: Oxford University Press, 2010).

12. Londa Schiebinger, *Plants and Empire* (Cambridge, MA: Harvard University Press, 2004), pp. 15, 27.

13. Kapil Raj, *Relocating Modern Science: Circulation and the Construction of Knowledge in South Asia and Europe, 1650–1900* (Ranikhet: Permanent Black, 2006), p. 58; see also Shruti Kapila, 'The Enchantment of Science in India', *Isis* 101, no. 1 (2010): 120–132.

14. Note by T. H. Holland, Revenue Dept., Agriculture Branch, proc. no. 3, August 1905, file 127, NAI (emphasis added).

15. A. Mackenzie Cameron to Lord Elgin, 10 July 1894, Elgin Papers, Microfilm No. 2031, Roll 7, NAI.

16. *Bharat Bandhu*, 12 September 1908, Native Newspaper Reports (NNR), Madras, 1908, p. 96.

17. After the great earthquake of 1897, the GSI promptly conducted a scientific investigation and its findings were published in the *Memoirs of the Geological Survey of India* 27, pt. II (1898): 46–272.

18. See I. H. Burkill, *Chapters on the History of Botany in India* (Delhi: Government Press, 1965).

19. Kumar, *Science and the Raj*, pp. 73–88; Sujaya Sarkar, *The Making of Geology in India, 1767–1856* (Kolkata: Progressive Publishers, 2016). For an interesting and unusual interface between geologists, ethnologists, archaeologists, and so on, see Pratik Chakrabarti, *Inscriptions of Nature: Geology and the Naturalization of Antiquity* (Baltimore: Johns Hopkins University Press, 2020).

20. H. Piddington, *On the Scientific Principles of Agriculture* (Tract for private circulation) (Calcutta, 1839), p. 18.

21. J. A. Voelcker, *Report on the Improvement of Indian Agriculture*, 2nd edn (Calcutta: Government Press, 1897), pp. 306–318. This remarkably honest report still has relevance.

22. 'It was settled in my time, that [the] Director of Agriculture was to be [a] "man of business" unacquainted with agriculture. He was to collect information and statistics to investigate markets and trade routes and complete reports on economic products but he was not to be a man who would tempt [the] Govt. to try agricultural experiments.' C. B. Clarke to I. H. Burkill, 26 March 1903, Letters to Burkill, folio 37, Royal Botanic Garden Archive (Kew Archive).

23. A. K. Bagchi, *The Political Economy of Underdevelopment* (Cambridge: Cambridge University Press, 1982), pp. 83–94.

24. *Amrita Bazar Patrika*, 24 November 1911, NNR, Bengal, 1911, p. 530.

25. The correspondence between the Committee and the Board can be seen at the Archive of the Royal Society, London and also at the Royal Botanical Garden Archive, Kew.

26. Deepak Kumar, *Science and the Raj* (Delhi: Oxford University Press, 1995), p. 111.

27. Kanai Lal Dey (who later chaired the Indigenous Drugs Committee) rued the fact that his son had failed in the entrance examination in history and geography but he had a remarkable taste for scientific subjects and could have passed in a science paper! Note dated 30 March 1875, Richard Temple Papers, Mss. Eur. F86/no. 214, IOR, The British Library.

28. Report of the Board of Education, Bombay, 1850–51, pp. 10–15, Maharashtra State Archive.

29. The *Gujarati Punch* of 11 December 1908 complained, 'While the whole country is ringing with the cry of more science in schools and colleges …

the Gujarat College Board has come to the curious and anachronistic decision that science should not be taught to BA student!' Native Newspapers Reports, Bombay, December 1908, p. 340.

30. Aparna Basu, *Essays in the History of Indian Education* (New Delhi: Oxford University Press, 1982), p. 40.

31. *The Athenaeum* no. 2019, 7 July 1866, p. 21.

32. Revenue Agriculture, Surveys, Prog. Nos. 25–33, September 1880, K.W., NAI.

33. Ibid., Prog. No. 25, September 1880, Pt. A.

34. For details on agricultural problems, see Prakash Kumar, *Indigo Plantations and Science in Colonial India* (Cambridge: Cambridge University Press, 2012); Smritikumar Sarkar, *Technology and Rural Change in Eastern India, 1830–1980* (New Delhi: Oxford University Press, 2014); Deepak Kumar and Bipasha Raha (eds), *Tilling the Land: Agricultural Knowledge and Practices* (Delhi: Primus Books, 2016).

35. *The Swadeshmitran*, 3 April 1905, Native Newspapers Reports, Madras, 1905. Another newspaper caustically remarked:

> The Pusa Institute is in the mountains, and the essays and the diagrams in the Agricultural Journal are mere hieroglyphics to the cultivators.

The Mahratta (English weekly from Poona), 1 December 1907, NNR, Bombay, 1907, p. 1722.

36. For a comprehensive discussion, see Roy MacLeod and Deepak Kumar (eds), *Technology and the Raj* (New Delhi: Sage, 1998); Tirthankar Roy, *The Economic History of India, 1857–1947*, 3rd edn (New Delhi: Oxford University Press, 2011).

37. For specific studies on the telegraph and the railways, see Deep Kanta Lahiri Choudhury, *Telegraphic Imperialism: Crisis and Panic in the Indian Empire, c. 1830–1920* (Basingstoke: Palgrave Macmillan, 2010); Michael Mann, *Wiring the Nation: Telecommunication, Newspaper-reportage, and Nation Building in British India, 1850–1930* (New Delhi: Oxford University Press, 2017); Ian J. Kerr, *Building the Railways of the Raj 1850–1900* (New Delhi: Oxford University Press, 1995).

38. Yet thousands of temporary workhands acquired new rudimentary technical skills from their experience of plate-laying, tunnelling, and bridgebuilding, and when the work was over, they were to prove of great value to the private engineering and bazaar industry. Ian Derbyshire, 'The Building of India's Railways', in Technology and the Raj, ed. Roy MacLeod and Deepak Kumar (New Delhi: Sage, 1998), pp. 193–277.

39. For an exciting study based on Indian language sources, see Aparajita Mukhopadhyay, *Imperial Technology and 'Native' Agency: A Social History of Railways in Colonial India 1850–1920* (London: Routledge, 2018), pp. 164–186. See also Ritika Prasad, *Tracks of Change: Railways and Everyday Life in Colonial India* (New Delhi: Cambridge University Press, 2015).

40. For details, see Suvobrata Sarkar, *Let There be Light: Engineering, Entrepreneurship and Electricity in Colonial Bengal, 1880–1945* (Cambridge: Cambridge University Press, 2020).

41. For a focused study on techno-scientific education, see S. N. Sen, *Scientific and Technical Education in India* (New Delhi: Indian National Science Academy, 1991); Suvobrata Sarkar, *The Quest for Technical Knowledge: Bengal in the Nineteenth Century* (New Delhi: Manohar, 2012).

42. P. N. Bose, *A History of Hindu Civilisation During British Rule*, Vol. III (Calcutta: Newman & Co., 1896), p. 98.

43. *Bengalee*, 25 March 1910, NNR, Bengal, no. 14 of 1910, p. 162.

44. For a lucid account of such technologies, see David Arnold, *Everyday Technology* (Chicago: University of Chicago Press, 2013). For rural technologies, see Sarkar, *Technology and Rural Change in Eastern India*.

45. Sarkar, *Let There Be Light*, pp. 203–231.

46. Ibid., pp. 166–172.

47. *The Swadeshmitran*, 13 February 1908, NNR, Madras, 1908, p. 98. Even after a century, this comment retains its relevance!

48. Revenue, Agriculture, nos. 18–19, February 1894, File 37, NAI.

49. Stephen, *A Meeting of the Minds*, pp. 761–767.

50. P. N. Bose (ed.), *Centenary Review of the Asiatic Society* (Calcutta: 1884), p. 101.

51. Brig. G. F. Heany Papers, Box V, Centre for South Asian Studies (CSAS), Cambridge; see also Shekhar Pathak, *Daastane-i-Himalaya* (in Hindi), Vol. I (Allahabad: Vaani Prakashan, 2021), Chapter 3.

52. For specific examples, see Joydeep Sen, *Astronomy in India, 1784–1876* (Pittsburgh: University of Pittsburgh Press, 2020), chapters 2 and 5.

53. J. W. D. Megaw, 'Confidential Note on the Working of the Panjab Medical Deptt.', 6 September 1928, India Health Department (IHD), 1.1, 464, India, Box 5, f.34, Rockefeller Archive Center (RAC), New York.

54. Cited in David Arnold, *The Tropics and the Travelling Gaze: India, Landscape, and Science 1800–1856* (Delhi: Permanent Black, 2005), p. 183.

55. Stephen, *A Meeting of the Minds*, p. 839. For a comprehensive account, see Henry Noltie, *Robert Wight and the Botanical Drawings of Rungiah and Govindoo* (Edinburgh: Royal Botanical Garden, 2007).

56. Pratik Chakrabarti, 'Medicine Amidst War and Commerce in Eighteenth Century Madras', *Bulletin of History of Medicine* 80 (2006): 1–38.

3

Lost in Religion and Translation

The time is now arrived, when every nation must either rise in the scale of civilization, or sink in the depths of contempt and misery. Prosperity in this age appears to be a term synonymous with civilization and the cultivation of the arts and sciences. Indeed, in every age they have been so more or less, but in the present their dependence on one another is too palpable to be overlooked by the most superficial observers. Let us only consider the pre-eminence to which England has arrived by the diffusion of knowledge among her inhabitants. Her astonishing machineries which have multiplied her means of acquiring wealth to an inconceivable degree, owe their origin to the cultivation of the arts and sciences. Is it not owing to the power which knowledge has given to the people of so small and so distant a country as England, that they have been enabled to conquer and keep possession of these vast territories far more congenial to the prosperity of the human race than the sterile soil of England? Why is it thought the most extravagant dream to impose that India should ever conquer England?

—*The Bombay Durpan*[1]

In Chapter 1 we have seen that pre-colonial India was no *tabula rasa*. It had a vigorous tradition at least in the realms of mathematics, astronomy, and medicine. But gradual colonization made a big dent. It brought forth a massive cultural collision which influenced profoundly the cognitive and material existence of both the colonizer and the colonized. This encounter was initially disturbing, even agonizing. Gradually, relations stabilized and the colonized recipients started examining what was living and what was dead in their system, and, under the new circumstances, what to accept and what not. A new stage was thus set at the end of the 18th century.

One Mirza Abu Talib visited England at the turn of the century, and wrote glowingly about the literary societies, theatres, mills, iron foundries, and the hydraulic machines that he saw there. Two Parsee visitors, Jahangir Nowrojee and Hirjeebhoy Merwanjee, devoted a full chapter to 'scientific institutions' in their travelogue.[2] The signs of wonder that Abu Talib or the Parsee cousins showed were not only spontaneous but also logical and natural. It was no slavish admiration because they did criticize certain elements of the social conduct and cultural values of the new masters. For a person raised in late-18th century India, social life in England appeared too different and unpalatable. In the same way, the European travellers who visited pre-Victorian India felt that Indian customs, their caste system, and their treatment of women were simply abhorrent. Both looked with amazement at each other. Both found the other exotic and largely not worthy of emulation.

When the British came, they were surprised by the elite Indian's knowledge capabilities and also shocked at their deficiencies. As a Victorian administrator wrote, 'We are not cleverer than the Hindu; our minds are not richer or larger than his'.[3] The early colonizers in India realized that they had to tread cautiously. In order to legitimize their own rule, they first had to delegitimize several pre-colonial structures and texts. For this, the condemnation of the immediate past was considered necessary. Indians were declared unscientific, superstitious, and resistant to change; India was 'identified with dirt and disease'. Travellers, scholars, and officials of both the Orientalist and Anglicist variety subscribed to this view. William Jones, the foremost Orientalist, declared that in scientific accomplishments, the Asiatics were 'mere children' when compared with the Europeans. Thus was established a paternalistic Raj that would be caring and dismissive at the same time. This sense of superiority came from the Western discourse on rationality and progress, and was promptly used to denounce whatever scientific knowledge, for example in astronomy and medicine, Indians could boast of.

Yet this denunciation was not total. Several early colonial scholars showed respect for certain indigenous scientific traditions and techniques. They wanted Western knowledge to permeate slowly and cause gradual displacement. The instance of L. Wilkinson, a British agent at Rewa, is simply exemplary. He encouraged established *jyotishcharya*s like Shubhaji Bapu (author of the *Siddhanta Shiromani Prakasa*) and Onkar Bhatt (author of *Bhugolsar*) to learn and appreciate European advances in astronomy. Bapu in turn trained a mathematical prodigy Sudhakar Dwivedi, who later wrote commentaries on the *Lilavati* and *Brahmasphuta Siddhanta* and also composed many original texts trying an assimilation of the old *siddhanta*s with modern knowledge.[4] They all justified Wilkinson's conviction that Bhaskar's *siddhanta* affords 'beyond all comparison the best means of promoting the cause of education, civilization, and truth amongst our Hindu subjects'.

Pure and unadulterated truth not only cannot be communicated with equal
facility, but is absolutely rejected by the mass of the Hindu population of
India … with the aid of the authority of the Sidddhantas, the work of general
and extensive enlightenment may be commenced upon at once, and will be
most readily effected, the truths taught by them being received with avidity.
To explain and correct their errors will at the same time be easy … How
readily may a knowledge of the science, as taught in the Siddhantas, be
recommunicated … to the Joshis [astrologer in rural centres] … They will
not stop in simply admitting what is taught in the Siddhantas. Grateful to
their European instructors for bringing them back to a knowledge of the
works of their own neglected, but still revered masters, they will in the fullness
of their gratitude, and from the exercise of their now improved powers of
understanding, also readily receive the additions made during the last few
hundred years in the science … What can be more flattering to the vanity of
the Hindu nation … than to see their own great and revered masters quoted
by us with respect, to prove and illustrate the truths we propound … Till
conviction of the truth of the Siddhantic system as to the size and shape of
the earth, is felt, the popular absurdities of the Puranic cosmogony will never
be abandoned.[5]

The New Interlocutors

An important section of Indians was quick to recognize the changes and new
opportunities. Ram Mohan Roy (1772–1833) stands tallest among them.
A remarkable polyglot, he had learnt classical languages and could cite from
the Vedas, the Quran, and the Bible with almost equal felicity. He believed
in the universality of truth but also recognized that its understanding was
conditioned by both time and place. He supported the Western concept of
reasoning and scientific thought, and tried to apply it in the Indian context.
In 1822, in his famous letter to Lord Amherst, he asked for teaching in
European sciences and arts. Unlike his Chinese contemporaries, Roy did not
call it 'new' knowledge but this is what he probably meant. He rather associated
it with a cultural–geographical area called the West. Western Europe was
definitely offering something new and different. Ishwar Chandra Vidyasagar
(1820–1891), another admirer of Western knowledge, wanted Indian students
to also study their own 'false system' in his Sanskrit College in Calcutta.
He wanted his students to learn different perspectives and then judge on their
own what appealed to them most. Ram Mohan Roy and Vidyasagar never
abandoned their ancient religion and inheritance; rather they emphasized those
aspects that were compatible with the tenets of the new scientific thinking. Both
were modernizers without losing their roots. In 1849, Vidyasagar published a

book in Bengali (*Jeebuncharita*) on the lives of Nicolaus Copernicus, Galileo Galilei, Sir Isaac Newton, William Herschel, Carolus Linnaeus, William Jones, and others. He wanted children to emulate the founders of modern science—the astronomers and mathematicians.

A great contemporary and friend of Vidyasagar was Akshay Kumar Datta (1820–1886). An exceptionally remarkable communicator and thinker, Datta tried to find an organic unity between science, society, and religion. Bal Gangadhar Shastri Jambhekar (1802–1846), who taught mathematics at Elphinstone College, Bombay, commenced his science popularization activities in both Marathi and English, and Master Ramchandra (1821–1880) who taught at the Delhi College began his mathematical researches from a 12th-century Indian text, Bhaskar's *Bij-Ganita*. All these early interlocutors exemplify a cross-cultural mentality and an exceptionally creative encounter. They were preparing the soil for cross-fertilization, and the seed they wanted to sow was a cross-breed.

Ram Mohan Roy and Vidyasagar were great social reformers. They worked for the abolition of *sati* (widow burning) and for widow remarriage, respectively. Unlike them, Bal Gangadhar Shastri Jambhekar and Master Ramchandra concentrated on mathematics teaching and science popularization. Jambhekar was the first Indian to become a professor of mathematics and astronomy. He taught at Elphinstone College, Bombay, and among his early pupils was Dadabhai Naoroji, the doyen of Indian nationalism. Jhambhekar worked for science learning through the local Marathi language. In 1836, he published the Marathi translation of a well-known English work on Mathematical Geography, to which he added an 'Essay on the System of Bhaskarcharya'. In 1842, he published in Marathi two books on the theory of equations, and differential and integral calculus. Jambhekar had translated the nosology of Madhav and anatomy of Susrut into English and advocated the dissemination of new medical knowledge through the means of local language. He wanted the native *vaidya*s to be taught Western medical and surgical practices as well. A little later, in Delhi, Master Ramachandra tried to revive the Indian spirit of algebra so as to resuscitate 'the native disposition'. Bhaskar was common to both Jambhekar and Ramchandra. To begin with one's own heritage was quite natural.

Indeed, this was the strategy advocated by the Orientalists as well. L. Wilkinson, British Resident and an astronomer at the court of Rewa, as mentioned earlier, found Bhaskara's works 'beyond all comparison, the best means of promoting the cause of education, civilization, and truth amongst our Hindu subjects'. Ramchandra, however, moved ahead and incorporated the post-Bhaskara 'advances' in his *Treatise on the Problems of Maxima and Minima*, published in 1850. His idea was to bridge the gap. But these efforts were aborted. An alien government, confident of its epistemic superiority (especially after Macaulay), would not allow the transplantation of modern science on an indigenous base. It seems that Master Ramachandra favoured English and at the same time wanted Western books to be translated into Urdu. He knew that English being a foreign language could never be fully adopted in India. He wrote articles like 'Galileo Sahib ka Hal' and 'Hal-i-Sir William Herschel' which were published in his Urdu journals *Fawaid-ul-Nazarin and Mohabb-e-Hind* between 1845 and 1855. He also authored 9 articles on medicine (*tibbiat*), and a few articles on *panchakki* (waterwheel), *risala-i-paimaish* (compass), and *ilm-i-tabai* (physics). In all, he published around 84 articles on different scientific topics aimed at popularizing science.[6]

Akshay Kumar Datta was unique as a communicator. He edited a famous monthly, *Tattwabodhini Patrika* and gradually introduced scientific curios in this magazine.[7] In 1855, he started a separate column, 'Vigyanvarta' (scientific news), compiled from leading international journals. The following year he published a monograph on matter titled *Padarth Vidya*. He wrote popular articles on geography, astronomy, geology, chemistry, and so on. Unlike his many illustrious contemporaries, he was probably more interested in the *brahmanda* (creation) than in Brahma (the Creator). He claimed, 'The entire universe is our religious scripture (*akhil samsar-i amader dharmasastra*). Pure knowledge is our teacher.' Datta even asked for translation of philosophers and scientists like Francis Bacon, John Locke, Sir Isaac Newton, and Pierre-Simon Laplace into Indian languages. He submitted a comprehensive scheme of education, free and compulsory, for the age group 4–14 (something which even free India has not been able to achieve!), and higher education including technical education in agriculture and industry for the age group 15–21. This was absolutely remarkable for the time in which he lived. Datta was not only a syncretist but much ahead of his time in many ways. No wonder his contemporaries hailed him as 'a sentinel of new knowledge'. But sometimes he was ridiculed as an atheist. Around the same time, a remarkable couple in Poona, Savitri Bai and Jyotiba Phule were questioning the *varnashram dharma* incisively. They had formed the Satyashodhak Samaj in 1873, and their emphasis on reason and truth in an utterly orthodox society was truly revolutionary.

Another multifaceted scholar was Rajendralal Mitra (1823–1891). Initially, he studied medicine but could not complete his course at the Calcutta

Medical College. He had innate linguistic skills and gradually mastered several classical languages. This made him the foremost Indologist of his time. But he never lost interest in the sciences. He edited two pictorial scientific periodicals, *Vividartha Samgraha* (1851–1859) and *Rahasya Sandarbha* (1863–1868), for which he wrote several articles relevant to courses in geography, geology, botany, and chemistry. Despite his love for Bengali, he was convinced that science education had to be delivered through the English medium, and 'for centuries to come, no vernacular substitute will supply its place'. He evinced interest in telegraph and photography, then cutting-edge technologies, and even devised a way to send telegraphic messages in Bengali. He prepared several atlases and pioneered thematic map-making (like physical, cultural, linguistic, and agricultural maps).

An extraordinary student of Calcutta Medical College, and one of the early Indians to talk in terms of sanitation, education, and public health, was S. Goodeve Chuckerbutty (1826–1874).[8] He was among the first four Indian medical graduates sent to England for higher studies in 1845. He was the first Indian to obtain an MD degree, and to join the coveted Indian Medical Service (IMS). On 8 January 1852, he gave a public lecture on the 'Sanitary Improvement of Calcutta' and dwelt upon the need for better sanitary habits, water pipelines, sewage, water tank management, and so on. He asked for strict legislation to stop adulteration in food items (how relevant even today in view of adulterated milk, spices, and anything edible!). He also talked about education, especially female education, and asked students to question their teachers and even parents. Later he spoke and wrote against the Revolt of 1857, dubbed it feudal, and called it 'a fight of ignorance and superstition against light'.[9] In such opinion he was not alone. The local intelligentsia did not support the Revolt of 1857, an uprising which many decades later came to be hailed as the First War of Independence.

The great poet Mirza Ghalib (1797–1869), who lived in Delhi, the epicentre of the Revolt, did not support the mutineers. After a visit to Calcutta in 1828, he sang *hosanna*s in praise of the power of steam, the new tools, and the new knowledge the British had brought. In 1855, when Sir Syed Ahmad Khan (1817–1898), a Muslim educationist and reformer, requested Ghalib to write a foreword for his edition of the *Ain-i-Akbari*, the poet admonished him in verse:

For such a task, of which this book is the basis, Only a hypocrite can offer praise …
Look at the Sahibs of England. Look at the style and practice of these,

See what Laws and Rules they have made for all to see. What none ever saw, they have produced ...
What spell have they struck on water. That a vapour drives the boat in water!
Sometimes the vapour takes the boat down the sea. Sometimes the vapour brings down the sky to the plains.
Vapour makes the sky-wheel go round and round. Vapour is now like bullocks, or horses.
Vapour makes the ship speed. Making wind and wave redundant.
Their instruments make music without the bow. They make words fly high like birds:
Oh, don't you see that these wise people Get news from thousands of miles in a couple of breaths?[10]

The would-be reformer probably did not contact the poet again!

Between 1860 and 1880, a number of cultural essayists tried to articulate modern scientific rationality in terms of indigenous traditions and requirements. Bankim Chandra Chatterjee (1838–1894), a Bengali novelist of high intellect and repute, for instance, wrote on *vijnan rahasya* (secrets of science), which appeared in *Banga Darshan* between 1865 and 1870. There are a number of direct references to Auguste Comte in his literary as well as discursive writings (for example, *Debi Chaudhurani* [1884] *and Dharmatatva* [1888]). Bankim urged Hindus to look to the West for knowledge about the phenomenal world in the physical sciences, and for knowledge about themselves in biology and sociology. His close friend Rajkrishna Mukherjee (1845–1886) regarded science as the key to man's emancipation from the forces of nature and was anxious to promote any doctrine which he thought might teach Hindus about science.[11] It was more a fear of Westernization than a fear of science that sometimes led Bankim Chandra to return to certain ancient theological concepts. In 1873, he rejected the Hindu concept of the Trinity as an aberration, but in 1875 he found Dasavatara close to Darwin's theory of natural selection. Hindu spiritualism finally sucked up many who ventured to travel outside its orbit. Islamic progressives faced a similar situation and fared worse. In 1877, one Maulavi Ubaidullah wrote:

The Mahomedans with their philosophy are exactly in the position of the school men of Europe, that is they have travelled half way towards actual civilization: consequently, when the modern reformed philosophy of Europe once gains an entrance to their minds, they will be able to make more rapid progress than their neighbour Hindoos. Among us a Newtonized Avicenna or a Copernicized Averroes may spring up, who may be able to criticise even sons of Sina and Rushd.[12]

The lure of inching towards 'actual civilization' and the hope of producing 'a Newtonized Avicenna or a Copernicized Averroes' present a curious mix of both self-criticism and a yearning for change (and also a hope, perhaps yet to be realized). They were all culturally rooted but they had the rational will to modernize, industrialize, and face the West without falling on their knees.[13]

The theme of the identity of the colonized on its own terms (that is, away from what the colonizers thought or dictated) also contained the seeds of decolonization. An imperial rationalist discourse showed Indians how rationalism could be turned against the Europeans themselves. Rationalism was seen as something inherent in human nature rather than a European 'patent' and as a mark of progress independent from Europeanization. Gradually colonialism came to be viewed as a cultural invasion of space, to be ended, neutralized, and rolled back.

Did the Indian elite, by presenting Europe and its ideas as a distinct and definable entity, contribute to the emergence of a belief which held India as 'somehow inferior'? Perhaps not. They did not see Europe as Asia's other. They neither emphasized nor de-emphasized the shared inheritance of mankind. They left these questions open. Admiration for the West was at no point unqualified. But they did accept what struck them as rational and useful. For example, Ram Mohan Roy talked of Europe's mastery over 'useful sciences' while Indian knowledge systems were conditioned by pre-Baconian medieval scholasticism; Jambhekar wrote in a similar language. He added useful arts, connected with the 'common purposes of life'.

Reason and Religion

Religion, of course, appears as a major obsession in almost every type of encounter—political, social, or cultural. When a Scientific Society was established in Bihar, its principal objective was

> that the inhabitants of India might learn the Western Sciences together with those of their Religion with ease and facility. It has been found by experience that in those who acquire Western Science by means of their country tongue, the effect of learning is deep and lasting and also others who live in their company acquire some information from them and therefore the benefits of knowledge can be readily spread and again when English is taught like a classical knowledge, higher sciences in English can also be acquired easily … There are 9 schools attached to the Society which impart education to hundreds of students of Mohammedan and Hindu creeds in the European sciences.[14]

But the society could produce only pleaders—no scientists!
Probably the best example of those who tried to synthesize reason with religion was Sir Syed Ahmad Khan. He wrote:

> The Qur'an does not prove that the earth is stationary, nor does it prove that the earth is in motion. Similarly, it cannot be proved from the Qur'an that the sun is stationary. The Holy Qur'an was not concerned with these problems of astronomy ... the real purpose of a religion is to improve morality.[15]

Here is the crux of Syed Ahmad's belief: 'the real purpose of a religion is to improve morality'. Let scientific truths be established by observation and experiment, he says, and not by 'attempting to interpret a religious text as a book of science'. This articulation was very significant. It defended new knowledge from obscurantist attacks in the name of religion and tradition, and at the same time protected indigenous culture and beliefs from colonial and evangelical onslaught. He even wrote a book on the life of the Prophet. Sir Syed's associate, Munshi Zakaullah (1832–1910) was even more emphatic. He wrote, 'God has given human beings the ability called reason to discover and comprehend the real world, and the application of this ability by human beings leads to the creation of knowledge'. To drive home the point he added, 'reason is to knowledge what sun is to light and eye to vision'.

Another important contemporary, Jamaluddin Afghani did not see any disjunction between Islam and science. He rather blamed the *mullah*s and *maulvi*s who were filled with superstition and vanity. To him the *ulema* represented a very narrow wick topped by a very small flame that neither lights its surroundings nor gives light to others. However, this does not mean that he accepted new researches emanating from the West.[16] While in India in 1881, Afghani wrote *Al-Raad al Dahriyyin* (The Refutation of Materialists to Counter the Spread of Naturalism, that is, *naychariyya*). He presented his opposition to Lamarckism and probably Darwinism in a simplistic way. He argued 'it would be possible that often in the passage of centuries a mosquito (*barghuth*) could become an elephant and an elephant, by degrees, a mosquito'. He cited the illustration of how the continuous cutting of a dog's tail for several centuries would produce a new generation of dogs without tails, and he related this to the Semitic practice of circumcision: 'Arabs and Jews have for several thousand years practiced circumcision, and despite this until now, not one of them has been born circumcised'![17]

When an oriental faculty was proposed in 1885 for Allahabad University, a petition drafted by Sir Syed was submitted. It enquired:

we wish to know what benefit will the University confer on the public and eastern sciences by establishing an oriental faculty, or to what use will it turn the eastern sciences and arts at the present day. We believe that an oriental faculty can do no good—secure no advantage to the public. It will only waste the time of those who may unfortunately fall into its snare—it may further be of use in helping *to fasten the hood of ignorance* tighter round our eyes or to precipitate our fall who stand dangerously on the brink of the abyss of darkness and ignorance.

To prove our statement conclusively we shall enumerate the various branches of oriental learning and try to discover [to] which branch or branches does the University of Allahabad propose to particularly direct its attention.

Is it to be astrology?—a science that teaches us the good or bad influence of the stars: informs us of the auspicious or inauspicious hours. Certainly, its cultivation will give prescience to the Government and enable it to manage the affairs of the country much better; while the people, knowing previously their own destiny, shall feel contented, and instead of grumbling at the conduct of the Government, they shall have to complain of their own ill fate.

Or is it to be astronomy? No doubt, if such be the case, the object is to revive the old Greek speculations on astronomy. And we shall see in our colleges the doctrine of [the] Ptolemic system taught over again, and find the illustrious names of Newton, Copernicus, and Kepler banished from the country forever. [18]

Perceptions no doubt were changing fast. Earlier Hindu social reformers have been referred to. By the mid-19th century, Indians exposed to modern medical knowledge and Christianity became assertive. S. C. G. Chuckerbutty, the first Indian to compete for and join the coveted Indian Medical Service, wrote,

[The Brahmanical system] may be a very praiseworthy exercise of self-denial but the philosophy it inculcates is a verbose and distorted philosophy, which consumes itself in its study and leads to no practical results … The Mahomedan system of education though hampered by no distinctions of caste, is nevertheless as defective as the Hindu. In this school lads are made to learn by rote voluminous compositions and these are mostly books of fable or of a dreamy morbid philosophy.[19]

Another doctor, Mahendralal Sircar (1833–1904), who had established the Indian Association for the Cultivation of Science (IACS) in 1876, criticized the Hindu ethos as 'a chaotic mass of crude and undigested and unfounded opinions on all subjects, enunciated and enforced in the most dogmatic way imaginable' and this, he thought, could be remedied only by 'the training which results from the investigation of natural phenomena'. In the mid-1880s, he treated a popular spiritual saint of his time Sri Ramakrishna for cancer. They discussed *jnana* and *vijnana* (knowledge and science), *para* and *apara* (sacred and profane) several times. The saint made it clear that his concepts were related to God and God alone and were different from the doctor's notions of knowledge and science. Sircar, though a believer, would never accept that *apara vidya* was inferior. He would retort,

> What is *para* and *apara* with regard to knowledge? What is higher or lower with revelation of truth? One will have to attain *para* through the *apara*. We can comprehend God, the primeval cause of the universe, more clearly through the truths we know directly from the study of the natural sciences.[20]

On one occasion when Sri Ramakrishna was explaining God with form and God the formless in terms of imagery—that is, the cooling influence of *bhakti* (faith) freezing part of the ocean of consciousness into ice of a definite shape, and the heat of *jnana* (knowledge) melting away the form of ice into formless Brahman (ultimate reality)—Mahendralal was impressed by the scientific part of the imagery and commented: 'Yes. When the sun (of knowledge) is up, the ice melts; and what is more, the heat of the sun turns the water into invisible vapour'.

Ramakrishna's famous disciple Swami Vivekananda stressed the need for modern science in India. He also tried to synthesize, 'It is not that secular and spiritual knowledge are two opposite and contradictory things … they are the same knowledge in its different stages of gradual development'.[21] He accepted the superiority of Western science and technology and wanted to reciprocate with higher religious and spiritual insights. So, the formula was, 'spirit' from the East and 'technology' from the West. But this was not acceptable to many others led by Dayanand and his Arya Samaj. They would claim India as the original homeland for both modern science and modern technology. Only the roots were forgotten and had to be rediscovered. Swami Dayanand tried to demonstrate that certain elements of modern science and technology could be found in the Vedas. For example, from the Vedic references to *taravidya*, *nauvimanavidya*, and *akarsana*, he deduced that the Vedic people knew about telecommunications, the construction of ships and aircraft, and also about gravitational attraction. Even in the 21st century there are many who believe in these claims. But the Arya Samajists vehemently opposed the Pauranic lore and Brahamnical *karmakand*. Lala Har Dayal wrote:

... a little science confers more happiness on mankind than all the piety of the middle ages ... Do not follow the old footsteps of the rishis. Benaras and Puri had their day. What is there in Benaras but fat bulls and fat priests? What is there in Puri but Cholera?[22]

Meghnad Saha (1893–1956), a pioneer astrophysicist, ridiculed the Hindu propensity to attribute all knowledge to the ancient Vedas—*sabai vede aache* (everything is in the Vedas). He was opposed to religion, not morality. A very caustic debate, unlike Ramakrishna and Mahendralal's jovial arguments, took place between Meghnad Saha and Anilbaran Ray (1890–1974). The latter argued:

M. N. Saha's opinions are not based on any original research; they are merely echoes of clichés uttered by ignorant and prejudiced western critics ... in order to understand the strength and effectiveness of Hindu religion and philosophy, one has to go back to the golden age of Hindu glory and prosperity, not to judge them by their present degraded standard. To evaluate a mango tree, one must take the best fruits, not the rotten ones.[23]

To this, Saha replied:

If the basic idea of the Western theory of evolution is contained in the Hindu theory of reincarnation or transmigration of souls, then poor Darwin loses all his claims to originality ... Aryabhatta (b.476) talked of the earth's rotation but he believed it to be the centre of the solar system. He might be called India's Copernicus but India most certainly did not produce any Kepler, Galileo or Newton.[24]

Yet there were exceptional men of genius who began with tradition, remained in tradition, and still transcended it. Srinivasa Ramanujan (1887–1920), for example, was an orthodox Brahmin but an unorthodox mathematician. Worshipping goddess Namagiri, Ramanujan remained all his life within his indigenous non-scientific tradition. But this regulated his personal life and behaviour, not his mathematics. As Edward Shils argues, 'a powerful mind is not bound entirely by its scientific tradition; nor is it entirely bound by the non-scientific traditions of the society in which it has grown up'.[25]

Any debate on reason and religion in the context of modern India must take into account the magnetic pull of tradition. In a subtle way, the colonizers themselves promoted this by heaping occasional praises on 'the spirit of the East', 'the Hindu Technology of Contemplation', and so on. Indians were shown as a superior civilization in spiritual matters. This was some, though poor, compensation for the loss of sovereignty. Indians themselves seemed to enjoy this distinction and it seems that Max Muller was discussed more than Charles Darwin. The positivists and the Brahmos emphasized the importance of reason and observation, though their reason was not without God and was mixed with a heavy dose of moral and spiritual teaching. In any case, modern science was not seen as an alien import. Darwinism, for instance, was imported readily and the theological issues at its heart did not cause ripples in India.

Islamic scholars also tried to show the origin of most, if not all, contemporary sciences in the Holy Qur'an. They were motivated by a wish to demonstrate compatibility (*muwafaqa*) between the Qur'an and modern Western science.[26] The new paradigms in science were quickly accepted and numerous popular articles traced the seeds of modern advancement in ancient texts. This was true of both the Hindus and the Muslims; all new concepts and new tools were to be seen in embryonic form in the holy books.

The Era of Translation

With classical languages like Sanskrit and Persian so well-entrenched in the indigenous education system, and several local languages and dialects, the question of the medium of instruction and the desirability of translations from English (the language of the new rulers) was bound to come up. Both the rulers and the local elite discussed it during the 1820s, but it raged during the early 1830s. This came to be known as the Anglicist–Orientalist controversy. There were several well-meaning British officials who thought Indian languages would be able to assimilate new knowledge and it will gradually filter down to all sections of society. In science and medical education, the problem was to find appropriate equivalents. John Tytler of the Native Medical Institution, for example, tried to prepare Arabic translations of a few European books. To translate one technical word of English, he meticulously searched Arabic lexicons, only to find that its counterpart did not exist. He concluded that translations were unprofitable and that it would consume years and years. He acknowledged that the Indian system though medieval and mostly archaic, did contain grains of truth also. But then in view of the insurmountable difficulties in translation, he agreed to throw the baby out with the bathwater.

This is exactly what the Anglicists were asking for, and Macaulay's Minute of 1835 stamped the supremacy of English in India, which continues even now. A modern medical college was established the same year in Calcutta. The 'Young Bengal' welcomed it with open arms. In other parts of India also, there was a craze for English education from the very beginning despite some British governors like Elphinstone championing the cause of Marathi.

In 1833, he had opened a medical school in Bombay in Marathi medium but it lasted for only six years.

This, however, did not mean that the vernaculars had no future. The missionaries continued to print in local languages. This is how they could enlarge their catchment area. Moreover, there were schoolbook societies in Calcutta, Agra, Bombay, and elsewhere which published books on geography, astronomy, algebra, sanitation, health, chemistry, and so on. In 1833, the young Derozians brought out a bilingual monthly called *Bignan Sar Sangraha* to spread scientific knowledge. Bal Gangadhar Shastri Jambhekar and Hari Keshav Pathare were doing the same in Marathi, writing tracts on chemistry and general science. Shubhaji Bapu wrote in Hindi on algebra and trigonometry while Onkar Bhatt was exposing Pauranic myths. A very popular book *Bhugolsar*, written in the teacher–taught dialogue style, was published by the Agra School Book Society in 1841. Herein the student enquires, 'How could the Great Vyasa be wrong when he wrote that the oceans are made of nectar and butter-milk?' The teacher replies, 'What Vyasa Muni was doing was in praise of God, he was not doing *Vigyan* [science]!'

An interesting dimension of these 'early stirrings' was that interlocutors like Jambhekar, Akshay Kumar Datta, and Ramchandra took to science popularization through their respective chapters of the Native Education Society, and published popular journals (the *Bombay Durpan* in English and Marathi, *Tattwabodhini Patrika* in Bengali, and *Mohabb-e-Hind*, in Urdu, respectively). They were avid translation enthusiasts. There were others who were trying to find, even coin, appropriate terms to facilitate proper translation. For example, Vidyasagar coined the Bengali or Indian equivalents of 74 technical terms, many of which survive even today. These include: *aviskriya* (discovery), *udvidvidya* (botany), *kusamskar* (prejudice), *kendra* (centre), *gavesana* (research), *grahaniharika* (planetary nebulae), *chhayapath* (milky way), *jyotirvidya* (astronomy), *durabiksan* (telescope), *dhatuvidya* (mineralogy, metallurgy), *visubarekha* (equator), *padarthavidya* (natural philosophy, physics), *paripreksita* (perspective), and so on. Ballantyne, who headed the Sanskrit College in Banaras, argued in favour of 'properly constructed Sanskrit terms'. Basalt he called *krishna-prastara* (that is, black rock) and iodine *aruna* (named after the colour of its vapour). In Bengal, Bhudev Mukhopadhyaya taught various scientific subjects such as zoology, optics, algebra, geometry, trigonometry, and so on, at Hooghly Normal school till 1856. He converted his class notes into the two-volume *Prakrtik Vijnan*. Years later, in Western India, B. P. Modak also advocated Sanskritized terms. But he did not hesitate to use even Pali or Persian words and retained English terms whenever he could not coin Marathi equivalents.[27] He used the word 'Shrishti Shastra' for physics instead of the popular word 'Siddha Padartha Vijnyan'. At Banaras, Sudhakar Dwivedi, a great Sanskritist himself, promoted popular Hindi.

In 1864, Sir Syed Ahmad Khan founded the Aligarh Scientific Society with prominent landholders as members. This society started a journal, organized popular lectures, and published books in Urdu on algebra, trigonometry, farming, sanitation, and so on. Its efforts did succeed in creating some awareness and inspired the establishment of the Bihar Scientific Society four years later. This society started schools in Muzaffarpur, Gaya, and Chapra; organized annual meetings; and published in Urdu a bi-monthly *Akhbar-ul-Akhyar*. These were very sincere attempts at science popularization, that too, without any official support. But they had certain inherent limitations. The grip of the *ulema*s and *moulvi*s was far stronger on the native mind.

In a meeting organized on 12 November 1867 by the Delhi Education Society on 'Learning European Knowledge Through Translations', an anonymous English priest argued that no society had gained knowledge through translations to which Ramachandra replied that Europe was enriched through translations as the centres of science had shifted from the Greeks to the Muslims. What Ramchandra probably did not realize then was that the translations in the Arab and the Mediterranean culture area were accompanied and often preceded by original research. Subsequent years were to prove the priest more correct, as the translation activities of Master Ramchandra and his more illustrious contemporary Sir Syed Ahmad Khan (and the Aligarh Scientific Society) were to end on a feeble note. As another great contemporary, Rajendralal Mitra, had also noted, 'I have the profoundest conviction that if the European Sciences are to be thoroughly studied, it should be through the medium of English, and for centuries to come, no vernacular substitute will supply its place.'[28] He was prophetic and had probably anticipated multilingual education! Later Jagdish Chandra Bose had to rue:

> I have a young assistant who helped me most efficiently in the construction of apparatus for the study of electric-radiation. He has a great enthusiasm for science, of which he gave proof by serving gratuitously in our laboratory for more than two years, though all this time he had to undergo great privations. The University has been hard on him; for though his scientific knowledge is considerable he could not master the intricacies of English grammar and idiom to entitle him to the degree of B.A., for which English is a compulsory subject, and unhappily a fatal one for the aspirations of many for university degrees.[29]

Two things are striking in any account of this period. First, it was an age of translations. The numerous schoolbook societies and scientific societies (Aligarh and Bihar, for example) were basically translation societies. Translations, no doubt, were very important and must have helped popularize certain scientific notions. But were they unwarranted foreign borrowings or improper assimilations? Translated terms were continuously contested and reformulated on the basis of epistemic, linguistic, and political concerns. A major lacuna was that they were not accompanied, except in one or two cases, by any original research. They remained mere translations—secondary, superficial, and of limited value. Second, in earlier transfers of knowledge, for example from Greek to Arabic, research 'preceded' or at least accompanied translations. This was not so with 'colonial transfers', at least in the case of India. It was at best a 'trial' transfer and in this sense, one could speak of the disintegration, not of the integration of knowledge.[30] Yet the penchant for translations must have done some good. Following Ballantyne's efforts, Rajendralal Mitra (the most active Indian member of the Asiatic Society) prepared 'a scheme for rendering European scientific terms in the vernacular'. In the vernaculars of India, 'untrammelled by any existing scientific literature', he could see the possibility 'to secure something thoroughly national and perfect'.[31] With limited and defective means, his intentions, however sound, were to remain utopian. But such efforts in different Indian languages continued and gained momentum, especially during the Swadeshi movement of the early 20th century.[32]

Adoption and Adaptation

A literal translation alone was not enough. Much more complex and difficult were the possibilities of adoption and adaptation of new ideas, especially in areas where traditions were very strong. For example, the Ayurvedic and Yunani medical traditions were not only strong but very popular. The germ theory of disease and its new medical tools had brought revolutionary changes. Was a grafting or assimilation possible? If Ayurveda had to remain in competition, then it had to 'borrow' (or imitate) and 'improve' on terms set by its epistemological 'other'. Some practitioners, of course, held out for *shuddha* (pure) Ayurveda. But the changes were unmistakable. How did indigenous practitioners cope with the changing times? To appreciate this, let us take a brief look at two pioneers who symbolized this struggle. They worked with two different systems at two distant places, yet were very close in both substance and method.

They were Hakim Ajmal Khan (1868–1927) of Delhi and Vaidya P. S. Varier (1869–1958) of Kottakal. Both came from physician families of high repute. Ajmal Khan's brother had established the Madrasa Tibbia (school of Yunani medicine) in 1883, and the whole family was engaged in promoting Yunani medicine. In 1891, Ajmal Khan prepared a catalogue of Arabic and Persian manuscripts on medicine. In 1897, he wrote a booklet in Urdu on the plague. In 1902, he started publishing a monthly medical journal, *Mujalla-i-Tibbia*. The same year P. S. Varier organized an Arya Vaidya Samajam, opened Arya Vaidyashala, and started a journal, *Dhanwantari*, to promote and analyse the strengths and weaknesses of the Ayurvedic system. The two seem not to have met or collaborated but were fired by a similar zeal. Both had open and eclectic minds, aware of the faults of their respective systems and willing to 'improve'. The Western system was not anathema to them, and both were keen to borrow and internalize what was good and beneficial from other systems without losing their own ground. Their works were culture-specific but not culture-blind.

Both Ajmal Khan and P. S. Varier were deeply engaged in the systematization and dissemination of what may be called 'traditional knowledge in a new light' and created institutions for the purpose.[33] To this Varier added the preparation and distribution of medicines on a commercial scale, while Ajmal Khan concentrated on education, synthesizing the different systems. The latter tried to bring both *hakim*s and *vaidya*s onto one platform and in 1910 organized an All India Ayurvedic and Tibbia (Yunani) Conference which became an annual event. Both he and Varier recognized that the future of indigenous systems depended upon their opening up and coming together. The strategies of both these prominent reformers were impacted by certain inherent limitations. They appealed to the landed aristocracy and enjoyed the patronage of local rulers (like the Nawab of Rampur, the ruler of Bhopal, and the Maharaja of Travancore). Their elitism was deliberate.

Unlike Ajmal Khan, P. S. Varier seems to have put more emphasis on the manufacture and sale of medicines than on teaching or research. He realized that Western medicines appeared more attractive to people because they were comparatively palatable, gave quick relief, and came without dietary restrictions. So, Ayurveda must change accordingly. After he had made adaptations to his drug products ensuring longer shelf life and quicker transportation, sales of Varier's medicines rose from 14,000 rupees in the period 1902–1906 to 170,000 rupees in 1914–1918.[34] Sales continued to increase, and it is still a flourishing house. By contrast, Ajmal Khan's educational efforts could grow only up to a point (his Tibbia College is now in a moribund state).

Whatever their limitations, both reformers enjoyed great esteem and a wide following. The question of indigenous medicine was not a question of medicine or medical science *per se*; it had become part of the upsurge of interest in India's cultural heritage, with all the accompanying political implications.

The Limitations of Education

There were four major educational questions that the colonial rulers had to contend with: why teach, what to teach, how to teach, and whom to teach? These questions still retain relevance and to some extent, are yet to be resolved. 'Why teach' was addressed with the 'moral development' and 'character formation' argument. Their hopes were pinned not on 'material' but 'moral' uplift. The 'new' education was expected to 'reform' and 'improve' the 'native' character. After all, it was a paternalistic Raj! The concept of 'order' was central to colonial policy in all areas of administration, including education. Knowledge was what the new education was supposed to give, but its underlying agenda was to improve conduct. The logic of the metropolis–colony relationship was not in favour of the latter getting anything like a higher form of scientific or technical education. What it got was some sort Colonies thrived on 'imitation'. How could it compete with the 'original'? Only hybridity was possible. It meant different things to different people. The term, technical education, thus generated much confusion.

'What to teach' was met with a strongly literary-leaning curriculum. This was what the Oxbridge tradition itself was. How could a colony get something different? Thus, a page of Shakespeare was considered worth hundred pages of Euclid. This literary bias helped produce numerous writers and lawyers. Scientific and technical education took a back seat. Yet, surprisingly enough, colonial India gradually produced more scientific pioneers than postcolonial India.

'How to teach' proved to be the hardest nut. It is yet to be cracked. What should be the medium of instruction, English or Indian languages? At what stage and how does one become bilingual or multilingual? The colonial state naturally foisted its own language and the Indian middle class took advantage of it. Imagine, had the Dutch colonized India, like Indonesia, and imposed the Dutch language, we would not have the same economic and academic advantage as we have today! On the question of the medium of instruction, almost all Indian leaders swore on Indian languages.

The question of 'whom to teach' was not that difficult. New education was meant for the dominant castes who could then be groomed easily as collaborators in the colonial project. Though the colonial officials talked of mass education, they had no real intention of educating the masses. They were here to rule, not to undertake philanthropy or social reform.

Why did Indian intellectuals put an unprecedented emphasis on cultural synthesis? The idea of a cultural synthesis gave them the best of both worlds. It enabled them to absorb culture shock and also promised a possible opportunity to transcend the barriers imposed by colonialism. Moreover, it also fitted well with the dominant Hindu doctrine of epistemological pluralism. So, the clamour for cultural synthesis grew. Bacon and Comte impressed the Indian mind. But how to integrate their experimental method and rationality into the Hindu 'science of spirit'? This the local thinkers were not clear about. They pursued a great variety of strategies—imitation, translation, assimilation, 'distanced' appreciation, and even retreat to isolation—but without much success. The perceived association of knowledge with jobs and power remained and still remains strong. Numerous magazines in different Indian languages were replete with instances of how scientific knowledge had brought unprecedented power to the modern West, and how the new knowledge would help revitalize Indian society. For example, Ramendra Sundar Tribedi (1864–1919) exhorted his young readers, 'Knowledge begets power. Try to gain knowledge, and you will become powerful'. The upper middle class benefitted, no doubt, but it did not lead to a genuine socio-economic transformation. For most among the middle class, education was merely a route to *chakari* (livelihood); they had no use for science and rationality that questioned the traditional ways that they were so comfortable with. Hence caste and gender discrimination and superstitions remained deeply entrenched in Indian society.

P. C. Ray once approvingly quoted Paul Deussen, 'Vedanta has proved the curse of material progress in India'.[35] Long ago, Marx had described religion as the opium of the masses. In 1926, Joseph Needham (who later edited magnificent tomes on science and civilization in China) called it 'a powerful antiseptic which preserves mummified customs that have long outlasted their usefulness and otiose dogmas that have long lost their vitality'.[36] He quoted Pascal's famous dictum: 'Two extravagances: to exclude reason, to admit only reason'. Are they *opposuit natura*? The debate continues.

Notes

1. 24 August 1832.
2. J. Nowrojee and H. Merwanjee, *Journal of a Residence of Two Years and a Half in Great Britain* (London: Murray, 1841).

3. John Seeley, *The Expansion of England: Two Courses of Lectures* (London: John Murray, 1883), p. 244.
4. Pandit Baldev Upadhyay, *Kashi ki Panditya Parampara* (in Hindi) (Varanasi: Vishwavidyala Prakashan, 1983), pp. 289–307; for this reference I am grateful to my student Ritesh.
5. L. Wilkinson, 'On the Use of the Siddhantas in the Work of Native Education', *Journal of the Asiatic Society of Bengal* 3 (1834): 504–519. Wilkinson expressed great enthusiasm over the response of Shubhaji Bapu and Onkar Bhatt and showered praises on them. *Calcutta Monthly Journal* 31(1837): 393.
6. For details on Master Ramchandra and other science popularizers, see S. R. Kidwai, *Master Ramchandra* (Delhi: Delhi University Publication, 1963); and Dhruv Raina and S. Irfan Habib, *Domesticating Modern Science: A Social History of Science and Culture in Colonial India* (New Delhi: Tulika, 2004); S. Irfan Habib and Dhruv Raina, *Social History of Science in Colonial India* (New Delhi: Oxford University Press, 2007).
7. In his *Patrika*, Datta argued:

> At present the education system is being sought only by a gang of clerks … Diffusion of technical knowledge among the labouring classes is necessary … Translation work has to be done carefully, and it should be free and simple so that even the lowest rungs of the society can understand it.

Benoy Ghosh (ed.), *Samayik Patre Banglar Samajchitra*, Vol. II (Calcutta: Bengal Publishers, 1964), p. 468.
8. Chuckerbutty had lost his parents at age 6, and at age 13, he served as a cook at a school in exchange for education in English. *The Indian Medical Gazette* 9, no 12 (1874): 330–331.
9. To quote this Indian pioneer of modern medicine:

> The war which has been raging during the last 14 months is not then the war of Europeans against natives, but that of ignorance and fanaticism against knowledge and religious toleration—a war in which the educated native has as great a stake as any European in the country.

S. C. G. Chuckerbutty, *Popular Lectures on Subjects of Indian Interest* (Calcutta: Thomas Smith, 1870), pp. 79–80.
10. The verses were in Persian. Cited in David Lelyveld, *Aligarh's First Generation* (Princeton: Princeton University Press, 1978), p. 73.
11. Geraldine Forbes, *Positivism in Bengal* (Calcutta: Minerva, 1975), pp. 132–134.

12. Cited in Deepak Kumar, *Science and the Raj*, 2nd edn (New Delhi: Oxford University Press, 2006), p. 80.

13. For an engrossing discussion, see Gyan Prakash, *Another Reason: Science and the Imagination of Modern India* (New Delhi: Oxford University Press, 2000).

14. Proceedings of the Annual Meeting of the Bihar Scientific Society, Gaya, 28 August 1874, R. Temple Papers, MSS. Eur. F86/No.214, IOR /BL

15. Quoted in P. Hoodbhoy, *Islam and Science* (London: Zed Books, 1991), p. 68.

16. Cited in, S. Irfan Habib, 'Reconciling Science with Islam In 19th Century India', *Contributions to Indian Sociology* 34, no. 1 (2000): 63–92.

17. Very interesting argument indeed! See A. A. Ziadat, *Western Science in the Arab World* (London: Macmillan, 1986), pp. 82–89.

18. Home, Education, proc. no. 19, November 1886, NAI. Interestingly enough, astrology is being taught at several universities in India at present with the approval and encouragement of politicians and even scientists.

19. Chuckerbutty, *Popular Lectures*, p. 79.

20. A. K. Biswas, *Gleanings of the Past and the Science Movement in the Diaries of Mahendralal and Amritlal Sircar* (Calcutta: The Asiatic Society, 2000), pp. 192–203.

21. *Complete Works of Swami Vivekananda*, Vol. IV (Almora: R.K. Mission, 1979), pp. 433–434.

22. Har Dayal, 'The Health of the Nation', *Modern Review* 12, no. 1 (July 1912): 43–49.

23. Anilbaran Ray, 'Modern Science and Hindu Religion', *Bharatbarsha* 26 (1939): 117–126.

24. Ibid., *Bharatbarsha* 26 (1939): 127–136.

25. Edward Shils, 'Reflections on Tradition, Centre and Periphery and the Universal Validity of Science: The Significance of the Life of S. Ramanujan', *Minerva* 29, no. 40 (1991): 391–419.

26. Muzaffar Iqbal, *Islam and Science* (London: Ashgate, 2002), p. 291.

27. A. S. Dhumatkar, 'Forgotten Propagator of Science: Kolhapur's Balaji Prabhakar Modak', *Economic and Political Weekly* 37, no. 48 (2002): 4807–4816.

28. For details, see Siddharth Ghosh, *Rajendralal Mitra* (New Delhi: Sahitya Akademi, 2002).

29. *The Electrician*, 19 February 1897, P. 545, Press clippings, File B, p. 115, Bose Institute, Kolkata.

30. Roshdi Rashed, 'Problems of Integration', in *Science and Empires*, ed. P. Petitjean, C. Jami, and A. M. Moulin (Dordrecht: Kluwer, 1992), pp. 76–77.

31. Rajendralal Mitra, *A Scheme for the Rendering of European Scientific Terms in the Vernaculars of India* (Calcutta: Asiatic Society, 1877), pp. 1–2.

32. Dhrub Kumar Singh, 'Hindi Protagonists of Science and Swadeshi in the First Half of the Twentieth Century', *Indian Journal of History of Science* 55, no. 3 (2020): 235–246.

33. Barbara Metcalf, 'Nationalist Muslims in British India: The Case of Hakim Ajmal Khan', *Modern Asian Studies* 19, no. 1 (1985): 1–28 and K. N. Panikkar, 'Indigenous Medicine and Cultural Hegemony: A Study of the Revitalization Movement in Keralam', *Studies in History* 8, no. 2 (1992): 283–307.

34. *Dhanwantari* no. 16 (1918): 58.

35. P. C. Ray, *Life and Experiences*, Vol. II (Calcutta: Chatterjee & Co., 1932), p. 259.

36. J. Needham, *Science, Religion and Reality* (London: Sheldon Press, 1926), p. 349.

4

A New Dawn

... despite the inherent submission to the foreign yoke—we have inherited a mind not inferior in its endowments to the mind of any nation on earth ... Science may be pursued for its own sake in the abstract, and for the mental pleasure it affords, and such pursuit is most laudable.

—Mahendralal Sircar [1]

... merely to revile the sciences by which the westerners have gained their victory in the modern world will not tend to relieve our sufferings, but rather will add to the burden of our sins ... Do not imagine that the day of the old village community was the Golden Age or that such a community was a paradise on earth ... instead of going back we should go forward, and using these tools of the modern world—the modern chaos if you like—rebuild therewith the old community life of the villages on a surer, a firmer and a sounder basis.

—Rabindranath Tagore [2]

The last quarter of the 19th century was simply remarkable. The seeds that had been sown earlier were beginning to sprout. A new middle class was finding its feet. New aspirations were in the air. The middle class was making new demands, even though India was now being controlled directly and more firmly by the Government in Britain. There were new schools, colleges, the telegraph, more railway lines, printing and publications, and so on, no doubt. Yet the flip side was heavier, for example, the economic drain, famines, severe pestilence, epidemics, and so on. It was during these difficult times that nationalism began to take root, and gradually flowered into a full-fledged national movement, not only for independence but reconstruction. It was also during this period that those who were to play a great role in different fields of life in the next century were maturing. The quest for identity had sharpened.

In terms of scientific knowledge, this quest had found early expression in the establishment of the Indian Association for the Cultivation of Science (IACS) by an eminent doctor, Mahendralal Sircar (1833–1904). In 1869, he had written an article, 'On the Desirability of a National Institution for the Cultivation of the Sciences by the Natives of India'. This title is extremely significant. He argued against the prevailing contention that the Hindu mind was metaphysical, and called for the cultivation of the sciences by 'original' research. He wrote, 'We want an Institution which will combine the character, the scope and objects of the Royal Institution of London and of the British Association for the Advancement of Science', and then added, 'I want freedom for this Institution. I want it to be entirely under our own management and control. I want it to be solely native and purely national'. In 1876, after a great deal of effort and controversy, the IACS was inaugurated in Calcutta. This event was no less important than the establishment, nine years later, of the Indian National Congress, a political forum that was to spearhead the national movement. The IACS was a cultural challenge and symbolized the determination of a hurt psyche to assert itself and stand on its own in an area that formed the kernel of Western superiority. Two years later, an unidentified Indian visitor in Paris wrote:

> We should do all we can to cultivate and master the physical sciences and make the most of these opportunities of acquiring them which have now been placed at our disposal. In the first place direct all our energies to be a 'scientific' nation under the guidance of the master minds of Europe and then we should have everything else we want.[3]

This association symbolized the search for an Indian identity in the world of science. Sircar had undertaken an extremely difficult job, and he himself grew a bit despondent as his age advanced. But his institution, despite the trying times, fared quite well during the first 25 years of its existence. It nursed and nurtured many scientific talents, and also popularized science. Sircar had heralded a dawn of which Jagadish Chandra Bose (1858–1937) and Prafulla Chandra Ray (1861–1944) were the early beams, and Chandrashekhara Venkata Raman (1888–1970) and Kariamanikkam Srinivasa Krishnan (1898–1961), the high noon.

In 1898, a proposal for the establishment of a research university with a grant of 3 million rupees came from J. N. Tata (1839–1904), a prince among Indian industrialists. Despite reluctance from the colonial government, and after much discussion and paperwork, this munificence finally led to the founding of the Indian Institute of Science in 1909.[4] During the course of more than a century of its existence, this institution has acquired cult status and represents probably the best of science in India.

Aspirational Milieu

No wonder, the turn of the century saw peoples' aspirations soaring high. In Bengal, a movement for *swadeshi* (self-reliance) had begun. In 1902, the Dawn Society was established which called for 'national' education in literary, scientific, and technical subjects. In the wake of the Partition of Bengal in 1905, a National Council of Education was formed. It formulated an ambitious educational scheme, free from European control, and aimed at a fusion between the best of the East and the West. One more society was formed calling for the promotion of technical education. The former set up the Bengal National College while the latter founded the Bengal Technical Institute. *Swadeshi* ideas symbolized the determination of the people in two fields: (*a*) The promotion of education along 'national lines and under national control' with special reference to the exact sciences and technology and (*b*) the industrialization of the country and advancement of materialism. *Swadeshi* (self-reliance) and *swaraj* (self-rule) were more than political slogans, rather they symbolized an intense yearning for change. As a result, the need to establish a three-dimensional system of education—literary, scientific, and technical combined—on national lines and under national control was felt. This took the shape of a national education movement and soon spread throughout the country.

The Great War had brought to the fore the inability of India to support war efforts through industrial production. India could only provide soldiers as cannon fodder. Hence, an Industrial Commission was appointed during the progress of the war itself. In its deliberations, the question of education, particularly technical education, came up. One of its members, Madan Mohan Malaviya (1861–1946) gave an exceptionally critical dissenting note.[5] Like his cultural predecessors who had rejected rationality as a Western import, Malaviya presented a nationalist critique of British economic policies in India, and stressed that India had remained deindustrialized. He knew that industry was no longer a mere tool of domination, it had become a discipline and, therefore, technical schools (with new curriculums) had become more important than factories. The British model was inadequate. The new icons were Japan and Germany, and the new watchword was science-based technology.

An interesting characteristic of the period was the cautious yet firm demands for industrialization. In industrialization lay salvation, the nationalists believed, but it was also thought necessary to avoid the pitfalls of blind imitation and crude industrialization. Efforts were to be made not to lose human, nay Indian, face. The colonizers had talked about moral regeneration for a long time.

This the nationalists viewed as propagandist in nature. Instead, they dwelt upon a 'synthetical' economic and industrial regeneration. This regeneration was not to be achieved at the cost of peasants and artisans. Whether it was the *Dawn Society Magazine* of Calcutta or the *Kayastha Samachar* (later the *Hindustan Review*) of Allahabad, or the *Swadeshmitran* of Madras, the tenor was the same—industrialization was in the national interest and should be conducted on national terms. Benoy Kumar Sarkar (1887–1949), an important interlocutor of the period, used interesting terms like 'mistrification' and 'factorification' (*mistri* refers to technicians) and called for *shilpa, banijya,* and *shilpalaya* (industry, commerce, and technical institutes).[6] The importance of artisans and technicians was thus brought into focus. The demand for chemical industries was ably advocated and pushed by scientists like P. C. Ray. All this had been preceded by a vociferous call for techno-scientific education. There was to be no diminution in that. Rather the new argument was that science should be taught in a scientific way and not by the literary method.

Noted individuals played a major role. P. C. Ray started the Bengal Chemical and Pharmaceutical Works (BCPW) to put scientific knowledge to immediate industrial use, to encourage the idea of self-sufficiency, and to provide employment to many science graduates. Himself a working scientist and deeply conscious of the industrial applications of science, he was one of the earliest to see it in its social context and to talk of its social relevance and accountability. Thanks to the technical support given by an Indian geologist P. N. Bose (1855–1934), Jamsetji Tata could establish a big steel factory in Singhbhum. An alumnus of the Bengal Engineering College, Rajendra Nath Mookerjee (1854–1936), formed an engineering firm which later grew into the famous Martin Burn & Co. The Bengal Engineering College welcomed electricity and started a course in electrical engineering. Its journal wrote:

> To run the machines of a factory, electricity plays the pivotal role by producing hundreds and thousands of horse-power. If one wants to talk with a friend, miles away from him, the remedy is [the] telephone—another offshoot of electricity. One cannot think without electricity in modern times.[7]

In the midst of this intellectual rigour, however, certain journals and many learned individuals showed streaks of revivalism. Going back to the distant past did entail the risk of unwarranted romanticism. An author who wrote extensively in Bengali on flora and fauna, Sarat Chandra Mitra (1863–1938), suggested that certain descriptions of animals discernible in ancient Indian texts corresponded to the ancestors of living creatures, actually seen by humans.

V. Narayanan Nair (1878–1959), a *vaidya*, wrote on bacteriology and infectious diseases from an Ayurvedic point of view. He believed that ancient Indian physicians were already acquainted with discoveries that were made with the aid of the microscope. Ramendra Sundar Tribedi (1864–1919) was a great science writer and had a remarkable cultural understanding. He criticized the content and quality of education in the *tols* and *chatuspatis*, but thought that these had at least some genuine respect for knowledge. Modern educational institutions failed to inculcate this genuine respect. They became what P. C. Ray later called *golam-khanas* (slave-factories) churning out munsifs, clerks, assistant surgeons, and overseers as per the requirements of the colonial job market. Tribedi would deny modern science any epistemic superiority, and would rather describe Western scientists in Hindu terms; for example, Copernicus as one with *dibyachakkhu* (spiritual vision), Newton as a *rishi* (sage), and Helmholtz as an *abatar* (incarnation).

A much more celebrated contemporary who appreciated modern science and technology was the soul-laureate of Bengal, Rabindranath Tagore (1862–1941). He wanted India to smell the Western repertoire of knowledge, taste it, and understand the nuances and differences within it. On one occasion he claimed to have 'read scientific books more than books of literature'.[8] In the 1890s, he wrote certain popular science articles in a Bengali journal *Sadhana*. He was a close friend of J. C. Bose and even raised funds for him from the Maharaja of Tripura to continue his researches in Europe. Both shared the *samkhya darsana* and looked for the unifying thread (*ek sute sakalam*). Tagore respected and remained in close touch with the rising scientists of India like P. C. Ray, C. V. Raman, M. N. Saha, and S. N. Bose. The poet was aware of the new developments in physics and had met Einstein and Heisenberg a couple of times during the 1920s. They discussed the nature of truth. For Einstein, scientific truth had validity independent of man's perception, while Tagore stressed man's perception and experience (*anubhav*) as the key to truth. Tagore probably appreciated Heisenberg's principle of indeterminacy more than Einstein's theory of relativity. In a poem titled 'One-upmanship' he refers to the intriguing relationship between Time and the measurement of Time:

'I am,' says Time, 'this world's Creator'.
'But I', says the clock, 'am your inventor!'

In a beautiful poem titled 'Paksi Manab' (Flying Man), he foresees an environmental crisis:

In the brutal roaring of an aeroplane we hear
Incompatibility with sky,
Destruction of atmosphere ...[9]

Like Gandhi, Tagore rejected not science but scientism, greed not technology. Both believed in the Upanishadic ideal of *ma gridah* (do not be greedy). Had he been opposed to mechanization, he would not have conducted agricultural experiments at Sriniketan; would not have invited an agricultural scientist, Elmhirst from the United States, nor would he have sent his son to study agriculture in Illinois.[10] His concern for rural society predates that of Gandhi. Though he lacked the Mahatma's charisma and mass appeal, his practical approach to the rural problem was both more realistic and more comprehensive. He was not enamoured of the magic of the *charkha*; he would advocate intelligent application of scientific techniques. But he shared the Mahatma's gospel of self-help and his faith in the dignity of manual labour.[11] Tagore had invited a Scottish polymath, Patrick Geddes to his abode Santiniketan to advise on curricula, and so on. Geddes would offer exact plans with diagrams and a heavy dose of scientificity. Tagore became cautious and remained reluctant. The Baul of Bengal refused to be 'disciplined'.[12] Both Gandhi and Tagore saw an efflorescence of Indian science. During their time, a galaxy of scientists emerged in India as seen never before nor afterward.

Numerous noted individuals, by raising their voices, had put pressure on both the government and society. The colonial government could afford to ignore them but the individuals kept organizing themselves professionally in small groups or under certain institutions. Together with the efforts to establish research groups and institutions, a major step in the professionalization of science in India came with the creation of the Indian Science Congress Association (ISCA) in 1914. Interestingly, this was started by two British scientists devoted to India, and Indian scientists responded with great enthusiasm. It was to serve as an important platform to catalyse 'community' consciousness as well as to unify the scattered specialist groups on a national scale during its annual conventions which took place in different parts of the country. During its formative period in the 1920s, the ISCA was instrumental in helping several science disciplines through its sectional committees. The scientific meetings of the ISCA provided an important professional forum for discussing advanced research in physics, geology, biology, and chemistry. Beginning with the formation of the Indian Botanical Society in 1920, the drive for the professionalization of science was further enhanced, and by the 1940s, 17 more societies and professional associations were created on an all-India basis covering all the major disciplines; these also launched journals in their respective fields.[13]

The Scientific Pioneers

A large number of Indian interlocutors, belonging to different disciplines and walks of life, contributed to the new quest for techno-scientific knowledge. Among those who were the first to take scientific research and teaching as their career were Pramatha Nath Bose (1855–1934), Jagadish Chandra Bose, and Prafulla Chandra Ray.

P. N. Bose specialized in geology at the University of London and later joined the Geological Survey of India (GSI). In 1886, he wrote a pamphlet on 'Technical and Scientific Education in Bengal' and a decade later published three volumes on *A History of Hindu Civilization during British Rule*.[14] Fierce nationalism had transformed a geologist into a historian. From physical mapping, he shifted to cultural contours. He held the Brahmanical system responsible for neglecting physical science 'to a most serious extent'. He argued:

> The decline [of Hindu civilization] was synchronous with the Mahomedan conquest and was no doubt facilitated by it. But Hindu civilization carried the germs of its decay within it. The caste-system upon which it is based, rendered its continued development an impossibility. The Brahmans were averse to material progress. They looked down with undisguised contempt upon arts and manufacture, upon, in fact, all occupations which had not spiritual or mental culture as their primary object. Wrapped up in severe philosophic contemplation, taking but little interest in the struggles after material progress carried on by the lower classes whom they looked upon as the vulgar herd, they carried mental science to a high pitch of perfection, while they neglected physical science to a most serious extent.[15]

But he would never agree with his (geological) Chief's perception of Indians as 'utterly incapable of any original work in natural science'. He could see no reason why 'with an improved system of scientific education, and with just and sympathetic treatment of the young men trained in India, they will not be able to take a place in the modern scientific world.' The Japanese 'instead of being thwarted, discouraged and set down as incapable, have been aided, encouraged and stimulated by their government to pursue science'. Bose only forgot to mention that Japan was not a colony! But he did realize (at his own cost) that just and sympathetic treatment was not always possible in a colony. Every concession had to be literally wrung. It was a struggle in slow motion but on a high pitch. In 1886, P. N. Bose asked for a science course at the FA (first arts; intermediate) level to facilitate early specialization. It was not till 1906 that an intermediate science course was introduced. He also pointed out the defects in the BSc course which in itself was divided into a literary and a scientific curriculum. The Presidency College had no chairs in botany, zoology, and geology. Officers of the GSI were asked to teach geology on a purely temporary basis. One could imagine what progress would come from such intermittent lectures. So was the case also in the Bengal Engineering College at Shibpur where chemistry, physics, geology, and metallurgy would be taught by the same teacher. He wanted science subjects to be taught with an eye to their application to industry. But at the same time, he warned against the dark side of industrialism in Europe, which was feeding the growing spirit of militarism and imperialism in the West. He would have preferred the cultivation of science and technology within the 'limits of intellectual culture'. Later the experience of the First World War made him revert to the propagation of ancient culture (as represented by India) which 'would rescue humanity from the morass of militarism, malevolence, destitution, disease etc.' Thus P.N. Bose wanted change and progress but on his cultural terms and without losing Indian values.

In contrast, the two most creative scientists that late-19th century India produced, J. C. Bose and P. C. Ray would fully accept the epistemic superiority of modern science and both treated education as the most effective vehicle for assimilation and gradual diffusion of new ideas. Both were well-steeped in Indian history and culture, and could discriminate between what was to be taken and what not. J. C. Bose was a bio-physicist who worked on electrical impulse and response in the living and the non-living. Unlike P. N. Bose and P. C. Ray, J. C. Bose did not undertake any investigation into the 'national memory' (that is, history). But he did try to identify his works with what he considered to be the greatest in his cultural inheritance. His propositions that life emerges out of non-life and that there exists an underlying unity between the living and the non-living were taken as scientific manifestations of the Samkhya philosophy. J. C. Bose used to quote from the Vedas and had a poetical flavour: he even gave Sanskrit names to his instruments and did not see any conflict between science and religion. Contemporary opinion did not consider this mystical or 'oriental', rather he was hailed as a syncretic mind.[16] His works were the first authentic rebuttal of the colonial view that Indians were incapable of original scientific investigation.

But his was not an ivory tower projection of education and research. He was convinced of the utilitarian value of science and wanted its widespread diffusion through proper science education. It had to be not only for the sake of scientific knowledge but also to harness the economic resources of the country and to show how to discriminate between industries which can and which cannot be profitably carried on under the climatic and other conditions prevailing in India. To achieve this were needed a satisfactory science course, good laboratories, and scholarships. Bose was particularly perturbed over the science curricula in Indian universities. At the graduate level in Calcutta University, for example, the vast area of acoustics, heat, light, electricity, and magnetism formed only half a paper! To add to the woes of the students, too many textbooks were prescribed. The result was they looked for help books. Second-hand knowledge thus took the place of 'living science'. Even this could not be put to any use because in the absence of any post-degree scholarship or employment, they would shift to a career in law or administration. Like his compatriots, Bose excelled in diagnosis but his solutions were limited and heavily dependent on the government. All through he remained a devoted researcher, not an activist.

P. C. Ray, on the other hand, showed a higher degree of social commitment. He was an educationist, a scientist, an entrepreneur, a Gandhian activist—all rolled into one. He did some original research on India's scientific heritage and attempted a social explanation of what went wrong, when, and how. Unlike Tribedi and others, he held the Indian social (caste) structure responsible for the cleavage between mental and manual work and the resultant stagnation. He wanted modern education to bridge this gulf. In his view, education has to be quality oriented; not for a degree but for the generation of employment and wealth. The average graduate was found to be 'a licensed ignoramus' and the degree itself served as a cloak to hide the degree-holder's ignorance. Higher education should be limited to only those who feel an instinctive call in that direction. The other great defect in his opinion was the undue stress on a literary curriculum. A Calcutta University student for a master of arts (MA) degree in 1930 had to attend 230 classes in English and only 65 in mathematics. He was equally unhappy about the intellectual narrowness of the specialist in science. He visualized a broad 'mental culture' in which science, literature, history, and philosophy were to be given almost equal attention. Apart from the defective curriculum, what hurt Ray most was the medium of instruction. He was convinced that learning through a foreign medium killed originality:

> Imagine for a moment what would happen if the English lad were compelled first of all to learn Persian or Chinese or say German or Russian and then had to read through the medium of such a tongue ... in India we have adopted the most unnatural system and have to pay a heavy penalty for it.[17]

Ray was not against English. He only asked for its late introduction after the mother tongue had laid the base. J. C. Bose held similar views and recalled with pride how his father had sent him to a 'vernacular' school. This did help him relate to his surroundings. But higher education and publication of research had to be in English—the language of the scientific world. They had no doubt about it. Further, existing institutions of science education and research had to be strengthened through fellowships, laboratories, and private donations. When J. N. Tata floated the idea of an Indian institute of research, Ray was reticent. He would have preferred private munificence to encourage existing institutions in different parts of the country rather than create one single island of excellence.

Another star in the firmament was Sir Asutosh Mookerjee (1864–1924)—a mathematician, lawyer, and educationist of high repute. Even while a young student between 1883 and 1892, he published 16 papers and three mathematical notes. As there was no research opening, he shifted to law, much to the regret of Mahendalal Sircar in whose association he used to give mathematical lectures. When in 1906, he was appointed the Vice Chancellor of Calcutta University, he transformed it from a mere examining body to a centre of high-quality research. Gradually he created a galaxy of professors—B. N. Seal (1864–1938), C. V. Raman (1888–1970), S. N. Bose (1894–1974), M. N. Saha (1893–1956), Ganesh Prasad (1876–1935), S. P. Agharkar (1884–1960), J. C. Ghosh (1894–1959), and many others.

Among the names mentioned above, the contributions of C. V. Raman, S. N. Bose, and M. N. Saha were and still remain simply matchless. Raman joined the IACS in 1907, three years after the death of Mahendralal Sircar. By that time, the association's laboratory had acquired instruments on sound, light, and electricity. It also had a workshop to make and repair instruments and other demonstration apparatus. Raman's initial publications were on acoustics. His experiments on Huygens' secondary waves attracted the notice of the Western scientific community. In 1913, he was offered the Palit Professorship at Calcutta University. He continued to work at the IACS, and in collaboration with some young and bright students and colleagues he could do outstanding research on physical optics, molecular diffraction of light, crystals, colloids, X-ray scattering of liquids, and so on. In 1928, he published a paper titled 'A New Radiation' in the *Indian Journal of Physics*.[18] This came to be known as the Raman effect and won him a Nobel Prize in 1930. In 1933, he left Calcutta for Bangalore to join the Indian Institute of Science as its first Indian director. At the IACS, he was succeeded by his close associate

K. S. Krishnan (1898–1961), who added crystal magnetism to the ongoing work on crystal optics. Krishnan was also the first to start work on low temperature physics and cryogenics.

Satyendra Nath Bose and Meghnad Saha were students of mathematics and began their career as lecturers in the applied mathematics department at Calcutta University in 1916. Soon they took to studying modern physics on their own. Saha specialized in thermodynamics, spectroscopy, and statistical mechanics, while Bose took to electromagnetism and relativity. Both of them were destined to make fundamental contributions in the fields of their choice. Saha gave the theory of thermal ionization which explained the physical conditions in stellar bodies. It is considered one of the 10 major discoveries in astrophysics. Bose formulated Bose Statistics which still plays a very vital role in the study of modern physics, in the fields of elementary particles and superconductivity. Meghnad Saha was both a thinker and a fearless man of action. Like his friend S. N. Bose, he was a devoted and inspiring teacher. Saha was not a man of vague ideas; he believed in making clear-cut plans and putting them to action. In 1934, he founded a journal called *Science and Culture*. As the national movement was in full swing, he wanted its leaders to be educated on the utility of science and technology for the economic development of the country. He emphasized the need for careful planning. Leaders like Subhas Chandra Bose and Jawaharlal Nehru listened to him. The result was the formation of a National Planning Committee (NPC) in 1938 under the umbrella of the Indian National Congress. Saha was the soul of this committee. A close contemporary was P. C. Mahalanobis (1893–1972), a physicist by training, a statistician by instinct, and a planner by conviction. He made significant contributions in the field of multivariate analysis and sample surveys, and introduced a new technique called fractile graphical analysis. He pioneered a new kind of knowledge which would prove to be crucial in planning the economic development of free India.

Science and the National Movement

For almost nine decades from its inception in 1885, the Indian National Congress was more than a political party; it was a movement which debated and deliberated upon not only political but also social and economic issues. It emerged as the most zealous vanguard of Indian interests. Whether it be education, health, agriculture, industries, or mining, the Congress touched upon several problems in its wide sweep. The very third session of the Congress in 1887 took up the question of technical education. K. T. Telang and

B. N. Seal showed how in the name of technical education, the government was imparting merely lower forms of practical training. In 1893, K. N. Bahadurji moved a resolution beseeching the government 'to raise a scientific medical profession in India by throwing open fields for medical and scientific work to the best talent available and indigenous talent in particular'.[19] The concern of the Congress for science started in response to the immediate exigencies of life in the country, such as the necessity of getting rid of, or, at least, coping with, the situation created by poverty, disease, and disasters like floods and famines. In 1896, when a famine had broken out throughout India, it urged:

> The true remedy against the recurrence of famine lies in the adoption of a policy which would enforce economy, husband the resources of the State, foster the development of indigenous and local arts and industries which have practically been extinguished, and help forward the introduction of modern arts and industries.[20]

Delivering the presidential address at the Congress session in 1901, D. E. Wacha said:

> ... it is idle to talk of mere small industries and carpentry and brick-making and so forth. If there is to be an industrial revival of a practical character which shall change the entire surface of this country, you will have first to lay the foundation of teaching in Applied Sciences. You cannot have the cart before the horse. Higher education must precede industrial development.[21]

For Wacha, technical education signified higher education. The Congress did not want the claims of higher education to be subordinated to those of primary education. In fact, it wanted the government to patronize both equally and effectively. The inadequacies of the medical service also attracted its attention. The Indian Medical Service (IMS) came under severe criticism.

In the first decade of the 20th century, amelioration was sought through the slogans of *swadeshi* (self-reliance) and *swaraj* (self-rule). The call for *swadeshi* preceded the call for *swaraj*. The Swadeshi movement of 1904–1905 conveyed to India and the world the determination of the people in promoting a kind of education that would be by the Indians and for the Indians. It was called national education and it was supposed to have more emphasis on techno-scientific knowledge. The new watchword was industrialisation.[22] These were more than political slogans, rather they symbolized an intense yearning for change. The 'new vision' of India that came be debated so intensely in the years to follow, had its beginnings in the last two decades of the 19th century. The quest for 'techno-scientific knowledge' preceded and facilitated the emergence of this 'vision'. At the Calcutta session of the Congress in 1901, an industrial exhibition was organized. The fervour was such that the Congress later sponsored an industrial conference on an annual basis. It also supported the 'national education' efforts which had begun as an integral part of the Swadeshi movement in 1905. Even in the midst of the First World War, the Congress continued the pressure. Its first example can be seen in the Note of Dissent submitted by Madan Mohan Malaviya as a member of the Indian Industrial Commission (1916–1918). His critique and suggestions remain valid even now.[23] He stressed that the British model was inadequate, and suggested specific measures for improvement. A decade before Jawaharlal Nehru, Malaviya had asked for 'an integrated economic development' based on new knowledge and technologies. Both, in their own way, realized the significance of modern technology as a new and strong linking of knowledge and power. The state was to play the most important role in this equation which, in turn, would make it all-powerful.

This was exactly the time that Gandhi appeared on the scene and took virtual control of both the Congress and the national movement. In the middle of growing demands for self-rule, democracy, industrialization, and development, Gandhi emerged as an extraordinary dissenter, with an extraordinary vision. He seldom used the terms science and technology. He was opposed to a machine-based civilization, but not machinery *per se*. Some of the very few occasions on which Gandhi touched on the issue of science and people directly were while he was talking to some students at Trivandrum in 1925, and when he visited the Indian Institute of Science at Bangalore in 1927. He said he was not an opponent or foe of science. He recalled how he once wanted to become a doctor but could not stand the idea of vivisection and retreated. He wanted to put certain limitations 'upon scientific research and upon the uses of science' in terms of humanity and morality. Moreover, he wanted science to be pursued for the sake of knowledge, accurate thought, and action. He cited how J. C. Bose and P. C. Ray pursued science for the sake of science and not for money or fame. Thereafter Gandhi would pose the most important question:

How will you infect the people of the villages with your scientific knowledge? Are you learning science in terms of the villages?[24]

There were no easy answers. The system prepared students (and still does) for an urban or industrial India or for a slot abroad. Gandhi was interested in something more than the political economy of his time; he was worried more about the distribution than about the generation of power or wealth. He warned his countrymen not to imitate Euro-America; he knew it would be virtually impossible and environmentally disastrous.

The national movement had generated a great deal of enthusiasm for independence as well as reconstruction. A clear direction came from the Lahore Congress, where Nehru talked not only about Purna Swaraj (complete self-rule) but also socialism and planned reconstruction. Taking advantage of this change, M. N. Saha persuaded the next Congress president, Subhas Chandra Bose, to appoint an NPC. Under Nehru's chairmanship, it began work in 1938 with 29 expert sub-committees dealing with different areas of national reconstruction. The onset of the Second World War and the Quit India Movement of 1942 disrupted this work. But soon it regrouped and by 1949, the NPC had published 27 volumes of reports, outlining a 10-year plan to be implemented by the government of free India.

There is one more dimension that has not received due attention until recent times, that of gender. Women in India have historically been excluded from knowledge generation and dissemination. Whatever knowledge they possessed was seldom acknowledged as knowledge. Science has always been considered masculine all over the world. A Western myth held that as women's brains developed, their ovaries shrank. In India many believed that girls who touched books would become widows. In the past, to think of a female Indian scientist was virtually impossible. It is only in the 20th century that a few women could get some training in physics and other basic sciences. In the field of medicine, of course, a very limited opportunity opened up in the 1880s and one finds some Indian women doctors like Kadambini Ganguli (1861–1923), Anandi Bai Joshi (1865–1887), and Hemvati Sen (1866–1933). The first medical school for women was opened at Ludhiana in Punjab in 1894. By 1929, 19 medical colleges and schools admitted women. The participation of women in engineering remained negligible till the early 1980s. It is only around the end of the 20th century that their enrolment has increased. Unlike the medical profession, engineering did not develop exclusive colleges for women.

The women's movement, as it developed during the 1920s and 1930s, saw education as a prerequisite for women's equality. Every cultural interlocutor and political activist of this period talked about it. However, the enrolment of girls in science education has remained dismal until recently. Notwithstanding the gender dichotomies in the nationalist discourse, women's education and aspirations surged ahead during the freedom struggle. We find such examples in scientists as Janaki Ammal (botanist, 1897–1984), Anna Mani (physicist, 1918–2001), Ashima Chatterjee (chemist, 1917–2006), and Lalita Chandrashekhar (physicist, 1910–2013). 'A self-conscious and self-confident identity' was emerging. Nevertheless, research institutions perpetuated 'their own gender biases'. Anna Mani could never earn a doctoral degree. Sunanda Bai, who had spent five years in Raman's laboratory and published 10 single-authored papers, committed suicide for reasons unknown. In 1939, Janaki Ammal wrote, '… because of its 'unscientific atmosphere—India is not a good place for scientific research—too much Red Tape in Government departments & Institutions'.[25] It seems that for social and cultural reasons also, women were unable to participate fully in science and remained in *the outer circle*. But after independence, the situation began to change, though many still feel and talk about the presence of a 'glass-ceiling'.

The most defining feature of the early 20th century was the beginning of the shift from colonial dependence to national independence. During the 1980s–1990s, several scholars tried to portray this shift in cultural and ideational terms.[26] Earlier this was done within the impact–response framework, which to some extent was useful.[27] But the colonial encounter was so complex and intense that no single framework could suffice. Unlike the previous studies that hovered around master–slave dialectics or the impact–response syndrome, the new microstudies emphasize the subsumed contradictions and disjunctions. As a result, the canvas has now been considerably enlarged; it involves studies on the power discourse as well as textual or prospographical analyses of cultural displacement and renegotiation. The cultural interlocuters of Victorian India themselves were no less aware of the contradictions and the dilemmas that they faced. Yet they had little choice but to work for both material benefits and traditional values. They wanted the best of both worlds, and in the process, they strove for more autonomy and power.

Notes

1. M. L. Sircar, *The Indian Association for the Cultivation of Science* (Calcutta: The Indian Association for the Cultivation of Science, 1877), p. 144.

2. 'Introduction by Tagore to Elmhirst's Lecture on the Robbery of the Soil', in *Poet and Ploughman*, by L. K. Elmhirst (Kolkata: Visva Bharati, 2008), p. 26.

3. *Tattwabodhini Patrika*, 1878, cited in Benoy Ghosh, *Samayik Patre Vamlar Samaj Chitra*, Vol. II (Calcutta: Bengal Publishers, 1964), p. 306.

4. For details on the British reluctance and Tata's dogged fight, see Deepak Kumar, *Science and the Raj*, 2nd edn (New Delhi: Oxford University Press, 2006), pp. 202–205.

5. Shiv Visvanathan, *Organizing for Science* (New Delhi: Oxford University Press, 1985), pp. 39–96.

6. B. K. Sarkar, *Education for Industrialisation* (Calcutta: Chatterjee & Sons, 1946), p. 3.

7. Cited in Suvobrata Sarkar, *Let There Be Light: Engineering, Entrepreneurship and Electricity in Colonial Bengal, 1880–1945* (Cambridge: Cambridge University Press, 2020), p. 41.

8. Letter to Hemantbala Devi, 19 April 1937, cited in William Radice, 'Particles and Sparks: Tagore, Einstein and the Poetry of Science', *India International Centre Quarterly* 25, nos 2–3 (1998): 131–150. See also Shiv Visvanathan, 'The Dreams of Reason: Rabindranath Tagore and the Invention of Science in India', *Economic and Political Weekly* 48, no. 47 (2003): 43–49.

9. Another poem critiquing big technologies:

> A rocket boasts: 'Watch what I do!
> I dare to hurl ash in the face of a star!'
> 'That', says the poet, 'won't get you far.
> The ash will fall back, right after you.'

Cited in Radice, 'Particles and Sparks'.

10. Deepak Kumar, 'Tagore's Pedagogy and Rural Reconstruction', in *Shantiniketan Hellerau: New Education in the 'Pedagogic Provinces' of India and Germany*, ed. Michael Mann (Heidelberg: Draupadi Verlag, 2015), pp. 309–330.

11. Krishna Kripalani, 'Foreword', in *Poet and Ploughman*, by L. K. Elmhirst (Kolkata: Viswa Bharati, 2008), p. x.

12. E. C. Dimock Jr., 'Rabindranath Tagore: The Greatest of the Bauls of Bengal', *The Journal of Asian Studies* 19, no. 1 (1959): 33–51.

13. V. V. Krishna, 'A Portrait of the Scientific Community in India', in *Scientific Communities in the Developing World*, ed. Jacques Gaillard, V. V. Krishna, and Roland Waast (New Delhi: Sage, 1997), pp. 236–280.

14. P. N. Bose, *A History of Hindu Civilisation during British Rule* (Calcutta: Newman & Co., 1896)

15. Ibid., vol. III, pp. ii–v.

16. Sometimes he did make tall claims. For example, according to a witness, on 6 December 1927, he announced that he had 'a wonderful drug that would alleviate human suffering'. His work on plant physiology was well recognized and he had worked on the reaction of stimulating and depressing drugs on the 'mimosa' plant, but no 'wonder drug' came. Heiser Diaries, 1927–1929, RG 12.1, RAC, New York.

17. P. C. Ray, *Life and Experiences of a Bengali Chemist*, vol. I (Kolkata: Asiatic Society (reprint), 1996), p. 289.

18. C. V. Raman, 'A New Radiation', *Indian Journal of Physics* 2 (1928): 387–398.

19. For the resolutions of the Congress, see A. M. Zaidi and S. Zaidi (eds), *The Encyclopaedia of the Indian National Congress*, vols I–V (New Delhi: S. Chand & Co., 1978), Vol. II, p. 406.

20. J. N. Sinha, 'Science and the Indian National Congress', in *Science and Empire: Essays in Indian Context (1700–1947)*, ed. Deepak Kumar (Delhi: Anamika Prakashan, 1991), pp. 161–162.

21. Zaidi and Zaidi, *Encyclopaedia of the Indian National Congress*, Vol. IV, p. 251.

22. Sumit Sarkar, *Swadeshi Movement in Bengal* (New Delhi: Peoples' Publishing House, 1973), p. 111.

23. Shiv Visvanathan has devoted a whole chapter to Malaviya's dissenting note in his *Organizing for Science*.

24. *The Hindu*, 19 March 1925, quoted in Raghvan Iyer (ed.), *The Moral and Political Writings of Mahatma Gandhi*, vol. 1 (Oxford: Clarendon Press, 1986), pp. 310–315.

25. The bureaucratic grip remained almost the same even after independence. In January 1955, Ammal wrote to a colleague abroad:

> I have been going through some difficult times over the sudden shifting of our laboratory from Calcutta to Lucknow and that in the middle of the growing season! All for the whims of one person—the [Joint] Secretary of our Ministry. It has upset my whole year's work on Nymphaea and Dioscorea. Now we have just 4 walls & no garden. However, one has to be prepared for all sorts of things in India.

For an in-depth study of Janaki Ammal and her time, see Savithri Preetha Nair, *Chromosome Woman, Nomad Scientist: E. K. Janaki Ammal, A Life 1897–1984* (London: Routledge, 2022).

26. Ashis Nandy, *Alternative Sciences: Creativity and Authenticity in Two Indian Scientists* (New Delhi: Allied Publishers, 1980); K. N. Panikkar, *Culture, Ideology, Hegemony: Intellectuals and Social Consciousness in Colonial India* (New Delhi: Tulika Publications, 1995); Tapan Raychaudhury, *Europe Reconsidered: Perceptions of the West in Nineteenth Century Bengal* (New Delhi: Oxford University Press, 1984).

27. B. T. McCully, *English Education and the Origins of Indian Nationalism* (New York: Columbia University Press, 1940); B. B. Misra, *The Indian Middle Classes* (London: Clarendon Press, 1965); R. C. Majumdar (ed.), *British Paramountcy and Indian Renaissance*, vol. 10 (Bombay: Bharatiya Vidya Bhawan, 1965).

5

Medical Knowledge and Public Health

To our national shame be it said that few, very few of the wonderful advances in the science of the healing art which have signalized recent years have been made by our country men. Even in tropical disease Frenchmen, Italians, Germans, Americans and even Japanese, are shooting ahead of us. We have to get a Koch to find for us the Cholera germ and a Haffkine to protect us from it, a Laveran to teach us what malaria is, a Kitisato to show us the germ of plague and a Yersin or a Haffkine to cure us of its effects.

—Patrick Manson [1]

Light comes from the East, but the light of medical science comes from the West. But our India ever ready to absorb the light from other sources, sometimes reflects but seldom radiates. In the domain of pure science under more favourable circumstances, we see already a radiant glow. In the science of medicine, if circumstances had favoured who knows we might not have had similar results. Each country is contributing its share to the common stock of medical knowledge but we have none to offer. We want a Professor Koch from Germany to tell us the cause of Asiatic cholera, and we are waiting for some other professor from somewhere else to find a cure for it.

—M. N. Banerjee at the Calcutta Session of the Indian National Congress in December 1901. [2]

Western medical ideas and practices occupied an extremely important place in the colonization of India. Western medicine functioned in several ways: as an instrument of control which would swing between coercion and persuasion as exigencies demanded, and as a site for interaction and often resistance. In its former role, it served the state and helped ensure complete dominance. The doctors who accompanied every naval dispatch from Europe emerged as powerful interlocutors (for both political and cultural purposes). They not only looked after the sick on ship and on land, but were also the first to report on the flora, fauna, resources, and cultural practices of the new territory. They were surgeon-naturalists and adventurer-scientists, roles in which they felt superior in their encounters with the medical practices of other people, although, intermittently, they did show respect for the latter. Increasingly, however, the colonial doctors developed into a cultural force. They began to redefine what they saw in terms of their own training and perceptions. Their work encompassed not only the understanding and possible conquest of new diseases but also the extension of Western cultural values to the non-Western world. [3]

The colonial discourse on medicine was mediated not only by considerations of political economy but also by several other factors. Polity, biology, ecology, the circumstances of material life, and new knowledge interacted and produced this discourse. The emergence of tropical medicine at the turn of the last century is to be seen in this light. It may be argued that tropical medicine itself was a cultural construct, 'the scientific step child of colonial domination and control'.[4] In the now burgeoning literature, terms like tropical medicine, imperial medicine, and colonial medicine have often been used interchangeably. But they have specific connotations. Tropical medicine and imperial medicine emphasize the tropics and the empire as units of analysis while colonial medicine stresses the colony. Each may attract different sets of questions. In tropical medicine, what ought to be the determining factor—climate, race, geography, or all taken together? What was carried over from the old medicine of tropical civilizations into the new tropical medicine? What attempts were made outside Europe to reconcile the older discourse of body humours and environmental miasmas with the new language of microbes and germs?

Marginalization

In travelogues and in colonial records, India was described as a vast pathological reservoir, overlaid perennially by a thick layer of maladies. The new code words were 'sudden', 'severe', 'decline', 'decadence', 'deterioration', 'degeneration', and, worst of all, 'putrefaction'. Against this backdrop, there were signs of some ambivalence and some appreciation of the indigenous ethos, at least until the mid-19th century. In this category come the works of J. Johnson (1813), B. Heyne (1814), H. Wilson (1825), W. Ainslie (1826), W. Twining (1832), G. Playfair (1833), J. R. Martin (1837, 1856), J. E. Royle (1837), T. W. Wise (1845), and many others. However, it was the culture of ancient India that began to receive some tributes. Medieval India, by contrast, came in for stinging criticism. Decadence and Muslim rule emerged as synonyms. Not many Indians would have agreed with these perceptions. But the educated Indians of the early and mid-19th century did show signs of restlessness and an acute sense of identity crisis. The language and practice of medicine were to play an important role in this.

Colonial hegemony rested upon baring the differences, real or assumed, and stamping its own supremacy. Differences were made to 'appear' great (though in some cases they were real enough). Medical discourse was an important tool to achieve this and at the same time a critical site of interaction and conflict. It was a double-edged weapon: it could distance and universalize simultaneously; one side emphasized the intrinsic difference between the two cultures while the other worked for scientific hegemony. It is, thus, not difficult to see the close relationship between the microparasites and the macro-parasites (that is, the colonizers).[5] Control over one was crucial to the success of the other. Yet, some argue that the role of medical discourse in the 'stabilisation of colonial rule was far more limited'. This role was conditioned and constricted by the values, opinions, and opposition of the indigenous society and the ground realities of the colonial economy.[6] This is a valid but limited argument. Parasitology had given many colonizers (especially those with lofty utilitarian views) a sense of purpose and a practical programme. It enabled and emboldened the colonizer, and sustained by this new will, the microscope supplanted the sword.

Even among the British officials, there were some who wanted the government to attempt a fusion of both 'both exotic principles and local practices, European theory and Indian experience', and thereby 'revive, invigorate, enlighten and liberalise the native medical profession in the mofussil'.[7] The establishment of Calcutta Medical College in 1835 was definitely a milestone, especially in the realm of anatomical knowledge. This college proved to be the pivot responsible for the dissemination of modern medical knowledge. Here medical education was imparted not only in English but in Bengali and Hindustani as well.[8] Its hospitals and dispensaries (called *daktarkhanas*) provided an opportunity for supplementing the pedagogic learning of medicine with clinical experience.[9] Yet there remained a lot to do to deal with dreadful diseases like cholera, malaria, pox, and plague.[10] These epidemics had an enormous impact on the economy and society of Bengal as in other parts of South Asia. The diseases were explained in terms of miasma, bad air, poor sanitation, contaminated water, and so on, of which the colonial officials had little knowledge or wherewithal to tame or control. Whenever reason failed, blame was put on superstition. As a Danish doctor noted, 'Superstition was extraordinarily strong among Indians, be they Christians, heathens or Muslims. Their doctors are just as superstitious …'[11]

As a critique argues, they were inclined to borrow but could not 'create a dialogue between the two epistemics'.[12] Long ago, a senior official of the Indian Medical Service (IMS) had written:

All the methods of scientific medicine are published and are available to the whole world; if the Hakims and Vaids have better methods we earnestly desire to know them and to adopt them. It is a great mistake to imagine that we are so blinded by prejudice that we refuse to investigate or accept useful remedies and methods merely because they are employed by the practitioners of other systems. Any useful method of treatment, from whatever source, is welcome by medical men of all sources. Quinine is a remedy which originated in Peru, mercury, arsenic and a host of other drugs were discovered by the ancient physicians of oriental countries.[13]

Co-opting the New Signs

From the Indian point of view, the mid-19th century was a period of looking for fresh opportunities and acquiring new knowledge. Syncretism, not revivalism, was the agenda. The emerging middle class was not blind to the fast-changing situation. Even some rulers were enlightened enough to see the new light. To illustrate, we take four relatively less known (though important) Indians from the three Presidency areas: Raja Serfoji (1798–1832, Tanjore), Bal Gangadhar Shastri Jambhekar (1802–1846, Bombay), S. C. G. Chuckerbutty (1826–1874, Calcutta), and Mahendralal Sircar (1833–1904, Calcutta).

Raja Serfoji, the last Maratha ruler of Tanjore, having surrendered real power to the British resident, spent his time in the pursuit of knowledge. Father Schwartz, a German missionary, was his friend, philosopher, and guide. Fascinated by the different systems of medicine, Serfoji had opened an institution for research in medical science and called it the Dhanvantri Mahal (abode of Lord Dhanvantri, the god of medicine). He assembled leading physicians there from the Ayurvedic, Yunani, Siddha, and Western systems. As a result of their interactions and investigations, the best among the tried and effective remedies were collected in a series of works named *Sarabendra Vaidya Muraigal*.[14] These were composed by the court poet in Tamil verse to facilitate easy memorizing and popularization. With the help of Father Schwartz and the British resident, Serfoji procured hundreds of European medical books and even surgical instruments. He already had a large collection of Tamil and Sanskrit manuscripts. Some of them dealt with diseases of animals and even birds. Ahead of his time, Serfoji also organized a hand-painted herbarium of medicinal plants in natural colours. In the eye wing of his Dhanvantri Mahal, he maintained a set of ophthalmic case sheets in an album, with authentic pictures of the eye and its defects, for research purposes. This is perhaps a very early example of 'methodical clinical research' under 'native' patronage, and must have induced the traditional physicians to take cognizance of

new therapies and methods. Serfoji appeared simultaneously in the roles of
practitioner and patient, diagnosing disease and judiciously moving between
medical systems in search of an effective cure. Moreover, this is an early
example of promoting plural medicine, making available to his people a range
of practical therapeutic options, including modern surgical skills.[15]

Serfoji was a man of resources with a genuine interest in medicine; a self-
taught doctor, he is said to have learnt the art of cataract removal. In contrast,
Bal Gangadhar Shastri Jambhekar was the first Indian to teach mathematics
at Elphinstone College in Bombay. He was also perhaps the first Indian to
start a journal for popularizing science (*The Bombay Durpan* in 1831), and
established the Native Education Society, which later did a commendable
job of translating some European works into Marathi, and Sanskrit works
(like the nosology of Madhav and the anatomy of Susrut) into English.
He wanted native practitioners to improve by studying 'anatomy from the
natural subject', even though touching a dead body was taboo at the time.
In 1837, the Bombay government sought his opinion on the desirability of a
medical school in Bombay and the nature of medical education to be given to
natives. In a written reply, Jambhekar asked for (1) the education of a limited
number of natives in all branches of the science, and (2) the dissemination
of the elements of medical knowledge among the *vaidya*s, *hakim*s, and the
community of the interior in general through the means of local language.[16]
This dissemination was to he achieved through translations or writing
synthetic books specifically for the purpose. Ordinary *vaidya*s and *hakim*s,
he felt, would respond better than the more 'learned' native practitioners,
as the latter were quite convinced of their own superiority and were unlikely
to compromise their status. Jambhekar wanted the government to go slowly,
without ruffling feelings, and be 'as little offensive as possible'. He argued
that the repugnance of the Brahmins towards dissection, and so on, could
he overcome 'by a little perseverance'. The Brahmins first shunned the Grant
Medical College in Bombay when it was established in 1845. The boycott
continued for more than a decade. But once they realized there was money in
modern medicine, they joined in hordes. How right this erudite *pundit* was!

S. C. Chuckerbutty came from a Brahmin family. He graduated from
Calcutta Medical College, and was one of the first four Indian medical
graduates sent to England in 1845 for higher studies. He was so much
charmed by Western values and people that he even embraced Christianity
before leaving for England, and put his teacher's name before his surname
(he became Soorjo Coomar Goodeve Chuckerbutty). Later he pronounced 'a
day in London' of more value than 'a month in Calcutta'. True to his training,

he lambasted indigenous practitioners: 'Every Boydo (*vaidya*) was a born Koberaj (physician) ... To suppose that a Boydo could not be a physician unless he passed an examination, was to question the ruling of Manu (an ancient law-giver)'. He was not in favour of medical education through Sanskrit or Arabic. He called it 'oriental mania'. But Chuckerbutty's perceptions changed later. He came to support the vernacular medium fully and criticized Calcutta University for representing 'only European opinion and interests' and ignoring 'the national element'. Long before social Darwinism became fashionable, he had attacked racialism:

> The inhabitants of the colder latitudes are white because the sun is less powerful on them ... In like manner the proteus, which dwells in caves, when exposed to the sun, becomes coloured, losing its former translucency of surface. The pride of colour, therefore, is as foolish in man as it could be in that humble creature.[17]

Mahendralal Sircar had studied medicine at Calcutta Medical College and enjoyed a stellar reputation as a doctor. He shunned orthodoxy, asked questions, and appreciated the plurality of therapeutic science. Faced with recurrent cholera outbreaks, he looked for remedies in homoeopathy, which Samuel Hahnemann (1755–1843) had pioneered in early 19th-century Germany. This shift was abhorred by his colleagues. But Sircar stood for a more 'plural encounter' between medical systems. He even delved into Ayurvedic texts and did not regard the system with contempt.[18] It was this non-parochial view and the desire to do something for his people and society that led him to think about the 'cultivation' of science in a land which had fallen 'fallow' for a long time. We have seen in Chapter 4 with what great difficulty he could establish the Indian Association for the Cultivation of Science (IACS) in 1876, and how he argued with Ramkrishna Parmahansa over the primacy of reason. He experimented with drugs himself:

> ... I made trial of drugs myself—preparations with my own hands—they acted marvellously in removing diseased conditions ... I made trials of other remedies such as Aconite, Belladonna, Nux Vomica ... I must say that I observed their unmistakable influence over disease, when administered after the principle of similarity of symptoms.[19]

We have thus seen the views of a native chief, a cultural interlocutor, and two 'modern' doctors. The first was action-oriented, the second persuasive, the third served the colonial state without being servile, and the fourth was a rebel *par excellence*. The emerging educated class showed great aptitude for change and new knowledge. But not the traditional *vaidyas*. The traditionalists were convinced that an alien government would not help them. Earlier the government had abolished medical classes at the Calcutta Madrasa and the Sanskrit College. Several thousand signatures were collected in protest. But nothing could stop, or even dilute, the Anglicists' victory in 1835.

In the average public esteem, however, indigenous practitioners continued to hold sway. In Calcutta, Gangaprasad Sen and Neelamber Sen were extremely popular.[20] They introduced fixed consultation fees, priced medicine, and the publication of sacred texts, with publicity through advertisements. Gangaprasad started the first Ayurvedic journal in Bengali, *Ayurveda Sanjivani*, and even exported Ayurvedic medicines to Europe and America. These were indications that certain European practices could be internalized and turned to the advantage of practitioners of indigenous medicine. Even at the conceptual level, the then reigning miasmatic theories and humoral pathology (of the *vaidya*s and *hakim*s) were not very incompatible. What Westerners were averse to was the oriental 'process', not its substance. Almost all of them did recognize the importance of and later emphasized the use of indigenous drugs.[21] But diagnostic procedures and, of course, surgery were to remain major areas of difference for a long time to come.

In 1896, Bhagvat Sinhjee, an Indian prince with training in modern medicine, wrote a history of Aryan medicine. With the help of certain texts, he argued that the Hindus knew that blood moved in blood vessels, but were ignorant of the particular course of its movement, which William Harvey was the first to demonstrate. He believed that European medicine owed much to the East, and with genuine enthusiasm concluded:

> The Indian Medicine deserves preservation and investigation. It is the business of all seekers after truth—be they Europeans or Hindoos—to take up the question in the spirit of fairness and sympathy. The revival of such a spirit will, it is hoped, lead at no distant date to a juster appreciation of Aryan Medical Science.[22]

Gananath Sen, an eminent Ayurvedic practitioner of the early 20th century, wrote a textbook titled *Sharir Parichay* (Introduction to Anatomy). He began with a complaint, 'Due to lack of anatomical knowledge, it is not possible to attain the desired knowledge in therapeutics too ... Primarily due to this fact, Ayurvedic practitioners have now become authority-less and unwelcome'. Then he unhesitatingly reproduced all the diagrams from either *Gray's Anatomy* or Cunningham's *Manual* and explained these diagrams in the language of ancient Ayurvedic texts in Sanskrit. He would argue that all these modern concepts remain 'hidden' in 'authoritative' ancient texts. He hardly realized that the language of modern anatomy had influenced him drastically and induced him to unabashed plagiarism.[23]

Medical Education

Earlier we have seen that India had a very strong medical tradition, which is still alive and flourishing. It continues to serve a large majority of the people. This would not have been possible without a system of education, however informal and sporadic it might have been. Ayurvedic education was imparted in *tols* run by eminent *vaidyas* while to some extent Yunani was taught in *maktabs*. This was largely empirical with the help of certain texts and commentaries. When the East India Company started oriental seminaries like the Sanskrit College in Banaras or the Madrasa in Calcutta, this kind of education was favoured. Those trained in modern medicine knew that the indigenous system was medieval but some of them also realized that it had grains of truth and did serve the people. With this pluralism in mind, a Native Medical Institution was established in Calcutta in 1822. But there soon emerged what came to be known as the Anglicist–Orientalist controversy. The Anglicists finally clinched it with Macaulay's Minute of 1835. They were convinced that the only way to combat disease was to weaken, if not eliminate, the base of the indigenous medical systems and patronize only their own system.[24]

When Lord William Bentinck opened Calcutta Medical College, there was great difficulty in finding sufficient students from the educated classes. Tempting facilities were offered but the higher-caste Hindus would not join; they especially objected to the anatomy classes and dissections. Eventually under the nurturing care of the Council of Medical Education, the lower-class Sudras were replaced by Brahmins, Kayasthas, and Baidyas.[25] Almost the same was the case when Madras got a medical college in 1835 and when in Bombay, the Grant Medical College was opened a decade later. The objectives were very clear; first, to train men to be hospital assistants and, second, to enable natives to become independent practitioners in the districts.

In Calcutta, the medical classes were of three kinds: (*a*) English class, (*b*) Bengali class, and (*c*) Hindustani class. Only those studying in the English class could hope to get the licentiate or bachelor in medicine degrees and this class was dominated by the Kayasthas. The Baidya caste preferred Bengali classes and the Muslims, Hindustani (Urdu medium) classes.[26] On 10 January 1836,

Madhusudan Gupta, a *pundit*, dissected a body to teach anatomy. This was done probably after a lapse of several centuries. A big taboo had been broken and this was hailed with a seven-gun salute from Fort William. As a mark of protest, a *vaidya* of high repute, Gangadhar Ray, is said to have left Calcutta in disgust.[27] Tension continued for a couple of decades but modern medical education had finally arrived.

After the Crown takeover in 1858, a number of medical schools granting a three-year licentiate degree were planned for Agra, Lahore, Nagpur, Sealdah, Dacca, Patna, Hyderabad, and so on. These schools required what the principal of Patna Medical School called 'nursing', 'special privileges', and 'monetary inducements.'[28] In 1886, it was found that while there was 'a large increase in the Calcutta Medical College and the Campbell School at Sealdah, the attendance at Patna fell from 151 to 92—a result ascribed to the backwardness of middle education in Bihar'.[29] Poverty was another reason; many could not afford the fees. In 1875, the Lahore Medical School reported that out of 28 native medical pupils, 21 were dismissed for 'idleness and incompetency'.[30] They were unable to read medical books in English and those in the vernacular were too few and elementary. Moreover, the curriculum was not uniform. Botany and zoology were not taught in these schools but chemistry, anatomy, and *materia medica* were taught. Training in surgery was rudimentary. The idea was to impart practical knowledge of the 'art' of medicine. This was done with an eye to promoting private practice in the *moffusil*. But the medical colleges were more rigorous in training and the bachelor in medicine course required five years, a year more than what was required even in London. The result was the three-year licentiate course became much more popular than the bachelor in medicine course. For newly trained Indians, research in medicine looked a distant dream; private practice was and still remains a far more lucrative option.

Research in Medicine

… as a matter of fact, research is discouraged, and too often in the IMS an energetic officer is at once dubbed a faddist and a nuisance. Originality is not encouraged, but rather the reverse, as is exemplified by the treatment which Maj. Ronald Ross received for the splendid work he did in India. 'It makes my blood boil to think of the way that the Government of India treated Ross', wrote a member of the IMS to me.[31]

Medical research in the modern sense may not have been on the agenda of the colonial government but they did encourage medical surveys and took prompt action when their own establishments and cantonments were threatened with disease outbreaks. Each Presidency had its own Medical Board, and it ran a well-oiled cadre, the IMS, while the Army had the Army Medical Department (AMD).[32] They all helped in the emergence of what came to be called tropical medicine.[33] The diseases this dealt with were supposed to be tropical in nature, and to know their causes and character was crucial to the existence of European armies, traders, and officials. This knowledge made them understand what impact hot climates had on the European constitution and whether the white races could survive in the tropics. In short, the Raj rested on this knowledge.

The members of the IMS were well-trained but were overburdened with hospital work and regular outbreaks of epidemics. So, focussed research in their own area was not feasible. But they did contribute enormously to botanical, geological, and meteorological knowledge, on which they could undertake research in their spare time or when they were deputed on government orders. Medical men like W. Roxburgh and N. Wallich enriched botanical knowledge as very few could do. Francis Balfour worked on the connection of meteorology with health. W. B. O'Shaughnessy had compiled *The Bengal Pharmacopoeia* in 1844, but is better known for introducing the telegraph in India. R. Royle and J. Falconer contributed to both botany and Himalayan geology. R. Tytler, who helped fight cholera at Jessore in 1817, was also accomplished in anatomy, surgery, and mathematics. But the field where he made significant breakthroughs was electro-galvanism, where he claimed to have made discoveries similar to those of Faraday! In addition, he had translated the *London Pharmacopoeia* into Urdu. There were numerous medical men who made significant contributions. They not only collected data but published with whatever limited analytical tools and resources they had.

In 1823, a Medical and Physical Society was established in Calcutta. Its purpose was to collect and publish original papers relating to medicine and surgery. This society even elected four Indians—Radhakant Deb, Ramcomul Sen, Madhusudhan Gupta, and Raja Kalikrishna Bahadur—as corresponding members in 1827, and they produced a few papers on indigenous drugs. In 1838, a similar society was formed in Bombay. Both societies published their *Transactions*. There were numerous other journals, in English as well as in Indian languages, which published articles of medical interest. All these journals had a great influence on the formulation of medical policy and practices in India. This signalled the beginning of a new kind of professionalization. Thanks to a greater acceptance of the print media, several issues like modern versus traditional medicine, allopathy versus homoeopathy, and miasma versus contagion were debated at great length and over a long period of time.

The earliest to catch the attention of the colonizers were venereal diseases and smallpox. Venereal diseases were called *firangi rog* as they were brought by the Portuguese. The European army and its cantonments suffered the most from these dreadful diseases. In fact, the earliest hospitals established by the Europeans were called lock hospitals, wherein the poor native prostitutes were kept for treatment under lock.[34] The treatment was mercury along with forced abstention from sex. Dozens of such hospitals functioned during the early 19th century. Syphilis ranked as one of the most destructive diseases that affected mostly White soldiers who were away from their families and were more prone to vices. Another big scourge which affected everyone was smallpox. For centuries, this was handled by a method called variolation which involved application of live pox pustules on healthy forearms after a little incision, followed by some dietary advice and worship of the Goddess Sitala. This gave some immunity but failures were frequent and it was not always easy to get live pustules. In 1796, Edward Jenner created the first vaccine, and within six years, vaccination was used in Madras. This was the first attempt at preventive public health which met with some acceptance and much resistance.[35] Touching the body later turned into control of the body. It involved a complex negotiation of different perceptions which continues even now.

Cholera, malaria, and plague were far more frightful. Between 1817 and 1865, cholera alone took about 15 million lives and for the period between 1865 and 1947, the toll was around 23 million.[36] Of all the diseases, malaria was most rampant and had the greatest political, agricultural, and military ramifications.[37] While malaria continued to pose a problem, plague became extremely virulent in the last decade of the 19th century. Both cholera and malaria were described as miasmatic. Weather, foul air, and devils were held responsible for these diseases. Malaria came from 'mal-aria' ('Bad air' in Italian). But the 1860s saw a revolution in medical thought. A French chemist, Louis Pasteur (1822–1895) proposed a germ theory of diseases which demonstrated microorganisms as the cause of diseases. Actually, during that period scientists were working on the notion of the species, trying to identify the origin of life. When Charles Darwin (1809–1882) went to the Galapagos islands and theorized on the evolution of species, Pasteur was riveted, turning to his microscope and revealing the origin of diseases in germs. This is how a new kind of cosmopolitan modern medicine was born.[38] The idea came from the chemistry of fermentation and the vaccine became its tool.

The epidemics were mass-killers, no doubt; even among the British troops, the casualty because of war was only 6 per cent, the rest died because of cholera, malaria, or plague. The names of three European medical scientists who worked in India are associated with these diseases—Robert Koch (1843–1910), Ronald Ross (1857–1932), and Waldemar Haffkine (1860–1930). They were the new 'scientific explorers' who played and tinkered with 'colonies' of microbes under their microscope. Robert Koch had developed the criteria and procedures necessary to establish that a particular microbe and none else caused a particular disease. In 1883, Robert Koch discovered the 'Comma' bacillus in Egypt, associated with cholera, and visited Calcutta's water tank the same year to confirm the discovery. This was an important contribution and helped to establish a germ theory of disease causation over the earlier miasmatic theories. The development and uses of germ theories varied across medicine, with different groups describing germs differently, depending on their interests, resources, and work.[39]

It was obvious now that a disease could be handled with biological intervention. Emphasis on vaccination meant restraint and handling of the body on some kind of a 'military' model. It also meant that hygiene would take a back seat. Even earlier, hygiene had always been on a 'missionary' mode marked by extreme denunciation of native habits and practices, which views were not unjustified. Hygiene was considered a personal and social problem, which a colonial state could easily wash its hands off. The indigenes were considered 'virus reservoirs', who could be treated and made productive through 'systematic quininisation' and later, vaccination. The germ theory seemed to provide a better option, and vaccines proved a boon to the state. In 1880, the British passed compulsory vaccination laws in India but their enforcement was not entirely feasible. Moreover, within the medical establishment itself, there were strong differences between the contagionists and the anti-contagionists. The former advocated segregation and quarantine, buttressing thus state power, and finally won the say. But even within those who knew how to 'fix' the germs, the dilemma remained as to what kind of germs to use, 'live' or 'dead'?[40]

While the bacteriological revolution was in the offing, India suffered a number of epidemics. A vicious cholera outbreak in 1861 made the government realize that segregation or palliatives were not enough; more knowledge about the disease itself was required. So, a Cholera Commission was appointed.[41] But no conclusive evidence on the cause of cholera could be found. This had to wait for two more decades. In 1872, the first Leprosy census was carried out, and the very next year Gerhard Henrik Hansen (1841–1912) detected 'rod-shaped bodies' on leprous nodules, which came to be known as *Mycobacterium leprae*. These he postulated to be the transmitting agents of the disease. Hansen's discovery of the *Mycobacterium leprae* was historic, leading to leprosy being called 'Hansen's disease'. But the government health officials continued to believe that air and soil were responsible for cholera. Only Francis MacNamara (1831–1899), professor of chemistry at Calcutta Medical College differed, and believed it to be water borne; he knew it was an intestinal bacillus. He himself contacted this disease and had to retire in 1876. He received no encouragement from his own government which ironically funded Robert Koch to visit Cairo and Calcutta, resulting in the discovery of the vibrio cholera. Had he been given the opportunity to visit cholera affected Egypt which he had requested, he might have been the discoverer of the bacillus, not Koch. Plague was another dreadful scourge. In 1894, Alexandre Yersin (1863–1943) isolated the bacillus of plague in the midst of a plague epidemic in Canton and Hong Kong. All this led to an unprecedented spurt in trials for new vaccines. This had significant implications for India and other colonies.

Medical Pioneers

Of all the medical men in India, only a select few like W. M. Haffkine, Ronald Ross, Charles Donovan (1863–1951), and Leonard Rogers (1868–1962) were obsessed with research and could make fundamental discoveries. Their work meant a lot for public health. In 1892, Haffkine perfected an attenuated cholera vaccine which gave satisfactory results on laboratory animals. He looked for field trials on humans. Lord Dufferin recommended him to India, a vast pathological reservoir ideally suited for 'controlled' experiments. Indians had used variolation (in which the virus came directly from the infected person) for smallpox for centuries. What Haffkine now offered was a virus at 'a given and fixed state of virulence' with the same safety and measurement as Jenner's calf-lymph or Pasteur's rabies emulsions. His new testing grounds were army cantonments, tea gardens, jails, pilgrim routes, and slums.[42] But the results were mixed and varied when doses differed or when it was administered before or during a cholera outbreak. In 1896, bubonic plague broke out in Bombay and Haffkine was asked to prepare a suitable vaccine which he did after a series of experiments on laboratory animals.[43]

Right from the beginning of the plague outbreak, Haffkine differed from the schemes of disinfection, segregation, and forced hospitalization which the government medical officials had launched.[44] This was apparently not liked by the officials. To Haffkine, the only plausible method to combat the epidemic was individual preventive treatment. The government would rather put the blame on the ignorance and insanitary conditions of the natives.[45]

The government had its own reasons to panic, and so had the people. They could hardly come to terms with each other. Certain measures evoked sharp opposition, even riots.[46] But there were many who came forward with little or some persuasion to accept Haffkine's prophylaxis. So, there was no single, homogenous response from Indian society. It varied from place to place, and time to time.[47] Haffkine himself had a fine understanding of Indian society. In a letter to a senior official (which for obvious reasons remained unanswered), he wrote:

> The natives here are, of course, not the prodigies of imbecility, superstition, and ingratitude which some good papers occasionally amuse themselves in representing them to be. Every civil surgeon or practitioner who has had an occasion of extracting a cataract or stone, or rendering any other good to a native, will say that such a description does not accurately represent him. Stories of superstitious fabrications attributed to the people are sometimes manufactured, sometimes only favoured and exaggerated, by an unwilling or incapable executive.[48]

Around the same time came an original discovery of everlasting value. In 1898, Ronald Ross (IMS, 1881) proved conclusively the relationship between malaria and the mosquito. Even in the midst of his fundamental work and much before he won recognition, Ross asked for different approaches to the study of bacterial diseases and that of animal parasites. He argued

> that a bacteriologist is not necessarily well-acquainted with the animal parasites, and that the tropical diseases due to animal parasites (malaria, dysentery, hepatic abscess, worm diseases, forms of diarrhoea) are just as important, if not more important than those due to bacteria (cholera, typhoid, leprosy, etc.). Hence Public Health Research work must split into various branches, each requiring different investigators.[49]

Gradually, Ross developed interest in the practical applications of his work, seeing malarial control as a matter of reducing the population of mosquitoes by destroying or treating their breeding areas. He argued, 'Rather than take so much trouble in protecting ourselves from the bites of these insects, would it not be better to get rid of them at once?'[50] This was a practical and preventive approach but it involved considerable expenditure and large-scale sanitary measures. No wonder the governments in India and in England preferred to ignore Ross.[51] Both Ross and Haffkine shared certain traits. They were actually aware of their own importance, they disdained the bureaucracy, and put a premium on 'men', not institutions. Ross wrote, 'we do not want laboratories, we want men'.[52] Haffkine would say, 'the worker is the chief item, not bricks and mortar, etc'.[53] Both believed in taking laboratory results to the common man; they believed more in prevention than in cure and sought active state intervention. As their expectations could not be fully met, both suffered exhaustion and frustration.

There was indifference on the part of government, no doubt, but no less inhibiting were the internal squabbles among the professionals. Ross had his own pangs of suffering but was lucky to get support from his peers in England; he won a Nobel Prize in 1902. Ross worked on aetiology; he unveiled the secrets of a parasite and its host (the female anopheles mosquito) while Haffkine's work was prophylactic. Unfortunately, Haffkine was not liked by many because he was a zoologist, not a doctor; moreover, a foreigner and not a member of the IMS. Of him, Ross once wrote:

> He is afraid that if the Institute takes me on, and then the theory fails, the Institute's reputation will suffer. He also seems to think that I have been theorising too much or talking too much. Haffkine who is to be the head of the Institute advises 'quiet pursuance of studies without stirring up exaggerated expectations and artificially exciting attention'. I am replying suitably and reminding him, very gently of the cholera inoculation business! In this world, it is necessary to excite attention, I fear.[54]

Even though Haffkine kept a low profile (he did not mix with his fellow Jews in Bombay), his close associates like H. Bannerman, J. Gibson, and R. Listen, whom he had brought from obscure field stations, betrayed him in subtle ways. He ran into trouble when in November 1902, in the village of Mulkowal (Punjab), 19 out of 107 vaccinated persons developed tetanus and died. Blame for this disaster was promptly put on Haffkine, the method of decanting in his laboratory, and the changes he had recently introduced in his vaccine-preparation method. 'Haffkine ought to be hung for his folly', screamed Lord Curzon.[55] 'If this appalling catastrophe comes out, there will be an end to all inoculation in India, and the cause of science will be set back for a generation'. Curzon gave his judgement when the incident had been barely reported and much before an enquiry could be held. Haffkine had to return to England in disgust and disgrace. Though he was exonerated and reinstated in 1907, he was no longer the same; he had turned to Zionism![56]

But there were some like Charles Donovan (1863–1951) and Leonard Rogers (1868–1962), stationed in Madras and Calcutta, respectively, who

carried the flame of research into the 20th century. In 1903, Donovan had
traced the cause of Kala-azar to a parasite (known as *Leishmania donovani*)
in the spleen of affected persons, and in 1904, Leonard Rogers showed by
culture that this parasite was a flagellate. Rogers had worked on leprosy and
believed in the institutionalization of medical research. In the first quarter of
the 20th century, there was some optimism in the air. It was claimed, 'it is by
no means an impossible task to make the tropics healthy … the mosquito is
no longer a nightmare, it can be got rid of'; similarly Rogers felt, 'leprosy can
be stamped out in the greater part of the British Empire probably within three
decades'.[57] After much lobbying and effort, he founded in 1914 the Calcutta
School of Tropical Medicine.[58] Thanks to his efforts and contributions from
the Rockefeller Foundation, in 1932, the All India Institute of Hygiene and
Public Health (AIIHPH) was established in Calcutta. This institute was
expected to undertake applied research and instruction in public health,
sanitary engineering, biochemistry, nutritional diseases, and so on.

How Public Was Public Health?

The Question is no less than this: How to create a public health department
for India—how to bring a higher civilization into India. What a work, what
a noble task for a government—no 'inglorious period of our dominion' but
a most glorious one.

—Florence Nightingale in 1864[59]

The celebrated Lady with the Lamp was caring and concerned. She would not
pour scorn, even in the face of disillusionment. She wanted the government
to take the lead and would encourage even small individual efforts.[60] Yet her
period unfortunately saw millions perishing in famines and epidemics. Why
did this happen, why was she ignored? Here one may ask, how 'public' was
public health? Currently it is defined as 'a grand social intervention' and also
as 'a historical, self-conscious social and scientific movement'.[61] Can this
definition be applied to a colonial situation? In Britain, Edwin Chadwick had
attempted an administrative and engineering solution to the problem of high
urban death rates. For funding, he coaxed Britain's towns to raise taxes and
this led to a political firestorm which ended his career.[62] Could there be a
Chadwick in colonial India?

Right from the mid-19th century, questions relating to public health
engaged both the official and public mind in India, and the debates
gradually became more intense in the wake of major cholera and plague
epidemics. These ranged from assertions of imperial altruism to allegations of

colonial callousness. One of the early Indians to talk in terms of sanitation and public health was again Soorjo Coomar Chuckerbutty. On 8 January 1852, he gave a public lecture on the 'Sanitary Improvement of Calcutta' and dwelt upon the need for better sanitary habits, water pipelines, sewage, water tank management, and so on. He sought strict legislation to stop adulteration in food items.[63] It was easier to explain certain things and make demands on an alien government than to effect real improvement. In view of the growing urbanization, agrarian distress, famines, and so on, the health situation remained bleak.

Unfortunately, public health remained limited to compilation of rather inaccurate vital statistics, vaccination, segregation, and so on. But even these were so wired in government machinery and 'so hopelessly tied in bureaucratic knots' that, as one foreign observer wrote, 'one doubts whether untangling can ever occur and the only hope is for a completely new system'.[64] Yet at the non-government level, certain new experiments were attempted. For example, in 1925, even a film on malaria was made by one Aurora Cinema Company of Baghbazar, Calcutta.

Another perceived difficulty was the process of Indianization that was taking place in the wake of the constitutional reforms of 1919. Senior European medical officers like L. Rogers, J. Megaw, and others were opposed to it and thought it would lower medical standards. But because of growing nationalist feelings, nothing could be done to retain the so called 'pristine purity' of the IMS. It is true that in the roll of honour of those who contributed fundamentally to modern medical knowledge, Indian names are almost missing. But one name shines through. This was Upendranath Brahmachari (1875–1946) who found a cure for the dreadful disease kala-azar (black fever). Its aetiology was first discovered by Leishman and Donovan in 1903. But no cure was in sight. A decade later Rogers introduced antimony treatment (*tarter emetic*) but this had serious toxic effects. After years of research, in 1921, Brahmachari produced the first organic antimony (stibalinic acid with urea). This urea stibamine worked miracles and saved lakhs of lives.[65] But it seems he was not above controversy. As a contemporary noted,

Brahmacharee was given a grant by the Indian Research fund. He ran on to von Hayden's urea and stibium work. As there are no copyright laws, he called the discovery his own and kept the formula secret. When the deception was discovered, he claimed he had worked out an important change in the process. He is said to have made several lakhs. Now another firm is making the product and Brahmacharee is suing.[66]

An area which received belated but considerable attention was female healthcare. Childbirth being an important attribute of a woman's body, what did the new medical knowledge and practices mean for the family, the government, and society at large? This was a period when both infant and maternal mortality were very high. Institutions like Calcutta Medical College and the Calcutta Municipal Corporation gradually transformed a female-oriented ritual into a medical event. In this transformation, the colonial government, its medical men, and the new *bhadralok* participated almost equally. The Countess of Dufferin Fund established in 1885 was a milestone. Women were now being encouraged to study and practice medicine. Kadambini Basu (1861–1923) and Hemabati Sen (1866–1933) were the pioneers of this change. Christian missionaries also played a significant role. Gradually even the rural *daktar*s began to prefer trained midwives over traditional *dhais*. Some licentiate doctors wrote articles and even books like Devendranath Roy's *Sochitro Dhatrishiksha* (Illustrated Guide to Midwifery) to 'convey the most baffling aspects of the subject in a lucid and intelligible manner'.[67] In the early 20th century, the knowledge of obstetrics and its tools (notably, forceps) made a big difference. Dr Kedarnath Das (1867–1936) was hailed as a great obstetrician. In 1928, he published a book titled *Obstetric Forceps: Its History and Evolution*. Women doctors wrote tracts and articles mostly of a primary and popular nature. Medical research was not for them, and 'no Science for Lady Doctors'.[68] The autobiographical works of two women doctors from two different parts of India, belonging to two different timeframes, demonstrate the fact that they were marginalized in the field of medicine: Dr Hemabati Sen and Dr Muthulakshmi Reddy (1886–1968), one from Bengal and the other from Madras, concentrated on the field of women and childcare.[69] In fact, Dr Reddy spent a great part of her life in the uplift of women and children.

Churns in Ayurveda–Yunani

The encounter between practitioners of indigenous medical systems and modern medical med produced hybrids known as *daktar*s who served best rural or *moffusil* societies.[70] They came from good families, had some kind of medico-scientific training, were sometimes fired with entrepreneurial zeal, and they invariably lauded cultural traditions. Yet they recognized:

> This is the age of science—goodbye to luck and fate. Man will fight death and disease. When he was helpless, he saw immortality in death, now he is looking for immortality in life ... Modern medical science is forging ahead; with the discovery of the microscope, the inner eye has opened, germs are being identified. The entire idea about causes of diseases is fast changing ...[71]

A recent work asks and probes a pertinent question: 'what is modern about modern Ayurveda?' The term 'encounter' probably has more political than cultural overtones. It offers 'the braiding of East and West around material objects and ideas' as a better explanation.[72] Ayurveda and Yunani practitioners drew their legitimacy from classical texts but their practice was always open to change. Especially under a formidable colonial impact, different medical ideas and even tools appeared and circulated. Thermometers, stethoscopes, microscopes, and vaccines had emerged and their utility and relevance could not be ignored even though they came from the West. These had to be accepted, internalized, or, to use a currently fashionable term, 'provincialized'. Miasmatic explanations, *tridosa*, and the germ theory could co-exist in the *daktar*'s mind. But this hybridization had its own dichotomies; it lacked coherence and organic growth. Nevertheless, Ayurvedic teachers and practitioners like Gangadhar Ray, Surendranath Goswami, Neelamber Sen, and Gananath Sen enjoyed iconic status. Numerous tracts, books, and journals dealing with medical and health issues were printed in Bengali.[73]

In the given scenario of complete hegemonization, the possibilities of intercultural interactions were rather limited. The indigenous systems felt so marginalized that they sought survival more in resistance than in collaboration. Total acceptance of new knowledge sometimes did mean total rejection of the old. Under such pressure, some of the 'old' withdrew into their own shell. Yet the majority of Indians had favoured revival and synthesis. There were several areas in which the Western and indigenous systems could collaborate but did not. The former put emphasis on the cause of the disease, the latter on *nidana* (treatment). Microbes and microscopes constituted the new medical spectacle. But the *vaidya*s emphasized the power of resistance in the human body. To them, the improvement of the *kshetra* (body of the patient) was far more important than the microbe and its destruction. The Westerners were forced to take cognizance of indigenous drugs, and the *vaidya*s took to anatomy, ready delivery of medicines, quick relief, and so forth. But the comparison ends here. Borrowed knowledge seldom develops into organic knowledge. This was true also of the hundreds of doctors produced by the government medical colleges annually. In the melee, some really good opportunities were lost.

Reflections in the 'Native' Press

In 1864, a Bengali magazine, *Somprakash* enquired why students, after studying Western medicine, had produced 'no new invention', 'no new medicine'. 'None of them after knowing the former system of therapy (*chikitsa*) have tried to examine the medicinal matters (*dravya*) ... they mainly concentrate on their fees.[74] Making money out of disease was true of European doctors as well. In 1854, one of them described his medical practice as 'killing and curing done by contract as it were'.[75] Still, practitioners of Western medicine were making steady inroads into public opinion.

In 1872, a Tamil journal noted that medical students in Madras were being 'complained of as incompetent and deficient'. 'In place of cramming these youths with the mysteries of a science and language foreign and distasteful, would it not be infinitely wiser, and better to encourage Native Doctors?' it asked.[76] In 1887, a Telugu weekly asked for both systems to be studied. 'Persons who are acquainted with practicing English medicine and chemistry, etc. should carefully study Hindu medical works and make experiments with their medicines and write books in the vernacular languages'.[77] Despite these demands, the indigenous system was gradually losing its traditional support from even the local chiefs and rajas. In 1874, a Malayalam journal reported that the Maharaja of Travancore, 'having examined various Hindu, Jaina and Turkish works', now preferred English doctors. It surmised that 'the time has come for the Hindu medical authorities to sink into obscurity before the English'.[78] Later, this turned out to be a false prophecy. For in the last decade of the 19th century, the revival of interest in Ayurveda was marked and widespread. Perhaps it had something to do with the emergence of the *swadeshi* spirit (self-reliance) and the political movements of the time.

Several outbreaks of plague, debates about the efficacy of the new vaccines in combating epidemics, the opening of bacteriological institutes (at Mukteshwar, Kasauli, Bombay, Coonoor, and so on), the policy of forced segregation, and compulsory vaccination were the critical areas where suspicion (bordering on hatred) of and social opposition (resulting sometimes in riots) to Western medicine were nursed. These made the traditional alternatives more exciting and trial-worthy. In 1896, a Tamil journal asked for the introduction of the native system of medicine in government medical colleges,[79] and 14 years later, a Calcutta daily repeated this never-to-be fulfilled demand.[80] A Telugu weekly wanted the government to spend on 'native drugs and recipes' just a tenth of what it spent on hospitals.[81] People were shifting from allopathic medicines in the wake of epidemics and forced vaccinations. Rumours were rife. One such rumour was:

> Since the germs were taken from cows, after taking it [the vaccine] one would contract small pox and after recovering, his (the patient's) face would be changed and he would have horns on his head.[82]

Even among Westerners, opinions were divided on the wisdom of opening bacteriological laboratories. Some reminded the government of the greased cartridges and the Mutiny of 1857. 'To introduce diseased animal matter into the very blood—this is sheer pollution in the eyes of thousands upon thousands of Indians'.[83] When Haffkine introduced the Pasteurian system of inoculation in Bengal in 1893, the journal *Vrittanta Chintamani* was among those that welcomed it.[84] But only six years later, in the midst of a plague outbreak, the same journal criticized the authorities for preventing native physicians from trying their medicine. 'The English doctors are too zealous and think that they have the monopoly of the knowledge of medicine', it argued.[85] Several journals pointed to the racial underpinnings of the government's policy. When British citizens were under no compulsion to accept vaccination, why should Indian subjects be made to do so? [86] When an advertisement appeared asking only Europeans and Anglo-Indians to apply for some assistant surgeonships, a daily asked, 'Why should preference be given to Europeans at the cost of Indians in the country of Indians?'[87] Another raised the interesting point of the great difference between 'the Englishmen's ideas of cleanliness and ours' (the former bathing only once in eight days!), and wanted questions of sanitation to be left to the Indians themselves.[88]

Possibilities for improvement were enormous. Suggestions poured in, but where was the will? Pilgrims to Mecca from Egypt and Indonesia were compulsorily vaccinated against smallpox and cholera. But this was thought impossible in India. Rogers' suggestion to inoculate pilgrims going to the Prayag Kumbh was considered by the Pilgrim Committee as 'impracticable, inexpedient, and even dangerous'. Had the practitioners of indigenous medical systems been co-opted, public health might have made more progress. After all, they remained popular even in the face of stiff competition and open hostility. Unfortunately, the modern medical men were too sure of their competence and superiority. The Bhore Committee of 1944 reinforced their convictions.[89]

Nevertheless, thanks to the new developments in medicine, health was poised to become a rallying point and a centre of cooperative action. Health was to come on the political centre stage in another sense also. A. V. Hill, who in 1944 reported on the state of scientific research in India, talked of a quadrilateral dilemma, that is, population, health, food, and natural resources. To him the fundamental problems of India were 'not really physical, chemical or technological, but a complex of biological ones referring to population, health, nutrition and agriculture, all acting and reacting with one another'.[90] Colonial India no doubt had its limitations. Could independent India meet the challenge?

Notes

1. P. Manson to Sir Charles Crosthwaite, 5 July 1897, Ross Papers, 02/027, Liverpool School of Tropical Medicine.
2. A. M. Zaidi and S. Zaidi (eds), *The Encyclopaedia of the Indian National Congress*, Vol. IV (New Delhi: S. Chand & Co., 1978), p. 144.
3. For a relevant collection of essays, see Deepak Kumar and Rajsekhar Basu (eds), *Medical Encounters in British India* (New Delhi: Oxford University Press, 2013).
4. Lenore Manderson, *Sickness and the State: Health and Illness in Colonial Malaya 1870–1940* (Cambridge: Cambridge University Press, 1996), pp. 10–14.
5. For elaboration, see William H. McNeill, *Plagues and Peoples* (New York: Anchor Books, 1976).
6. For details, see David Arnold, *Colonizing the Body: State Medicine and Epidemic Disease in Nineteenth-Century India* (New Delhi: Oxford University Press, 1993); Mark Harrison, *Public Health in British India: Anglo Indian Preventive Medicine, 1859–1914* (Cambridge: Cambridge University Press, 1994); Anil Kumar, *Medicine and the Raj: British Medical Policy in India, 1835–1911* (New Delhi: Sage, 1998).
7. W. Adams, *Report on Vernacular Education* (Calcutta: Government Press, 1868), pp. 322–323.
8. Jayant Bhattacharya, 'Encounter in Anatomical Knowledge: East and West', *Indian Journal of History of Science* 43, no.2 (2008): 163–209. For tables on the number of students at this college, and so on, see Poonam Bala, *Imperialism and Medicine in Bengal: A Socio-historical Perspective* (New Delhi: Sage, 1991), pp. 135–140.
9. Srilata Chatterjee, *Western Medicine and Colonial Society: Hospitals of Calcutta, 1757–1860* (Delhi: Primus Books, 2017), pp. 215, 282–288.
10. Kabita Ray, *History of Public Health: Colonial Bengal 1921–1947* (Calcutta: K. P. Bagchi, 1998); Mridula Ramanna, *Western Medicine and Public Health in Colonial Bombay, 1845–1895* (Hyderabad: Orient Longman, 2002); M. Harrison and B. Pati (eds), *The Social History of Health and Medicine in Colonial India* (London: Routledge, 2008); Arabinda Samanta, *Living with Epidemics in Colonial Bengal, 1818–1945* (New Delhi: Manohar, 2016).
11. N. T. Jensen, 'The Medical Skills of the Malabar Doctors in Tranquebar, as Recorded by Surgeon Folly in 1798', *Medical History* 49 (2005): 489–515.
12. K. N. Panikkar, 'Indigenous Medicine and Cultural Hegemony: A Study of the Revitalization Movement in Keralam', *Studies in History* 8, no. 2 (1992): 283–307.
13. J. W. D. Megaw, Inspector General, Hospitals, Note dated 6 September 1928, 1HD, 1.1, 464 India Box 5, folder 34, Rockefeller Archive Center (RAC).

14. G. Ganapathi Rao, 'Dhanvantari Mahal', *Journal of the Tanjore Saraswati Mahal Library* 30 (1977): I–IV. Numerous books, instruments, and medical case sheets survive as the Modi Raj Records at the Saraswati Mahal Library, Thanjavur.

15. Savithri Preetha Nair, 'Diseases of the Eye: Medical Pluralism at the Tanjore Court in the Early Nineteenth Century', *Social History of Medicine* 25, no. 3 (2012): 573–588. For more details, see Savithri Preetha Nair, *Raja Serfoji II: Science, Medicine and Enlightenment in Tanjore 1798–1832* (New Delhi: Routledge, 2012).

16. Home, Public, No. 18, K.W. Pt A, 18 July 1838, NAI.

17. S. C. G. Chuckerbutty, *Popular Lectures on Subjects of Indian Interest* (Calcutta: Thomas Smith, 1870), pp. 56, 85, 138.

18. Dhrub Kumar Singh, 'Choleraic Times and Mahendra Lal Sarkar', *Medizin Geshellschaft und Geschichte* no. 24 (2005): 207–242.

19. Cited in Shinjini Das, 'Debating Scientific Medicine', *Medical History* 56, no. 4 (2012): 463–480.

20. Chuckerbutty records that one of his serious patients asked for Neelamber Sen. When he arrived, people lined up to see him. The patient could not be saved but the day and hour of death foretold by the *vaidya* proved to be correct. Chuckerbutty, *Popular Lectures*, p. 139.

21. W. B. O'Shaughnessy (Professor of Chemistry, Calcutta Medical College, 1835–1849) had compiled a *Bengal Pharmacopoeia* to facilitate greater use of locally available drug materials and reduce expensive imports from Europe.

22. Bhagvat Sinhjee, *A Short History of Aryan Medical Science* (London: Macmillan, 1896). A review of the work appeared in *The Athenaeum* no. 3634, 19 June 1897.

23. Gananath Sen, *Sharir Parichay* (Calcutta: Kalpataru Ayurveda Bhavan, 1924), pp. 1–2. I am grateful to a fellow scholar, Jayant Bhattacharya, for this pertinent point and the reference.

24. For a stinging criticism, see C. E. Trevelyan, *On the Education of the People of India* (London: Longmans, 1838), pp. 200–205.

25. Patrick Hehir, *The Medical Profession in India* (London: H. Frowde and Hodder & Stoughton, 1923), p. 11, Mss.T.3358, IOLR/BL.

26. For caste-wise data, see *Report of the Medical College of Bengal for the Years 1848–53* (preserved at the Calcutta Medical College Library).

27. B. Gupta, 'Indigenous Medicine in Nineteenth and Twentieth Century Bengal', in *Asian Medical Systems: A Comparative Study*, ed. Charles Leslie (Berkeley: University of California Press, 1977), p. 371.

28. Municipal Department, Medical Branch, nos. 80–82, August 1875, Pt. A, Bihar State Archive, Patna.

29. *Report on the Administration of Bengal, 1885–86* (Calcutta: Government Press, 1887), p. 317.

30. Home, Medical, nos. 96–101, October 1877, NAI.

31. J. D. B. Gribble, 'The London School of Tropical Medicine', *East and West* 1, no. 13 (1902): 1417–1433.

32. For the most authoritative document on the IMS, see D. G. Crawford, *A History of the Indian Medical Service, 1600–1913*, 2 volumes (Calcutta and Simla: Thacker, Spink & Co., 1914); Donald McDonald, *Surgeons Twoe and a Barber: Being Some Account of the Life and Work of the Indian Medical Service 1600–1947* (London: Heinmann, 1950); see also O. P. Jaggi, *Medical Education and Research* (Delhi: Atma Ram & Sons, 1979).

33. For extensive debates on the tropics and imperial expansion, see Roy MacLeod and Milton Lewis (eds), *Disease, Medicine and Empire: Perspectives on Western Medicine and the Experience of European Expansion* (London: Routledge, 1988); David Arnold (ed.), *Warm Climates and Western Medicine: The Emergence of Tropical Medicine, 1500–1900* (Amsterdam: Rodopi, 1996); also, Mark Harrison, *Climates and Constitutions: Health, Race, Environment and British Imperialism in India, 1600–1850* (New Delhi: Oxford University Press, 1999); David Arnold, *The Tropics and the Travelling Gaze: India, Landscape and Science, 1800–1950* (Ranikhet: Permanent Black, 2006); Pratik Chakrabarti, *Medicine and Empire 1600–1960* (London: Palgrave Macmillan, 2014).

34. A study so far unsurpassed on this theme is K. Ballhatchet, *Race, Sex and Class Under the Raj: Imperial Attitudes and Policies and Their Critics, 1793–1905* (London: Weidenfeld and Nicolson, 1980).

35. For details, see Sanjoy Bhattacharya, Mark Harrison, and Michael Worboys, *Fractured States: Smallpox, Public Health and Vaccination Policy in British India, 1800–1947* (Delhi: Orient Longman, 2005); also, Harish Naraindas, 'Care, Welfare, and Treason: The Advent of Vaccination in the 19th Century', *Contributions to Indian Sociology* 32, no. 1 (1998): 67–96; Niels Brimnes, 'Variolation, Vaccination and Popular Resistance in Early Colonial South India', *Medical History* 48 (2004): 199–228.

36. David Arnold, *The New Cambridge History of India: Science, Technology and Medicine in Colonial India* (Cambridge: Cambridge University Press, 2000), p. 81.

37. As Ross wrote before discovering the malaria parasite,

> ... it renders large tracts of fertile country more or less uninhabitable, impedes cultivation, planting and public works and is often the most

serious enemy which armies in the field have to contend against. On the whole then I think we are justified in claiming that the malaria-question is quite as important a matter as famine and plague.

R. Ross to P. Manson, 13 June 1897, Ross Papers, 0/1099, Liverpool School of Tropical Medicine.

38. To know about the bacterial explanations and the larger sociopolitical context, see Michael Worboys, *Spreading Germs: Disease Theories and Medical Practice in Britain, 1865–1900* (Cambridge: Cambridge University Press, 2000).

39. For Indian examples, see Pratik Chakrabarti, *Bacteriology in British India: Laboratory Medicine and the Tropics* (Rochester: Boydell and Brewer; University of Rochester Press, 2012).

40. Pratik Chakrabarti, '"Living Versus Dead": The Pasteurian Paradigm and Imperial Vaccine Research', *Bulletin of the History of Medicine* 84, no. 3 (2010): 387–423.

41. This marked the beginning of a number of commissions that gradually became a hallmark of both pre-independence and post-independence governments (for example, the Leprosy Commission, Famine Commission, Plague Commission, Education Commission, Agriculture Commission, even a Knowledge Commission!).

42. W. M. Haffkine, 'A Lecture on Vaccination Against Cholera', *The British Medical Journal* 2 (1895): 1541–1544.

43. Unlike his anti-cholera serums in which 'living' (though 'fixed') viruses were used, his anti-plague vaccine was completely devitalized with no 'living' plague bacillus.

44. Haffkine Papers (HP), Ms. Var 325 file 332, f. 364.9, Hebrew University Library & Archive, Jerusalem.

45. To this Haffkine's reply was, 'would it be practical and helpful if, upon a visit to the poor of London, in connection with some misfortune, one suggested to them, as a remedy, to lift their lot from the condition they were in?' Haffkine to the Secretary of State, 19 September 1911, HP, f. 388.2.

46. For details, see I. J. Catanach, 'Plague Policy and Popular Unrest in British India', *Modern Asian Studies* 22, no. 4 (1988): 723–755; I. J. Catanach, 'Plague and the Tensions of Empire 1896–1918', in *Imperial Medicine and Indigenous Societies*, ed. D. Arnold (New Delhi: Oxford University Press, 1989), pp. 149–171.

47. R. Chandavarkar, *Imperial Power and Popular Politics* (Cambridge: Cambridge University Press, 1998), pp. 234–265.

48. Haffkine to H. Butler, 21 April 1911, HP, f. 407.2; later he recounted:

The people in Dharwar not only came forward in thousands to be inoculated when the efficacy of the method was explained to them, but they paid for the inoculations.

Haffkine Papers Mss. Var. 325.78. This holds a lesson for those handling vaccinations to combat the Covid 19 pandemic of 2020–2021.

49. R. Ross to P. Manson, 13 June 1897, Ross Papers, 01/126, Liverpool School of Tropical Medicine Library, Liverpool.

50. R. Ross, *Mosquito Brigades and How to Organise Them* (London: George Philip, 1902), pp. 15–20. Even a century later, a vaccine against malaria was not considered feasible. In 2020, it was reported that a research team at Oxford is close to perfecting this vaccine.

51. As Ross himself lamented, 'Instead of using me for the large sanitary schemes as I desired, my countrymen offered me only three minor occupations—to teach students, to dissect parasites, or to prescribe pills. The British are a practical people; they seldom actually kill the goose that lays the golden eggs; they force her to lay goose's eggs!' R. Ross, *Memoirs* (London: John Murray, 1923), p. 468.

52. R. Ross to P. Manson, 10 May 1898, Ross Papers, 02/155, London School of Hygiene and Tropical Medicine, London

53. Note dated 10 July 1913, Haffkine Papers, f. 443.5 Hebrew University Library, Jerusalem.

54. R. Ross to P. Manson, 9 December 1897, Ross Papers, 02/137, London School of Hygiene and Tropical Medicine.

55. Curzon to G. Hamilton, 27 November 1902, Curzon Papers, Mss. Eur. P111/161, p. 380.

56. Deepak Kumar, 'Colony Under a Microscope', *Science, Technology and Society* 4, no. 2 (1999): 240–271.

57. Leonard Rogers on the British Empire Leprosy Relief Association, 1924, Rogers papers, PP/Rog C/13/175, Wellcome Institute for History of Medicine (WIHM), London.

58. Helen Power, 'The Calcutta School of Tropical Medicine: Institutionalizing Medical Research in the Periphery', *Medical History* 40, no. 2 (1996): 197–214.

59. F. Nightingale, *How People May Live and Not Die in India* (London: Longman, 1864), p. 16. In this 18-page pamphlet, Nightingale talks only about the health of the army!

60. Thirty years later, Nightingale supported one Dr Dhurandhar (then Sanitary Commissioner at Baroda State), who tried to promote public awareness in villages through magic lantern slides showing 'the horrible microscopic life

in impure air, polluted water and decaying animal and vegetable matter'. In a letter to G. Birdwood, a senior IMS official, dated 23 April 1894, she wrote: 'I need not remind you that the pious Hindu will put a veil over his face to avoid swallowing a gnat and does penance if he accidentally eats a weevil in his rice. To show him therefore microbes and Bacilli in impure air and water would have a strong effect on him'. Birdwood Papers, India Office Records MSS. Eur. F216/75.

61. Simon Szreter, 'Rethinking McKeown: The Relationship Between Public Health and Social Change', *American Journal of Public Health* 92, no. 5 (2002): 722–732. I am grateful to Dr V. K. Yadavendu for this reference.

62. For details, see C. Hamlin, *Public Health and Social Justice in the Age of Chadwick* (Cambridge: Cambridge University Press, 1998), pp. 1–14.

63. Chuckerbutty, *Popular Lectures*, pp. 56–60.

64. Diary of J. B. Grant, March 1940, R.G. 12.1 RAC.

65. A. K. Dutta, 'Upendranath Brahmachari in Pursuit of Kala-azar', in *History of Medicine in India: The Medical Encounter*, ed. C. Palit and A. K. Dutta (Delhi: Kalpaz Publications, 2005), pp. 138–155.

66. Note dated 25 February 1926, Heiser Diaries 1925–26, RG 12.1, p. 403, RAC, New York.

67. Two important books have come on this theme. See Sujata Mukherjee, *Gender, Medicine and Society in Colonial India: Women's Health Care in Nineteenth and Early Twentieth Century Bengal* (New Delhi: Oxford University Press, 2017); Ambalika Guha, *Colonial Modernities: Midwifery in Bengal, 1860–1947* (London: Routledge, 2018).

68. Geraldine Forbes, 'No Science for Lady Doctors: The Education and Medical Practice of Vernacular Women Doctors in Nineteenth Century Bengal,' in *Women and Science in India: A Reader*, ed. Neelam Kumar (New Delhi, 2009), pp. 3–20.

69. T. Raychaudhuri and G. Forbes (ed.), *The Memoirs of Hemabati Sen* (Delhi: Roli Books, 2020); S. Muthulakshmi Reddy, *My Experience as a Legislator* (Madras: Current Thought Press, 1930).

70. For a scintillating description, see P. B. Mukharji, *Nationalizing the Body: The Medical Market, Print and Daktari Medicine* (London: Anthem Press, 2009). This book brings out relatively unknown but interesting medical interlocutors like Moulvi Tamiz Khan (?–1882), Anandacharan Khastgir (1830–1890), Nabinchandra Datta (1852–1920), and Narendranath Datta (1884–1948).

71. Tarashankar Bandyopadhyaya, *Arogyaniketan*, trans. Enakshi Chatterjee (New Delhi: Sahitya Akademi, 1996), pp. 162, 297.

72. P. B. Mukharji, *Doctoring Traditions: Ayurveda, Small Technologies, and Braided Sciences* (Chicago: University of Chicago Press, 2016), pp. 2–34.

73. For relevant extracts, see P. K. Bose (ed.), *Health and Society in Bengal: A Selection from Late 19th Century Bengali Periodicals* (New Delhi: Sage, 2006). Hygiene as ideology and practice is discussed in Srirupa Prasad, *Cultural Politics of Hygiene in India, 1890–1940: Contagions of Feeling* (London: Routledge, 2015), pp. 89–109.

74. Benoy Ghosh, *Samayik Patre Vamlar Samaj Chitra*, Vol. IV (Calcutta: Bengal Publishers, 1964), p. 505.

75. W. Walford, *The Autobiography of an Indian Surgeon* (London: Nicholson, 1854), p. 94.

76. *Sukirthavachani* (Tamil), 17 August 1872, Native Newspaper Reports (NNR), Madras, January 1872 to February 1874, p. 67.

77. *Vivekavardhani* (Telugu), August 1887, NNR, Madras, 1887, p. 138.

78. *Paschima Taraka* (Malayalam), 30 June 1874, NNR, Madras, 1874, p. 53.

79. *Swadeshmitran* (Tamil bi-weekly), 21 April 1896, NNR, Madras, 1896, p. 109.

80. *Daily Hitavadi* (Calcutta), 6 July 1910, NNR, Bengal, 1910, p. 807.

81. *Rajayogi* (Telugu weekly), 1 December 1895, NNR, Madras, 1895, p. 379.

82. K. C. V. Raja, 'Vasoorikerivekkal', *Mangalodayam* (Malayalam) No. II, Trichur, 1910, p. 2.

83. *The Kathiawar News* (Anglo-Gujarati bi-weekly), 27 January 1897, NNR, Bombay, 1897, p. 93. *The Suryodaya Prakasika* (Kannada weekly) of 1 June 1904 alleged that for the Kasauli laboratory thousands of cattle had been killed, 'to the great detriment of agriculture', NNR, Madras, 1904, p. 209.

84. *Vrittanta Chintamani* (Kannada weekly), 9 August 1893, NNR, Madras, 1893, p. 202.

85. *Vrittanta Chintamani*, 18 January 1899, NNR, Madras, 1899, p. 28.

86. *Hitavarta* (Calcutta), 27 July 1911, NNR 31, Bengal, 1911, p. 95.

87. *New Times* (Karachi), 25 April 1923, NNR, Bombay, 1923, para. 6.

88. *Vijaya* (Tamil daily), 23 March 1910, NNR, Madras, 1910, p. 580.

89. A prominent member of this Committee was Sir Weldon Dalrymple Champneys (1892–1980). In a lighter vein he composed:

       My name is – er-Eustace, As you see
       I'm a fine specimen of the Master Race
       You may think my conversation inane,
       But to manage these dirty Indian does not need a brain!

     Champneys Papers, GC/139/H. 2/10, Wellcome Institute, London.

90. A. V. Hill, *The Ethical Dilemma of Science and Other Essays* (New York: Rockefeller Institute Press, 1960), p. 375.

6

Science for Development

The real question is not one of quantitative adjustment and balancing of various incongruous elements and methods of production, but a qualitative change-over to something different and new, from which various social consequences flow. The economic and political aspects of this qualitative change are important, but equally important are the social and psychological aspects. In India especially, where we have been wedded far too long to past forms and modes of thought and action, new experiences, new processes, leading to new ideas and new horizons, are necessary.

—Jawaharlal Nehru[1]

The outstanding difficulty is not so much that only a very small percentage of the Hindu population is literate, but rather that only a very small percentage of the literate minority is able to read a journal like Science and Culture and to understand its rational and scientific message. The peace, security and prosperity of India will not be advanced by metaphysical and religious discussions but by the wise application of scientific and rational methods. For the sake of India's freedom, we hope that the Hindu audience of Science and Culture will increase considerably.

—George Sarton[2]

During the 19th century, the British colonial records and tracts talked about improvement, for example, 'the moral and material improvement of the natives'. In the next century, the discourse changed to development. A very interesting and ambiguous term, it is still in vogue. Is development an ideology, is it growth, or a process, or a tool to achieve certain ends? Whichever way one looks at it, the economic parameters based on technological sophistication and scientific research weigh heavier. The buzzword now is sustainable development. Techno-scientific knowledge, without doubt, occupies a central role in this discourse. M. Visvesvaraya (1860–1962), engineer extraordinaire, was probably the first Indian to talk about planned development in 1918. He had built the Krishna Raja Sagara dam in Mysore with remarkable tenacity.[3]

He gave the slogan, 'Industrialize or Perish'. Years before him, a British official, Alfred Chatterton had pleaded for and written pamphlets and books on the use of machines, small industries, irrigation, and so on. The Swadeshi movement itself had put great emphasis on industrialization with the help of new tools and knowledge. Educated people had begun to ask for an all-embracing 'socio-cultural transformation'. *Suraj* (good rule, which many genuinely believed the British provided) was to be replaced by *swaraj* (self-rule) which, coupled with *swadeshi* (self-reliance), constituted a *weltanschauung* powerful enough to transcend the barriers imposed by colonial rule. Jawaharlal Nehru was to play the role of a great catalyst in this debate, even at the risk of dissenting firmly with his guide and mentor, M. K. Gandhi.[4]

In tropical climates, agriculture and health are the most crucial areas. They impact on the very survival of the people, what to say of development. The turn of the 20th century saw India ravaged by famines and pestilence. Advances in solar spectrography and meteorological researches had shown a link between sun-spot activities and the onset or lack of rains, thereby causing famine and epidemic-like conditions. Norman Lockyer, founder of the celebrated journal *Nature*, in a report to the Indian Famine Commission of 1880, had pointed out that the famines in Madras since 1801 could be correlated very closely with sun-spot minima.[5] Such researches helped administrators like Curzon to exclaim with impunity, 'Britannia rules the waves, not the solar flames' and thus insulate the government from any responsibility! He thought of India's economic problems as being eternal, 'not to be solved by a batch of industries or a cluster of polytechnics'. 'They will scarcely produce a ripple in the great ocean of social and industrial forces', he added.[6] But the people of India were not pessimistic. They continued to ask for both industrial and agricultural education.

A little later, the British government itself began show signs of what some scholars call 'constructive imperialism'. A Board of Scientific Advice was established in 1904; the great Royal Society of London subsequently formed an Indian Advisory Committee to give scientific advice on Indian resources. In 1911, an Indian Research Fund Association came up. The Indian Science Congress Association (ISCA) was established in 1914. Two years later, in the midst of the Great War, an Industrial Commission was set up. Around the same time, an Agricultural Research Council was formed. The Reforms of 1919 acceded to the Indian nationalists' long-standing demand for Indianizing medical and educational services. An Agricultural Commission was instituted in 1928 for agricultural improvement. There was no dearth of advice and recommendations but all this was certainly not enough to effect any substantial change in the material conditions of the people. Rather, because of recurrent epidemics and food-shortages, both mortality and poverty grew. As a consequence, the national movement entered an intense phase of non-cooperation and civil disobedience. The government could weather it with some compromises but it would always end up throwing its hand down. The Great Depression of the late 1920s was a good excuse to do so. For many ills, the blame could easily be put on Indian habits and culture. As a British Surgeon General wrote, 'the Indians breed like rabbits and die like flies'.[7]

There was an undeniable conflict of interest between India and Great Britain. British capital, imported into India for the promotion of British enterprise, inevitably received preferential treatment, not by law, but certainly from British officials. This was natural. The standard official argument was that the country had no potential to absorb technically qualified personnel. They thought of India's economic problems as being eternal and cultural. This was deeply resented by Indians. Indians not only demanded distinct institutions devoted to technical and industrial education; they also wanted the existing university structure to be expanded to both liberal and technical education. They wanted even more in terms of policy-planning, asking for a share in its formulation and implementation. Science and technology alone were not enough. As a journal asked, 'Does the problem of Indian agriculture begin and end only with the knowledge and use of scientific methods of agriculture?'[8]

Furthermore, public health continued to be a major problem. Millions perished during the influenza pandemic of 1918–1919. An official report says:

> The hospitals were choked so that it was impossible to remove the dead to make room for the dying … the burning ghats and the burial grounds were literally swamped with corpses … the depleted medical service, itself sorely stricken by the pandemic, was incapable of dealing with more than a minute fraction of the sickness requiring attention; every household was lamenting a death, and everywhere terror and confusion reigned.[9]

Even in such a serious situation, some thought excessive reliance on medical intervention 'one-sided' and 'dangerous'. For example, J. D. Megaw, who in the early 1930s was the Director General of the Indian Medical Service (IMS), argued:

> Suppose for a moment that the public health services of India were to achieve complete success in stamping out malaria, cholera, small-pox, tuberculosis, and all other great killing diseases of India, and suppose that nothing was done to increase the production of food or to restrict the growth of [the]

population, the inevitable result would be the replacement of the tragedy of
death from disease by the greater tragedy of death from starvation.[10]

If medical intervention was no panacea, many thought that the control of
disease would promptly raise the standards of living and reduce fertility. Yet
the situation was always too dismal to warrant optimism. So, the standard
official argument was that public health depends not only on the control of
preventable disease, but also on the state of nutrition and general economic
conditions. To quote Megaw again, 'a public health policy must be worked
out in terms of agricultural and industrial production; it must look ahead and
take into account the maintenance of a proper relation between the number
of the people and the available supply of the necessities of life'.[11] This indeed
was a tall order. The colonial government had neither the intention nor the
wherewithal. To growing demands for greater indigenization, the government
responded with retrenchment (vide the Inchcape Committee Report, 1923).
With the advent of the Great Depression, agriculture and public health were
early casualties.

Industrialize or Perish: Reflections in the Indian Press

As an Indian newspaper noted in 1911,

> whenever the interests of the English merchants clashed with those of
> the Indians, it has always been the latter that had to go to the wall—
> notwithstanding the strenuous support of the whole executive machinery of
> the Empire from the Viceroy up to the King-Emperor himself. In view of this
> unfortunate circumstance, self-help and self-reliance seem to be the only ways
> left for the furtherance of the industrial good of India.[12]

An Industrial Conference held at Ootacamund in 1910 asked for the
establishment of model factories attached to institutions imparting technical
education. This was rejected by the government 'on the pretext that these factories
would be detrimental to private enterprise'.[13] A committee of this conference,
however, did not recommend training of Indian youth abroad. This was
strongly criticized by an influential journal, *Swadeshmitran*, which argued:

> The committee says that there is no use of sending our young men to foreign
> countries. This is wrong, for it is only by thus sending hundreds of young
> men that Japan rose to prominence. At present, thousands of Chinese are
> learning the industries in Japan. There are many good results arising out of
> our young men going to foreign countries for the purpose of general education

and industry. In the first place, young men who go to foreign countries return with a widened intellect, a fresh experience, courage and self-respect. Those can never go in vain at any time. The first and foremost thing in this matter is the hope that we can earn much by means of the industries. At present, our men think that they can amass wealth by holding appointments, by instituting false proceedings in courts, by alchemy, by finding out hidden treasure and by practicing as a lawyer and as a doctor, by gambling. Our young men must understand that industries alone are the real sources of wealth and that all other means will tend to destroy it.[14]

The *Hitvarta* (a Calcutta journal) ascribed the poverty of India to the undeveloped condition of its industries, and to the fact that it exported only raw materials while importing manufactured goods from foreign countries. It enumerated the following difficulties which were in the way of the advancement of Indian industries:

1. Indians had to import machinery from foreign countries at considerable cost.
2. They had to incur several times more expenses in setting up and working the machines in India than were incurred in European countries.
3. There was a great want of capital.
4. There was no arrangement in the country for scientific training.
5. There was indifference on part of the government.[15]

As discussed, there was an undeniable conflict of interest between India and Great Britain, with British capital receiving preferential treatment from British officials in India. As a Calcutta daily argued,

> Blood is always thicker than water and intimate social intercourse between the British officials and the British exploiters in India naturally helps British enterprise to the prejudice of Indian enterprise ... In view of these patent facts how can it possibly be held that the want of national sovereignty and independence does not stand in the way of India's scientific advancement so far as the application of science to industries is concerned?[16]

A contemporary journal noted with regret that, 'a handful of Whites have the audacity to say ... that people should wait for higher technical education till there are sufficient factories in India to employ those who have taken such education.'[17] What colonial India could honestly boast of was a battery of officials who would produce reams of reports and contradictory assessments. Reports of several commissions were seldom meant for even partial, much less full implementation. The famous Industrial Commission Report on which Madan Mohan Malaviya had given a dissenting note, also met the same fate. In 1923, a Bombay journal noted:

> Four years have passed since the publication of the report and all we have got is a glowing array of Directors and Assistant Directors of Industry who justify their existence by doling out bits of information with regard to the possibilities of this industry here and that industry there. An industrial service without a polytechnic institute is possible only in India![18]

The demands of Indian reformers for distinct institutions for technical and industrial education and expansion of the existing university structure to both liberal and technical education formed part of an agenda for the comprehensive reconstruction of the country. Each and every institution was expected to play a role, more so institutions of higher learning. As a Bengali journal noted,

> The noble task of building the nation is a high prerogative of the University. Literary as well as scientific and vocational education of all kinds should engage the earnest attention of the Universities. The spread of technical education should be as much within its province as to encourage original research and scientific investigation. Indeed, the spheres of the activity of the Universities should be considerably enlarged and be made sufficiently elastic to embrace all the varied domains of human culture and thought and at the same time to encourage industrial and scientific education which alone can increase the wealth of the land and find a remedy for the growing poverty of the peoples.[19]

Impetus for Modernization

By the mid-1930s, the long-drawn freedom struggle had begun to yield significant results. India had by then entered a phase of transition from dependence to independence. National leaders began to visualize how independent India would look and what steps were to be taken. Gandhi, the undisputed leader of the national movement, held a different view. He argued, 'to industrialise India in the same sense as Europe is to attempt the impossible'. To an extent, he was right. Where were the resources? P. C. Ray, an outstanding scientist with great social commitment who knew that the *djinn* of industrialization could not be bottled any more, accepted the Gandhian logic. He wrote:

> During my recent tours in Saran, Meerut, etc., the miserable-looking clumps of sugarcane made me almost weep. No less primitive was the method of

expressing the juice and of boiling it down over naked fire. No wonder that the planters of Java following the scientific methods of agriculture and of expressing juice from the cane and boiling it in vacuum pans are ousting the former ... Industrialists now-a-days talk of mass production, but in India we have to count [the] population in masses ... The hatred of machinery, the hatred of capitalism which burns so strongly in Gandhi is the reflection of the hate of millions of Indian peasants and handworkers whose traditional basis of existence was completely destroyed by capitalism and who were excluded from the possibility of existence on a capitalist basis as a factory proletariat.[20]

Ray knew the realities of rural life. He realized that the *charkha* enabled a rural woman to clothe herself. This small easy machine not only helped generate a little extra money but also gave dignity. During a severe draught in Khulna district in 1923, Ray tried to introduce tractors for tilling but soon realized that this would displace human hands, make them idle, and induce them to migrate to the cities. The project was abandoned. Agricultural experts like James Mackenna also felt that agriculture would be ruined if the *ryots* used heavy machines. It was argued that 'if agriculture be carried on with the help of machinery, the poor *ryots* will be deprived of even the wages they are getting at present for working in the field'.[21]

Ray's illustrious Nobel laureate contemporary, Rabindranath Tagore was no less interested in rural amelioration. Unlike his peers (for example, R. C. Dutt), he took the peasant question far beyond theoretical debates on the rights and duties of various categories of *ryots*. He visualized it not in isolation but as a component of the entire rural landscape. He was a 'ploughman's poet'.[22] Like Gandhi, Tagore also wanted to empower the weak, but probably more than Gandhi, he trusted and emphasized the role of 'proper education' to achieve this. How to empower the villages? How to formulate an education which would cater to the needs of any child in rural India? Thus, was born the Sriniketan experiment in 1912. Tagore was pro-science, pro-innovation, and pro-development. Unlike Gandhi, he supported the increasing use of machines. He once remarked: '... steam and electricity shall be our nerve and muscle'.[23] To raise crops on small, fragmented land, with time-honoured ploughs, was as good as trying to fill a 'bottomless pit'. He asked for amalgamation of fragmented land, common use of tractors, and collective agriculture on scientific lines. He advised cultivation of vegetables and cash crops and asked the *ryots* to try crop rotation and even multiple cropping. He knew how difficult it was to initiate peasants into new practices. No farmer surviving at a low subsistence level would take any risk of crop failure or more debt. Tagore found a way out in cooperative societies. He started *krishi* banks and initiated what is today known as microfinancing. In this, Tagore was a pioneer and much ahead of his contemporaries.

Similarly, many like Meghnad Saha, pioneer astrophysicist and well-known for his deep social commitment, wanted India to choose 'the cold logic of technology', and not the vague utopia of Gandhian economy. The 1930s was a remarkable decade. After provincial autonomy was introduced in 1935, independence looked within reach and the country began to experience an unprecedented interest in national reconstruction. The necessity of planning was thought about earlier also; M. Visvesvaraya and G. D. Birla had written about it.[24] But immediate inspiration and models for planning came from the Union of Soviet Socialist Republics (USSR). Two things were very clear; that reconstruction required planning, and that it needed science and technology. So, in 1937, the Indian National Congress appointed a National Planning Committee (NPC) to prepare a comprehensive and integrated plan for reconstruction, in which science and technology were to play a principal role. The NPC started its massive exercise with its 29 sub-committees clustered into eight groups, and despite the intervention of World War II, the Quit India movement, and so on, its deliberations continued. The NPC placed special emphasis on large-scale industrialization, accorded agriculture the status of an industry, and made recommendations to promote animal husbandry and dairying, horticulture and fisheries, irrigation, soil conservation, and afforestation. The areas that it touched were incredibly vast. As Nehru noted,

one thing led to another and it was impossible to isolate anything or to progress in one direction without corresponding progress in another. The more we thought of this planning business, the vaster it grew in its sweep and range till it seemed to embrace almost every activity. That did not mean we intended regulating and regimenting everything but we had to keep almost everything in view even in deciding about one particular sector of the plan.[25]

The NPC itself had laid bare inherent tensions and contradictions. Gandhians like J. C. Kumarappa and S. N. Agarwal preferred traditional technology and village industries, and attacked the NPC. Within the Congress, younger leaders leaned towards modern science, technology, and heavy industrialization. Some wanted to follow the socialist path, others favoured capitalist models such as that envisaged in Purshotamadas Thakurdas's 1944 *Plan for Economic Development of India* (popularly known as the Bombay Plan). This Plan also was not averse to the concept of planning; what it advocated was some kind of a 'Buddhist' middle-path between state-led planning and private enterprise.[26]

Indian public opinion was markedly divided on whether to adopt socialist methods or accept the capitalist model. Socialism and the Russian model looked promising and exciting for India's progress, but this ideology lacked roots in Indian soil which had been traditional and feudal for long. Capitalism, on the contrary, had many takers among the urban upward social groups. No wonder, the capitalist model of progress found instant sympathizers in the government as well as among an influential section of society. A third group wanted progress the Gandhian way, through traditional knowledge and skill. But to many, Gandhi's politics were convenient, but his economics were not.

Gandhi's own political heir and independent India's first Prime Minister, Jawaharlal Nehru, differed with his mentor. For Gandhi, the individual, society, and technology formed one whole, in a similar manner as did religion, politics, and constructive work. Keeping them separate or autonomous was to him inconceivable. In a letter to Nehru in September 1945, Gandhi talked about the necessity of escaping the 'moth-like circling'. 'When the moth approaches its doom, it whirls round faster and faster till it is burnt up'. To this Nehru replied:

> I do not think it is possible for India to be really independent unless she is a technically advanced country. I am not thinking for the moment in terms of just armies but rather of scientific growth. In the present context of the world, we cannot even advance culturally without a strong background of scientific research in every department.[27]

Nehru was fond of science and put a premium on scientific temper. Socialism fascinated him and the Russian Revolution fired his optimism. Where Gandhi was unquestionably a traditional *sanatani*, Nehru became a 'humanist' who resented being neatly categorized within the four corners of a single 'ism'.[28] His preferences were all for science and for scientific method. Nehru was very clear and convinced on this point:

> It is the scientific approach, the adventurous and yet critical temper of science, the search for truth and new knowledge, the refusal to accept anything without testing and trial, the capacity to change previous conclusions in the face of new evidence, the reliance on observed fact and not on pre-conceived theory, the hard discipline of the mind—all this is necessary, not merely for the application of science but for life itself and the solution of many of its problems.[29]

But he also understood and appreciated the limitations of science in elaborating questions like the purpose of life or providing clues to absolute truth.

His curiosity and fascination for science were child-like but he explained some of the recent advances in science in his letters to his daughter (February to July 1933 from Dehradun Jail) like an accomplished and devoted science popularizer.[30] He looked into the history of the sciences; cited examples of how dogmas were fought; reasoned about the relations between science and religion; discussed Darwin, Einstein, and Pavlov; pondered over the good and bad applications of science; and what is unique, exulted in seeing women as doctors, teachers, and engineers.[31] In September 1933, Nehru wrote to Aldous Huxley refuting his characterization of Congress views as anti-science. He clarified that the Mahatma had never asked the Congress to accept or adopt all his ideas nor were his views anti-science.[32] Despite fundamental differences, Nehru defended Gandhi. On science, he became almost lyrical in his message to *Science and Culture* (a journal founded by M. N. Saha in 1935):

> Science is the very basis and texture of life today and without it we perish, or what is even worse, slide back to barbarism. Science does not mean the thousand and one applications of it that we see today, but even more so the scientific and rational approach to all problems of life. Science has made great progress in the West and raised the standard of living in some countries to unprecedented heights. And yet that very science has failed to solve the major problems of the age and we see war with all its horrors ravaging the world. Thus, science destroys itself if it is not extended to the political, economic and other fields of human life and endeavour. It would appear that science today is in a position to solve all these problems, or most of them, and to create conditions of well-being and progress for all humanity. Yet though we swear by science and accept it advantageously for many purposes, still the habit of unscientific approach remains. Vested interests, superstitions and out-of-date customs prevent the full application of the scientific and the rational method.[33]

Many Indian scientists and technologists sought solutions to the country's problems, but their methods differed. P. C. Ray saw the remedy in *swadeshi* and the *charkha*, while Visvesvaraya demanded rapid industrialization through the use of Indian capital and enterprise. The Bombay Plan asked for a shift from an 'over-agriculturalized' economy to an industrial economy, and this had to be done with help from Indian capital. Visvesvaraya's approach was an early instance of the technocratic thinking that became the centrepiece of public policy in modern India.[34] Meghnad Saha also insisted on industrialization but under the aegis of the government. So did Nehru. This was the crucial difference between the advocates of the Bombay Plan and those of the NPC.

Scientists like Shanti Swaroop Bhatnagar (1894–1955) and Homi Jehangir Bhabha (1909–1966) preferred to build centres of excellence in frontier areas of scientific research. Bhatnagar was to build a chain of laboratories under the aegis of the Council of Scientific and Industrial Research (CSIR) in 1942. Bhabha played a greater role in independent India, pioneering nuclear technology. He saw a source of power in the controlled release of fission, while Saha saw power in the huge rivers of India. Bhabha argued for the quick importation of overseas industrial models for adaptation in India, thereby gaining time and leverage. Saha believed in the development of India through a wholly independent science and technology firmly embedded in socialist economics. Although socialism remained an ideal for many (including Nehru and Saha), a version of democratic socialism with a mixed economy was accepted by national leaders as the basis for future development. Saha resented this dilution, and even called the Congress leaders 'puppets in the hands of big industrialists'. He and Nehru gradually drifted apart. Nehru leaned more towards Bhatnagar and Bhabha, which led to government-controlled industrial and defence research. Another trusted scientist was the physicist, statistician, and planner, P. C. Mahalanobis (1893–1972), who pioneered new kinds of knowledge in the field statistics which were crucial in planning the economic development of free India. Besides significant contributions in the field of multivariate analysis and sample surveys, and introducing a new technique called fractile graphical analysis, he also founded in 1931 the Indian Statistical Institute.[35] On him Nehru depended for planning work, and both treated planning as 'science in action'. By 1950, Indian leaders had made a conscious decision to modernize, and the dilemma of the previous decades virtually ended.

There were a few others who not only made outstanding scientific contributions, but were also great institution-builders. They were Debendra Mohan Bose (1885–1975) and Sisir Kumar Mitra (1890–1963). Debendra Mohan Bose initially worked with J. J. Thomson at the Cavendish Laboratory and later in 1918 obtained his Ph.D in Berlin under the guidance of Max Planck. He was the first to make the Higgs boson particle visible. His dissertation was on the passage of alpha- and beta- particles through gases. His significant research work using the cloud chamber and magnetism in India and abroad, established him as an internationally reputed physicist. He is also known for Welo-Bose's rule, Bose's theory of magnetism, and the discovery of a new photo-effect in chemicals.[36] On the demise of his illustrious uncle, J. C. Bose, he took charge of the Bose Institute. Later, in a series of articles published in *Nature*, he, in collaboration with Bibha Choudhuri, identified a cosmic particle having a mass close to 200 times the mass of an electron (the mu-meson). Many believe that they missed the Nobel Prize for this discovery because of their lack of access to modern scientific tools. In spite of painstaking and tedious experiments done by Bibha Chaudhuri, she is little known and less discussed in the scientific community.[37]

Sisir Kumar Mitra obtained a D.Sc. from Calcutta University in 1919 on the 'interference and diffraction of light'. But soon while at Sorbonne and Nancy, he changed his line of research and worked on the propagation of radio waves. On returning to Calcutta University in 1923, he started teaching wireless and even constructed a radio transmitting station. This was a unique attempt. Within a decade, a Radio Research Committee was formed and later in 1949 he founded an Institute of Radio Physics and Electronics.[38] All India Radio owes its origin to this scientist.

Last Flicker

In the early 1940s, despite the raging Second World War, the British government in India made some level of contribution by forming several expert committees. It suddenly realized that it was possible to outmanoeuvre the Congress by attempting, 'regardless of conventional financial restraints', a 'complete overhaul of India's national life', with the British playing the post-war role of a 'bold, far-sighted and benevolent despot'. This was the last flicker of what may be called 'constructive imperialism'. In early 1945, an Industrial Research Planning Committee headed by Shanmukham Chetty made 64 recommendations. 'The first and most important desideratum', in its view was 'an effective liaison between university, industry and research institutions'. So was recommended a National Research Council which would organize and maintain national laboratories, coordinate research activities of all institutes, and function as a national trust for patents. A committee to discuss medical issues was formed under Joseph Bhore and a very comprehensive report was prepared. The modern All India Institute of Medical Sciences (AIIMS) owes its origin to this report. Similarly, the N. R. Sarkar Committee was formed to discuss technical education. It recommended the establishment of an All India Council for Technical Education (AICTE) and also an Indian Institute of Technology (IIT) on the pattern of the illustrious Massachusetts Institute of Technology (MIT).

An interesting development in 1944 was to bring A. V. Hill, the then Secretary of the Royal Society, to report on science in India. He spoke of a quadrilateral dilemma, that is, population, health, food, and natural resources. To him, the fundamental problems of India were 'not really physical, chemical or technological, but a complex of biological ones referring to population, health, nutrition and agriculture all acting and reacting with one another'. So, Hill recommended the creation of a central organization for scientific research with six research boards, covering medicine, agriculture, industry, engineering, war research, and geographical and botanical surveys. He felt that under a central organization, these subjects would be treated with 'some degree of uniform encouragement'. This obviously meant 'regulation' and 'centralization', which he would have never recommended to his own government in Britain.[39] Such advises came in profusion. Surveys were conducted in various departments and plans drawn, but where was the political will to implement them? The fact that the intentions of the government were largely unreal soon became evident when constitutional hindrances came in the way of translating these plans into reality. The Department of Planning and Development was wound up and its head, Sir Ardeshir Dalal had to resign in disgust!

Hill was also worried about the state of university education, especially when faced with the superior facilities at the newly established government-run laboratories and institutes. He could foresee that the university system would become 'sterile' in the absence of adequate funding and talent. He was a close friend of S. S Bhatnagar who was spearheading the expansion of the CSIR. Bhatnagar assured him that while the university system would decline (because they 'are having vice-chancellors not on the consideration of their attainments but of their political affinity'), his laboratories would remain centres of excellence.[40] This is exactly what happened in a few decades.

The Second World War had brought unprecedented trauma and loss of men and material, no doubt, but it also led to extensive scientific activities in basic research and great innovations in areas like industry, defence, medical science, transport and communications, and agriculture. Wars have always been recognized as great catalysts leading to massive plans of reconstruction. Could India benefit from this? No, Indian scientists were kept at bay. Like the First World War, the second one also treated and consumed Indian soldiers as cannon fodder. As a critique puts it, 'the influence of colonialism was so deep rooted and crippling that even one of the most powerful catalysts to science and technology—the war—failed to take them out of the colonial rut and put them on a natural course of progress'.[41]

After Independence

In August 1947, independence came after decades of struggle, but unfortunately, in the midst of a bloody partition. The task of reconstruction was enormous and expectations high. The mantle fell on the cabinet headed by Jawaharlal Nehru. Unlike some of his colleagues, Nehru was fond of scientific knowledge and put a premium on scientific temper. Nehru also understood the flip side of science. It turned humans into 'almost a geological force, changing the face of the planet earth chemically, physically and in many other ways'. But control over nature does not mean control over one's self. Still, optimist that he was, Nehru felt, 'perhaps new developments in biology, psychology, and the interpretation of biology and physics, may help man to understand and control himself more than he has done in the past'.[42] This remains a valid hope for many of his succeeding generations!

On numerous occasions, opening various of institutions, addressing scientific gatherings, conferences, and so on, during his prime ministership (1947–1962), Nehru underscored one point repeatedly, that is, scientific temper as a way of life, as 'an approach to life and all life's problems'. The importance and urgency he attached to it can be gauged from the fact that in the very next week after independence, he placed scientific research under his own 'personal charge'. A decade later came the nation's declaration of faith in science in the shape of the Scientific Policy Resolution adopted by parliament on 4 March 1958. It promised *inter alia* 'to foster, promote and sustain, by all appropriate means, the cultivation of science, and scientific research in all its aspects—pure, applied and educational'. The party and the parliament stood behind the new helmsman. In fact, the manifesto of the Congress party for the first national government in 1945 itself had declared scientific research as 'a basic and essential activity of the state' to be 'organized and encouraged on the widest scale'.[43] Nehru's stamp was unmistakable.

Nehru kept his doors always open to those scientists who wanted to build institutions, like S. S. Bhatnagar (Director General, CSIR) and Homi J. Bhabha (Director, Tata Institute of Fundamental Research). The chain of laboratories established under the CSIR between 1947 and 1954 was known as the result of the 'Nehru–Bhatnagar Effect'. Nehru fondly called Bhatnagar 'a live-wire'. This close alliance between Nehru and scientists in industrial research and atomic energy probably had a negative influence on other sectors. For example, agricultural scientists were not given the same prominence. Agriculture may have advanced a great deal had Nehru evinced the same interest in the Indian Council of Agricultural Research (ICAR) as he did in the CSIR and Department of Atomic Energy (DAE). B. P. Pal (1906–1989) was then experimenting with wheat genetics and breeding but he was no Bhatnagar. Similarly, the university sector also suffered relative neglect. Many good scientific workers moved out of universities to mission-oriented government laboratories and institutes. Universities worldwide are the basic source of scientific talent. Thanks to the 'Nehru–Bhatnagar Effect', Indian universities suffered silently, facing a bleak prospect. Even Hill was alarmed to see 'the great developments in Government research laboratories in India', and warned Bhatnagar 'lest by getting all the best people away from the universities you may dry up the source of scientific talent, or at least training, for the next crop of scientists'.[44] How correct he was!

Very striking is Nehru's repeated call for a scientific temper. Rational thinking was an article of faith for him. This was not something new to Indian thought. Right from Gautam Buddha to Vivekananda and Tagore, rational thinking has been valued. Nehru took a nuanced view of our religious and philosophical heritage, and its points of conflict with science. He was not opposed to or against religion, he simply wanted to encourage curiosity and free will. Scientific temper is the temper of a free man, he argued, and reiterated this at every session of the Indian Science Congress. Following this vision, the Indian Parliament adopted the Scientific Policy Resolution of 1958, which mandated that 'it is only through the scientific approach and method and the use of scientific knowledge that reasonable material and cultural amenities and services can be provided for every member of the community'.[45]

After independence, Nehru had adroitly perfected the art of mixed economy and mixed politics. He tried to combine Gandhi and Visvesvaraya; however, he could finally do justice to neither. Another casualty in an era of mixed policies was the traditional distinction between pure and applied science. S.S. Bhatnagar, Homi Bhabha, and many others looked for a composite structure that combined the two. Bhatnagar, practical chemist that he was, argued that 'applied science had been neglected by the universities', and lamented that while India had many distinguished scientists, 'there are comparatively few scientific processes named after Indians and still [fewer] articles of utility which are in use which can be said to have been manufactured by us'.[46] But to 'purists' like Meghnad Saha, pure science was the seed of applied science, and 'to neglect pure science would be like spending a large amount on manuring and ploughing the land and then omit sowing of any kind'. S. N. Bose and C. V. Raman had similar views. Academic science still held a greater appeal for the Indian mind. In the mid-1950s, a brilliant physicist, G. N. Ramachandran (1922–2001) explored the beauty and order of protein structures, and came up with what is known as the Ramachandran Plot in 1963. Around the same time, an astrophysicist Vainu Bappu (1927–1982) developed the Wilson–Bappu Effect and built the first indigenous large optical telescope. A little later, J. V. Narlikar (b.1938) was to offer the Hoyle–Narlikar theory of gravity.

Govind Swarup (1929–2020) created not only a school of radio astronomy but established giant telescopes in Ooty and Poona. They were also remarkable institution-builders. Some individual sparks are still there and will keep coming, but the soil seems to have fallen fallow.

The notion that science and technology were two sides of the same coin had two interesting results for a country emerging out of the colonial yoke. First, it meant assigning a far greater authority and responsibility to the state. Second, in the name of coordinating the two, the tendency in practice was to centralize. Greater emphasis was put on institutions than on men and ideas. Freedom and democracy should have led to decentralization and upward mobility. But the results were exactly the opposite. The postcolonial state in India emerged no less centralized, bureaucratized, and top-heavy than the colonial state. A new scientocracy had taken over.

Nehru's period was also significant for it not only witnessed the end of the dualism and vacillation of earlier periods but also the laying down of specific policies and establishment of new institutions (like the IITs) as instruments of implementation. Nehru's personal popularity among scientists was legendary. In 1947, he even presided over the 34th session of the ISCA, an honour yet to be bestowed on any other politician. Henceforth he was invited to inaugurate the Science Congress every year. The scientists themselves wanted to hear the voice of the nation and feel reassured, while for Nehru, it was personal satisfaction. Sometimes he softly demurred; at the 44th ISCA session in Calcutta he said, 'I consider this a great privilege and honour for a variety of reasons although I sometimes fear that repetition of a practice makes it rather stale'. But this practice evoked a sharp response from C.V. Raman, India's only 'Nobel' scientist:

> Can you give me the example of any other country in which the Science Congress is inaugurated by a politician? Every year, for 17 years continuously, the organizers of the Indian Science Congress could think of only Prime Minister Nehru to inaugurate it ... How self-respecting scientists could go on listening to piffle spouted by politicians in a 'Science Congress' is something which I have never been able to understand.[47]

Agriculture and health proved to be Nehru's Achilles heel. The end of British rule did not end hunger in India. Eradication of hunger did form part of the core agenda of the new government's food policy. However, malnutrition was (and still is) rampant. During the mid-1950s, an acute shortfall in the foreign currency reserves and drought in the eastern part of India severely impacted the economic stability of the country. Experts saw the growing population dangerously running out of food. It was argued that if the government took away land from the better-off farmers, it would only decrease production because the poor would not have the facilities to cultivate properly. India till then had a very limited capacity of producing chemical fertilizers and most farmers lacked the means to purchase expensive inputs. The government had to appeal to the United States for food grains which came partly gratis and partly as a soft loan under the PL 480 scheme. This eased the situation but probably made Indian officials a little complacent. Nehru remained jittery about the food situation.

Closely related to the issues of hunger and malnutrition, was the question of health. The NPC and the Bhore Committee had given useful recommendations. In 1949, the Indian Research Fund Association of 1911 was renamed the Indian Council of Medical Research (ICMR). This became the nodal agency responsible for all medical and health issues. This council took a dozen medical research institutions under its wing. In coordination with state governments, several practical measures were taken. Thanks to DDT (dichlorodiphenyltrichloroethane), malaria was brought under some control. Again, vaccines sharply reduced deaths by cholera and smallpox. The death rate had fallen to 21.6 per cent for the period 1956–1961, and life expectancy had risen to 42 years. However, tuberculosis continued to be a major threat. To make recommendations for the future path of development of health services, the Mudaliar Committee was set up in 1959. But implementation suffered both for want of funds and lack of commitment on the part of several stakeholders. The result was that private medical practice developed as the core of the health sector in India. It began as an 'enclave', and then gradually penetrated the hinterland. Health was soon to become big business.

Around the same time, relations with neighbouring countries and the situation on the border were far from satisfactory. Hence, steps had to be taken to increase India's capacity in the production of defence equipment. A Defence Research and Development Organisation (DRDO) was set up in 1958 for research in the manufacture of missiles, armaments, explosives, and other defence-related equipment. In the late 1940s itself, Nehru, Saha, and Bhabha had recognized the importance of nuclear energy. They were convinced that nuclear energy would bring about a global revolution in the economic and political spheres, along with strengthening the nation's defence capabilities. The constitution of an Atomic Energy Commission in 1948 and the establishment of the DAE, again under the direct charge of the prime minister, are proof of their foresightedness. In August 1961, at the prime minister's urging, the government identified an area known as 'space research and the peaceful uses of outer space', and placed it within the jurisdiction of the DAE. This gradually evolved into the Indian Space Research Organisation (ISRO). A close collaborator of Bhabha, Vikram Sarabhai (1919–1971) was given the responsibility to chart an ambitious rocket programme which later reached great heights. But on ground level, defence preparedness was poor and this was terribly exposed during the Sino-Indian war of 1962.

National reconstruction as well as national defence were daunting, and it seems Nehru did not have a free hand; he had to make choices with caution. In the midst of the Nehruvian heyday, he is reported to have confessed to a noted scientist, J. D. Bernal:

> Most of my ministers are reactionary and scoundrels but as long as they are my ministers, I can keep some check on them. If I were to resign, they would be the government and they would unloose the forces that I have tried ever since I came to power to hold in check ... I have to work with the people who are actually influential in the country. They may not be the kind of people I like but it is the best I can do.[48]

Nehru's daughter, Indira Gandhi was expected to continue her father's policies. Despite a continued emphasis on industries and higher education, it must be noted to the eternal credit of Mrs Gandhi that henceforth, government thinking took a definite turn towards rural India. For the first time, in 1971 (despite the Indo-Pak War over Bangladesh and the economic strain caused by the refugee influx), India's national expenditure on research and development in agriculture was on par with that on atomic energy. Under the Fifth Five Year Plan, it rose higher than expenditure on defence and atomic energy. Experiments were made for introducing fertilizers, irrigation techniques, hybrid seeds, and for plant and soil development. Under the remarkable and selfless leadership of C. Subramaniam (1910–2000), India was soon to reap the benefits of the Green Revolution. But *rural* India needed (and still needs) more than agricultural experiments.

Lal Bahadur Shastri, who had a short stint at the helm after Nehru, wanted agricultural work to be undertaken on a war footing. To Subramaniam, the state of national emergency warranted, more than ever, that Indian agricultural scientists conducted research on the new seed varieties from Mexico. He confidently declared that given the right type of political and administrative support and academic freedom, India's research workers could convert theoretical knowledge into tangible advances in the food sector. A close confidant of Subramaniam and a crucial actor in the introduction of dwarf varieties in India, M. S. Swaminathan (b. 1925) pointed out how rapid advances in agronomic practices, especially in fertilizer application and water management, were making possible the obtaining of very high yields in the range of 5,000 pounds per acre from the Mexican dwarf varieties of wheat. In the successful trials conducted at farms in Delhi, Uttar Pradesh, Punjab, and Bihar, Swaminathan saw a great possibility of solving the food situation. Indira Gandhi gave the scientific community the full support necessary to implement the 'Green Revolution' technological package in India. As the scientific experts persuasively argued in favour of a technical solution to the food problem, the juggernaut of the Green Revolution rolled over. It did give good quick results but later also led to deterioration in soil quality as well as depletion of the water table. Hunger was treated primarily as a problem of low-yield which it was not. It was also a problem of distribution. But now an era of capital-intensive agricultural modernization had set in.

In the late 1960s, the 'Green' Revolution did help augment food production and stave off famine-like situations. It was characterized by breakthroughs in hybrid seeds, extensive irrigation, and the use of nitrogen-based fertilizers. At the time many could not anticipate, much less appreciate, its ecological implications. Later the clamour for sustainability gained momentum and ecological concerns came to the fore. M. S. Swaminathan, one of the pioneers of the Green Revolution, now advocates a gradual and calculated move towards an Evergreen Revolution. This basically means a multipronged approach involving the sciences of agronomy, nutrition, environment, and even sanitation. But one thing seems missing; that is, the centuries-old need for land reforms. This is what an agricultural chemist, J. A. Voelcker had advocated in his Report on Indian Agriculture submitted in 1892 which the then colonial government had promptly shelved. He had argued that the Indian farmers had centuries of experience but no capital and no land reforms. He called for a total overhaul of the revenue system and landholdings if the lot of the farmers had to be improved.[49] In the 1930s, an important peasant leader, Chotu Ram from undivided Punjab voiced similar concerns; decades later even the 'much-maligned' Mandal Commission had asked for it. Nehruvian India made some half-hearted attempts. Discontent simmered, which led to the emergence of sporadic but powerful subterranean armed movements. Contemporary India is still struggling with the pains and pangs of an ever-growing agrarian unrest and farmers' suicides. The solution lies in a judicious mix of technology, ecology, and welfare economics. As Swaminathan puts it, sustainable agriculture needs to adopt the 5Es (that is, ecology, economics, energy, employment, and equity).

As the years rolled on and Mrs Gandhi rose in strength, she did try to put emphasis on cutting-edge knowledge. Addressing the American Association for the Advancement of Science, she outlined how apart from agriculture and rural crafts, Indian science covers a wide spectrum, 'encompassing work in some frontier areas of atomic energy, and fundamental research in mathematics, particle physics, molecular biology and so on'.[50] To the question why India, still struggling with basic needs, should step into frontier areas of science and technology, she argued:

> ... new knowledge is often the best way of dealing with old problems. We see our space effort as relevant for national integration, education, communication, and the fuller understanding of the vagaries of the monsoon which rules our economic life. Mapping from the sky also gives information about natural resources. Oceanography augments food and mineral supplies. Modern genetics open out vast possibilities. Knowledge cannot be fragmented. How can one say which kind of knowledge is immediately applicable? Also, can we compel our scientists to be content with repeating the work of others?[51]

This was indeed a succinct portrayal of a developing nation's perspective. But she did not stop here; she enquired why and how '95 percent of the world's R & D [research and development] is still confined to the industrialized nations'. 'Almost 60 percent of this is military-oriented and of the rest, a good part of even basic scientific and engineering research is directed to problems specific to advanced economies', she argued. But she herself yielded to military pressure when in 1974 she opted for a nuclear test that was carried out at Pokhran. When China exploded the first bomb in 1960 or so, Pandit Nehru refused to follow suit. His daughter probably did this more to divert attention from internal problems and domestic unrest. Under her leadership, Vikram Sarabhai carried on the work of Bhabha and pioneered an eminently successful satellite programme. Our education and communications systems today owe much to these space initiatives.

The West was not favourably disposed to India's nuclear energy and space programmes. But pioneers like Homi Bhabha and Vikram Sarabhai remained steady and resolute and the nation stood behind them. The cultivation of nuclear science or space research was not for the sake of glamour or exclusive knowledge. As Bhabha quipped, 'there is no power so costly as no power'. Probably this meant both industrial and military power.[52] The objective was independence from foreign sources of nuclear-power technologies and also satellite launches. The nuclear and space programmes, whether intended or not, provided the country with nuclear weapons and strategic nuclear delivery vehicles.

The rationale was provided by the future combination of energy, telecommunications, and other development requirements in the civilian sector, and strategic necessities in the defence sector.[53] After Bhabha's sad demise in an air crash, Sarabhai virtually ran both the departments of atomic energy and space research. In 1970, he presented 'a 10-year profile' on both departments. Its objectives were far too ambitious. In the space area, for example, the profile involved going from Rohini rockets to Geosynchronous Satellite Launch Vehicles (GSLV) in 10 years![54] This nevertheless reflected the optimism and confidence of the Indira years. The result was the Pokharan atomic experiment in 1974 and the launch of Aryabhatta in 1975. GSLV, of course, had to wait for almost three more decades.

Another distinctive feature of Mrs Gandhi's period was the total integration of science and technology into the Fifth Five Year Plan. At the discussions on the approach to the fifth plan, Mrs Gandhi made it very clear that 'science and technology should not be looked upon as a separate subject or sector, but as powerful tools which permeate all aspects of our thinking and action'.[55] It was this approach which finally culminated in the Technology Policy Statement in 1983 which aimed at 'the development of indigenous technology and efficient absorption and adaptation of imported technology appropriate to national priorities and resources'.[56] The nation sought 'technological advancement not for prestige or aggrandizement but to solve our multifarious problems and to be able to safeguard our independence and our unity'. New technology missions were launched, with multiagency participation, to provide science and technology inputs for meeting immediate needs in critical areas such as drinking water, literacy, pulses and edible oils, immunization, and rural communication.[57]

Perhaps the most distinctive and ironically less-known feature of Indira Gandhi's leadership was her concern for environmental degradation and her efforts at conservation. Her critics may have denounced her so-called authoritarian style of functioning, the Emergency, and so on, but her concern for poverty alleviation and sustainable development were honest and genuine. She strove for a balance between nature, power, and science. Mahesh Rangarajan, a noted environmental historian, cites interesting and relatively unknown examples from Mrs Gandhi's life and career to show her care and concern even under most the trying circumstances.[58] For example, she addressed the first meeting of the National Committee on Environmental Planning and Coordination (NCEPC) on the day (6 December 1971) the Indo-Pak War began. Later in the midst of the Shimla Agreement discussions in May 1972, she sent off an urgent letter to the chief minister of Bihar asking him to stop the diversion of forest land for a development project. Incredible indeed!

During the early 1980s, one may see a gradual but sure shift towards neoliberal policies. The focus was to be more on wealth creation than distribution. Critics pointed to the increasing disparities between the urban rich and rural poor as result of science-and-technology-based developments. Even the Green Revolution which had definitely lifted the country from droughts and virtual begging for food came under the scanner. The 'top–down' approach or 'trickle-down' theories which the country had witnessed since Macaulay's time, again showed their limitations, if not total failure. This decade also saw the emergence of critical voices, analysing and assessing the consequences of the Nehruvian vision, and the technology-based model of social development. It also led to the search for compatibility between economic development and environmental sustainability. Anil Agarwal, a noted environmentalist, pleaded for a holistic understanding of the interconnectedness between different natural resources, their access and ownership, and popular participation in their management. Many well-meaning people joined him to shape the *Dying Wisdom* campaign. In the midst of protecting forests, the tiger, and Silent Valley, the government failed to protect the neighbourhood and its environment from polluting industries. The Bhopal gas tragedy was waiting to happen. It killed and maimed several thousands.

Politically also, the country was in turmoil. The violent unrest in Punjab finally claimed Mrs Gandhi's life in 1984, and the baton passed to the young and techno-savvy Rajiv Gandhi. He was probably the first to talk about the 21st century and India's place in it. He fired the imagination of the nation and won a landslide victory in 1985. In his first broadcast to the country on 12 November 1985, he said:

> As we build today so will be the tomorrow. Together we build for an India of the 21st century ... How are we going to prepare the nation to meet the challenges of the next century, to meet the challenges of the latest technology, as it comes? Development has to mean absorption of the most modern techniques at the most basic levels in our society.[59]

In 1986, the young Gandhi introduced a National Education Policy which emphasized inclusive education and took literacy to a much higher level. He ushered in a computer revolution and a paradigm shift in telecommunications. Technology missions were given top priority and they boosted the economy as nothing else had done in previous eras. The setting up of the Centre for

Development of Telematics (C-DoT) and its success in telecom switching, were strong steps towards self-reliance. The success of companies like Reliance, Infosys, and so on was scripted in the 1980s. Nehru had talked of a scientific temper, now the discourse was on knowledge economy and knowledge society. The stage was set for the forthcoming debates and initiatives on liberalization, privatization, and so forth. Sectors like oil, infrastructure, and so on, were to get quantum leaps while moral values nosedived.

The stage was thus set for an unprecedented boom in information technology and allied service sectors. The neoliberal policies of the 1990s and the new century under successive prime ministers facilitated the growth of a middle class enamoured of the new knowledge economy and new knowledge society. It cared less if some poor farmers committed suicide and the divide between the rich and poor grew as never before.

Liberalization and the Tilt towards Technology

Since the adoption of the new economic policy in 1991, there has been a drastic change in the Indian economy. With the arrival of liberalization, the government has reordered business transactions with fewer restrictions. For developing countries, liberalization opened economic borders to foreign companies and investments. This led to discussions on how to bring about technological change in less developed countries. How to bring faster productivity growth? What would be the practical difficulties? The tilt towards technology was now obvious. And science as 'public good' had suddenly become science as a 'market good'.

Nowhere is this more obvious than in the emergence of Bengaluru and Cyberabad as the symbols of India's soft power. The offices of India's glamorous IT companies look 'like twinkling towers of innovation'. But in reality, they are not. They are, like 'plastic fruit', mere imitation. Outsourcing is neo-colonialism, aided and abetted by a new kind of technology-driven 'platform capitalism'. It is said that data is the new oil, and whoever controls data will control human lives in myriad ways. No wonder, 'crony capitalism' thrives.[60] Would there arise a new East India Company powered by artificial intelligence, using optical fibres and satellites as its mercenary tentacles?

Today's quest for knowledge is shorn of any moral or social values. Students emerging from our distinguished engineering institutions seldom opt for manufacturing units or research labs; finance or sales attracts them more. Our forefathers knew how to grow sugarcane, so when sugar was considered a high-end product in the international market, they were uprooted from their villages and sent to far-off Fiji, Trinidad, or Mauritius. They were called coolies. Now software is the high-value product and the new techno-coolies equipped with degrees from prestigious institutions and eyes on pay-packages jump into it. And they do not have to be uprooted! They practise this new skill in companies that take advantage of the time-zone, paying a dime for what would have cost a dollar in the other hemisphere. For the companies, the watchword is profit and profit alone. Public resources (even airwaves) are ripped at a pace which could easily shame the buccaneers of the East India Company. Governments are willing partners in this game.

Politics apart, one lesson that one may draw from the above discussion is that in independent India and in many developing countries, technology unfortunately masquerades as science. In sharp contrast to the early 20th century, when scientists like J. C. Bose, S. N. Bose, C. V. Raman, or M. N. Saha were eulogized for their fundamental contributions, today nuclear or missile engineers are hailed as scientists. In political circles, the respect for science is so low that if a minister is transferred from the petroleum or health ministry to the ministry of science and technology, it is considered a demotion. Even technology is taken as spectacle, and people in power seem to revel in technology demonstrations. On 7 September 2019, the then chairman of ISRO was seen crying on the shoulders of the prime minister over the failure of a moon-lander named Vikram. Can one imagine Vikram Sarabhai doing so? Technology is scientific knowledge, not an event, much less a spectacle. When faced with non-academic pressure, some self-respecting scientists prefer to resign. Dr Gagandeep Kang, a rotavirus-vaccine pioneer and the first woman from India to be elected a Fellow of the Royal Society, left the directorship of a prestigious transnational research institute recently (July 2020) when the ICMR Committee that she headed for examining the suitability of Covid 19 vaccines was suddenly disbanded in the midst of the pandemic. There is no denying the fact that the research climate in India is rough. Budding scientists who left the shores early for the United States or United Kingdom like S. Chandrasekhar, Hargobind Khurana, Abdus Salam, or more recently, Venkat Ramakrishnan won great laurels including the Nobel Prize. The last one could even become President of the Royal Society, truly the rarest of rare honours.

We need to realize that complete identification of science with technology does no good to science, or to technology. Earlier, the economy used to drive technology; now technology drives the economy. In this mega metamorphosis, curiosity-oriented research has been pushed to the background. In its place now we have big, heavy-budget, mission-oriented programmes (for example, space-, nuclear-, or defence-related missions). However, 'little yet ambitious laboratories' spread all over the country will be no less useful than large establishments. The country needs scientific temper and intellectual curiosity more than the technological gadgets that originate elsewhere and are promptly imported or assimilated. There is no doubt that certain technologies satisfy immediate needs but at the same time they also create new problems to solve, for which another kind of technology is required. One innovation has within it the need and seed of another innovation. This perennial cycle requires and involves extensive institutionalization. Independent India has responded well to this need. You think of any theme or problem and you have an institution devoted to it! We have achieved quantitative expansion, no doubt, but what about qualitative upgrades?

The qualitative change will come only through curriculum development and self-evaluations within the academic community. The state can only be a facilitator; it cannot enforce academic churning. The British colonizers had fostered the concepts of 'state' science and 'state' scientists. They needed these for their own distinctive requirements. Independent India should have changed from its colonial legacies. But unfortunately, the concepts of state science and state scientists have entered the Indian psyche deeply. The Indian elite revels in technology demonstrations so ably provided by organizations like DRDO and ISRO. These are important for national security, no doubt, but useful science and innovations can also come from the 'little' laboratories that function under a crumbling university system. Without strengthening university education manifold, Indian science will continue to remain in the backwaters, and Indian scientists will have to continue to look for patron saints in the West for their survival.[61] On a broader social level, scientific temper remains elusive even today, in spite of the fact that there is tremendous growth in science and technology and dependence on it for the growth of the country's economy.[62] Certain dogmatic beliefs and falsehoods are being spread continually, ironically, through the means of modern science and technology, and that too, even on academic platforms like the Indian Science Congress. People who have vested interests in perpetuating the existing social consciousness, continue to oppose the basic tenets of a scientific temper. In 2017, about 12,000 scientists marched all across India in protest not only against funding cuts but also for an end to the 'propagation of unscientific, obscurantist ideas', noting that 'untested and unscientific ideas are being introduced into the school textbooks and curricula'. Hope lies in going back to the values and ethos seen during our freedom struggle. Those who know little about it, may acquire power for other reasons, but will eventually lead India to another kind of subordination, both internal and external.

Notes

1. Jawaharlal Nehru, *The Discovery of India* (Reprint) (New Delhi: Penguin, 2004), p. 451.
2. G. Sarton, 'Freedom of India and Science' *Isis* 38 (1948): 244.
3. As folklore remembers him:

    You built the dam at Kannambadi
    And breathed life into crores of people
    May hundreds of inspirations like you be born
    O embodiment of Kaveri, Visvesvaraya.

4. Nasir Tyabji, *Forging Capitalism in Nehru's India: Neocolonialism and the State, c. 1940–1970* (New Delhi: Oxford University Press, 2015), pp. xiii–xxviii; Benjamin Zachariah, *Developing India: An Intellectual and Social History* (New Delhi: Oxford University Press, 2005), pp. 1–24.
5. A. J. Meadows, *Science and Controversy: A Biography of Sir Norman Lockyer* (London: Macmillan, 1972), p. 127.
6. Curzon's speech at the Asiatic Society, Calcutta, 26 February 1901; Home, Education, proc. Nos. 11–12, May 1901, Pt. B, NAI.
7. J. D. Megaw to W. S. Carter, 29 October 1928, IHD, 1.1 464 India Box 5 F.34, Rockefeller Archive Center (RAC), New York.
8. *The Mahratta*, 24 October 1926, Native Newspaper Reports (NNR), Bombay, 1926, pp. 1173–1174. These questions retain their relevance in post-independence India, and were raised time and again in critique of the much-feted Green Revolution in the 1970–1980s.
9. Norman White, *A Preliminary Report on the Influenza Pandemic of 1918 in India* (Simla: Government Press, 1919), pp. 8–9, cited in Chinmay Tumbe, *The Age of Pandemics, 1817–1920* (Noida: Harper Collins, 2020), p. 131. This reminds one of a similar death-dance in the summer of 2020 in North India.
10. J. D. Megaw, 'Medicine and Public Health', in *Social Service in India*, ed. E. Blunt (London: Her Majesty's Stationery Office, 1938), p. 186. The Rockefeller doctor in India also agreed with him. 'The time is bound to come when food supply will not be sufficient; the only solution is birth control; this can be done by a) later marriage b) contraception; it is up to the Indian statesmen to apply the remedy. The population has increased by 10% in the last decade.' Dr Heiser with his experience of both China and India found Indians much inferior to the Chinese. The Heiser Diary, R.G.12.1, f. 173, Rockefeller Archive Centre.
11. Ibid.

12. *Mysore Star*, 13 February 1911, NNR, Madras, 1911, p. 271.
13. *Swadeshabhimani*, 23 December 1910, NNR, Mangalore, 1911, p. 22.
14. *Swadesamitran*, 8 January 1910, NNR, Madras, 1910, p. 102.
15. *Hitvarta*, 25 May 1911, NNR, Bengal, 1911, p. 648.
16. *Amrita Bazar Patrika*, 13 October 1923, NNR, Bengal, 1923, p. 927.
17. *Jam-e-Jamshed*, 9 August 1922, NNR, Bombay, 1922, p. 796.
18. *Bombay Chronicle*, 21 May 1923, NNR, Bombay, 1923, p. 503.
19. *Bengalee*, 28 January 1922, NNR, Bengal, 1922, pp. 87–88.
20. P. C. Ray, *Life and Experiences of a Bengali Chemist* (Calcutta: Chatterjee & Co., 1932), pp. 370–387.
21. *Kanara Leader*, 21 September 1926, NNR, Bombay, 1926, p. 1075.
22. Tagore's understanding of rural problems came from his *zamindari* experiences at Shilaidaha and Patisar during the 1890s. He saw villagers steeped in poverty, ignorance, and superstition, succumbing to disease and natural calamities. There was no help. For details, see Bipasha Raha, *The Plough and the Pen: Peasantry, Agriculture and the Literati in Colonial Bengal* (Delhi: Manohar, 2012).
23. Suvobrata Sarkar, 'Domesticating Electric Power', *Indian Economic and Social History Review* 52, no. 3, (2015): 357–389.
24. For incisive details on capital, planning, and the state, see M. Visvesvaraya, *Planned Economy for India* (Bangalore: Bangalore Press, 1934); Bipan Chandra, *Nationalism and Colonialism in Modern India* (New Delhi: Orient Longman, 1987); Aditya Mukherjee, *Imperialism, Nationalism and the Making of the Indian Capitalist Class* (New Delhi: Sage, 2002).
25. Nehru, *The Discovery of India*, p. 436.
26. Medha M. Kudaisya, *Tryst with Prosperity: Indian Business and the Bombay Plan of 1944* (Delhi: Penguin, 2018), pp. xxvii–xxxiii.
27. Jawaharlal Nehru, *Selected Works*, Vol. 14 (New Delhi: Nehru Memorial Fund, 1993), pp. 554–557.
28. B. G. Gokhale, 'Nehru and History', *History and Theory* 17, no.3 (1978): 311–322.
29. Nehru, *The Discovery of India*, p. 570.
30. Baldev Singh (ed.), *Jawaharlal Nehru on Science and Society* (New Delhi: Nehru Memorial Museum and Library, 1988), pp. 3–14.
31. Unlike the majority of his countrymen, Nehru happily lived with a single girl child! This personal example was conveniently ignored by his people.
32. For an interesting discussion, see Shambhu Prasad, 'Towards an Understanding of Gandhi's Views on Science', *Economic and Political Weekly* 36, no. 39 (2001): 3721–3732.
33. *Science and Culture* 8, no. 1 (1942), reprinted in Singh, *Jawaharlal Nehru on Science and Society*, pp. 28–29.

34. For details, see Aparajit Ramnath, *The Birth of an Indian Profession: Engineers, Industry, and the State 1900–47* (New Delhi: Oxford University Press, 2017).

35. C. R. Rao, 'Prasantha Chandra Mahalanobis', *Biographical Memoirs of Fellows of the Royal Society* 19 (1973): 455–492.

36. S. C. Roy and Rajinder Singh, 'D. M. Bose and Cosmic Ray Research', *Indian Journal of History of Science* 50, no. 3 (2015): 438–455.

37. See Rajinder Singh and S. C. Roy, *A Jewel Unearthed: The Story of an Indian Woman Scientist* (Mumbai: Ebenezer Printing, 2020).

38. J. A. Ratcliffe, 'Sisir Kumar Mitra', *Biographical Memoirs of Fellows of the Royal Society* 10 (1964): 221–228.

39. A. V. Hill to S. S. Bhatnagar, 21 June 1948, Hill Papers, AVHL II, Churchill College, Cambridge.

40. S. S. Bhatnagar to A. V. Hill, 18 May 1951, ibid.

41. Jagdish N. Sinha, *Science, War and Imperialism: India in the Second World War* (Leiden: E.J. Brill, 2008), p. 192; see also Jagdish N. Sinha, 'Science and Culture Under Colonialism: India Between the World Wars', *Indian Journal of History of Science* 39, no. 1 (2004): 101–119.

42. Singh, *Jawaharlal Nehru on Science and Society*, p. 35

43. Cited in V. V. Krishna, 'Changing Policy Cultures, Phases and Trends in Science and Technology in India', *Policy Cultures* 28, no.3 (2001): 179–194.

44. A. V. Hill to S. S. Bhatnagar, 11 May 1951, A. V. Hill Papers, AVHL II, Churchill College, Cambridge.

45. Gauhar Raza, 'Revisiting the Scientific Policy Resolution Debate', *Journal of Scientific Temper* 2, nos. 1–2 (January–April 2014): 5–9.

46. S. S. Bhatnagar, 'Indian Scientists and the Present War', *Science and Culture* 6, no. 4 (1940): 194–195.

47. Cited in Rajendra Singh, 'Indian Science Congress Association and the VIPs', *Current Science* 84, no. 12 (2003): 1498–1499. This practice continues even now and Raman's criticism is still valid.

48. Jawaharlal Nehru to J. D. Bernal at a meeting in Beijing in 1954. See *Bernal Papers*, MSS. Add. 8287, Box 48, B. 3.349, Cambridge University Library.

49. J. A. Voelcker, *Report on the Improvement of Indian Agriculture*, 2nd edn (Calcutta: Government Press, 1897).

50. Indira Gandhi, 'India and the World', *Foreign Affairs* 51, no. 1 (1972): 65–77.

51. Indira Gandhi, 'Scientific Endeavour in India', *Science* (New Series) 217, no. 4564 (1982): 1008–1009. The gulf which she had so astutely perceived was to widen even more under her successors in the years to some.

52. Robert S. Anderson, 'Cultivating Science as Cultural Policy: A Contrast of Agricultural and Nuclear Science in India', *Pacific Affairs* 56, no. 1 (1983): 38–50.

53. R. C. Thomas, 'India's Nuclear and Space Programme: Defence or Development?', *World Politics* 38, no. 2 (1986): 315–342.

54. Ashok Parthasarathi, 'Leadership in Science and Technology: Some Aspects of the Indian Experience', *Economic and Political Weekly* 36, no.40 (2001): 3843–3851.

55. Ashok Parthasarathi, *Technology as the Core: Science and Technology with Indira Gandhi* (New Delhi: Pearson, 2007), p. 52. This volume is full of interesting anecdotes.

56. Technology Policy Statement, Department of Science and Technology, New Delhi, 1983; Pawan Sikka, 'Technology Policy in India: Key Issues and Future Perspectives', *International Journal of Services Technology and Management* 2, nos. 3–4 (2001): 388–401.

57. S. Mohan and Ashok Jain, *India: 50 Years of Independence 1947–97: Science and Technology* (New Delhi: B. R. Publishing, 1999), p. 84.

58. Mahesh Rangarajan, 'Striving for a Balance: Nature, Power, Science and India's Indira Gandhi, 1917–1984', *Conservation and Society* 7, no. 4 (2009): 79–92.

59. David Dickson, 'Gandhi Shakes Up Indian Science', *Science* (New Series) 230, no. 4729 (1985): 1016–1017; see also Pawan Sikka, *Rajiv Gandhi's Modern India: Development with Science and Technology* (New Delhi: Kalpaz Publications, 2007).

60. As a recent critique points out,

> People do not understand that being pro-market is to believe in competition, which helps keep prices low, raises the quality of products, and leads to a 'rule-based capitalism' that serves everyone. To be pro-business, on the other hand, means to allow politicians and officials to retain power over licences, which distorts the market's authority over economic decisions, and leads to 'crony capitalism'.

Gurucharan Das, 'Introduction', in *Tryst with Prosperity: Indian Business and the Bombay Plan of 1944* by Medha M. Kudaisya (Delhi: Penguin, 2018), p. xxvi.

61. P. Majumdar and D. K. Mukherjee, 'Mega Science vs. Small Science: Remarks on Scientific Research in India', *Current Science* 114, no. 5 (2018): 953–955.

62. Navneet Sharma, Yusuf Akhtar, and S.A. Mir, 'Science Education in India: A Misnomer of Scientific Temper', *Journal of Scientific Temper* 8, no 3–4 (2020): 135–145.

A Bibliographical Note

As this short book is meant for undergraduate and postgraduate students, and also for lay persons, I have tried a judicious mix of both archival and secondary sources. For the colonial period, the archival sources are immensely rich. Files from the Home Public, Home Education, Health, Agriculture, Municipal, and other departments survive in different archives within the country, especially at the National Archives of India (NAI). The Native Newspaper Reports open a window to local opinion. The private papers of the colonial scientists who worked in India are well preserved at different British archives. Important among these are papers preserved at the Centre for South Asian Studies (CSAS; Cambridge), the Cambridge University Library, the National Library of Scotland, the Wellcome Trust Library, and the India Office Records (IOR) at the British Library. The Haffkine papers are preserved at the Hebrew University Library, Jerusalem, while relevant references on diseases and epidemics can be found also, at the Rockefeller Archive Center (RAC) in Sleepy Hollow near New York City. Taken together, these materials provide good insight into why and how certain developments took place, the roles played by certain individuals, and the impact that all this had on our society. During the last four decades or so, a large number of books have been published on issues relating to science and society in the context of modern India. Some of these are listed below according to the chapters in which they appear.

The Inheritance

D. M. Bose, S. N. Sen, and B. V. Subbarayappa's (eds), *A Concise History of Science in India* (New Delhi: Indian National Science Academy, 1971) presents in a chronological framework, techno-scientific activities through the ages. Debiprasad Chattopadhyay has emphasized socio-economic factors while writing a history of science in ancient India; see his *History of Science and Technology in Ancient India: The Beginnings* (Calcutta: South Asia Books, 1986). For discussions on the medical legacy, Charles Leslie (ed.), *Asian Medical Systems: A Comparative Study* (Berkeley: University of California Press, 1976) and Dominik Wujastyk, *The Roots of Ayurveda: Selections from Sanskrit Medical Writings* (New Delhi: Penguin, 1998) are important. So are two of K. G. Zysk's books, *Medicine in the Veda: Religious Healing in the Veda* (Delhi: Motilal Banarsidass, 1996) and *Asceticism and Healing in Ancient India: Medicine in the Buddhist Monastery* (New York: Oxford University Press, 1991). For Yunani practitioners, see Seema Alavi, *Islam and Healing: Loss and Recovery of an Indo-Muslim Medical Tradition, 1600–1900* (Ranikhet: Permanent Black, 2007); and Muzaffar Iqbal, *Islam and Science* (London: Ashgate, 2003).

For mathematics, see G. G. Joseph, *The Crest of the Peacock: Non-European Roots of Mathematics* (Princeton: Princeton University Press, 2011) and for astronomy, M. S. Sriram, K. Ramasubramanian, and M. D. Srinivas (eds), *500 Years of Tantrasangraha: A Landmark in the History of Astronomy* (Shimla: Indian Institute of Advanced Study, 2002) and Joydeep Sen, *Astronomy in India, 1784–1876* (Pittsburgh: University of Pittsburgh Press, 2020). Scholars like Dharampal, *Indian Science and Technology in the Eighteenth Century* (New Delhi: Impex, 1971); Ahsan Jan Qaisar, *The Indian Response to European Technology and Culture* (New Delhi: Oxford University Press, 1982); Irfan Habib, *Technology in Medieval India* (New Delhi: Tulika, 2008) and Harbans Mukhia (ed.), *History of Technology in India,* 2 vols (New Delhi: Indian National Science Academy, 2012) have contributed to detailing India's techno-scientific history in the pre-colonial period.

The Age of Exploration and Consolidation

Satpal Sangwan has outlined the beginning of colonial science in India and its gradual maturation through surveys, scientific training, and indigenous initiatives [*Science, Technology and Colonization* (Delhi: Anamika, 1991)]. In the field of botany and environmental sciences, Richard H. Grove, *Green Imperialism: Colonial Expansion, Tropical Island Edens and the Origins of Environmentalism, 1600–1860* (Cambridge: Cambridge University Press, 1995), and on the work of the Trigonometrical Survey, Matthew H. Edney, *Mapping an Empire: The Geographical Construction of British India, 1765–1843* (Chicago: University of Chicago Press, 1997), offer important insights. P. Petitjean, C. Jami, and A. M. Moulin (eds), *Science and Empires* (Dordrecht: Kluwer, 1992) and Deepak Kumar, *Science and the Raj* (New Delhi: Oxford University Press, 1995; 2nd edn, 2006) have provided in-depth analyses of colonial policies, education, and research.

Once a less-explored field for the history of science, the period of Company rule in India has of late been the focus of several interesting and important studies. Mention may be made of David Arnold, *The Tropics and the Travelling Gaze: India, Landscape and Science, 1800–1950* (Ranikhet: Permanent Black, 2005); Deepak Kumar, Vinita Damodaran, and Rohan D'Souza, *The British Empire and the Natural World: Environmental Encounters in South Asia*

(New Delhi: Oxford University Press, 2010); Anna Winterbottom, *Hybrid Knowledge in the Early East India Company World* (Basingstoke: Palgrave Macmillan, 2016); Vinita Damodaran, Anna Winterbottom, and Alan Lester (eds), *The East India Company and the Natural World* (Basingstoke: Palgrave Macmillan, 2014); Matthew H. Edney, *Mapping an Empire: The Geographical Construction of British India, 1765–1843* (Chicago: University of Chicago Press, 1999); and Nilanjana Mukherjee, *Spatial Imaginings in the Age of Colonial Cartographic Reason* (London: Routledge, 2020). Prakash Kumar, *Indigo Plantations and Science in Colonial India* (Cambridge: Cambridge University Press, 2012); Bipasha Raha, *The Plough and the Pen: Peasantry, Agriculture and the Literati in Colonial Bengal* (New Delhi: Manohar, 2012); and Deepak Kumar and Bipasha Raha (eds), *Tilling the Land: Agricultural Knowledge and Practices* (Delhi: Primus Books, 2016) discuss issues related to agriculture.

There exist several studies on specific aspects of 19th-century technology. On shipping, Henry Bernstein's *Steamboats on the Ganges* (Bombay: Allied Publishers, 1960); on the technological importance and economic impact of colonial canal irrigation, Ian Stone's *Canal Irrigation in British India: Perspectives on Technological Change in a Peasant Economy* (Cambridge: Cambridge University Press, 1984); on the telegraph, Deep Kanta Lahiri Choudhury's *Telegraphic Imperialism: Crisis and Panic in the Indian Empire, c. 1830–1920* (Basingstoke: Palgrave Macmillan, 2010) and Michael Mann's *Wiring the Nation: Telecommunication, Newspaper-reportage, and Nation Building in British India, 1850–1930* (New Delhi: Oxford University Press, 2017), deserve mention. For a more general discussion see, Roy MacLeod and Deepak Kumar (eds), *Technology and the Raj* (New Delhi: Sage, 1998); Tirthankar Roy, *The Economic History of India, 1857–1947*, 3rd edn (New Delhi: Oxford University Press, 2011); and Suvobrata Sarkar, *The Quest for Technical Knowledge: Bengal in the Nineteenth Century* (New Delhi: Manohar, 2012).

Two books by Daniel R. Headrick, *The Tools of Empire: Technology and European Imperialism in the Nineteenth Century* (New York: Oxford University Press, 1981) and *The Tentacles of Progress: Technology Transfer in the Age of Imperialism, 1850–1940* (New York: Oxford University Press, 1988); and Michael Adas's *Machines as the Measure of Men* (Ithaca: Cornell University Press, 1989) offer a provocative, though a Eurocentric view of 19th- and early 20th-century technology. Roy MacLeod and Deepak Kumar's edited volume, *Technology and the Raj* (New Delhi: Sage, 1998; reprint Delhi: Aakar Books, 2022) presents a more structured and critical interpretation of the theme. Recently, an altogether new perspective has been put forward by David Arnold, *Everyday Technology* (Chicago: University of Chicago Press, 2013). Unlike the big technologies (railways, hydraulic dams, and so on), which were mostly state-sponsored, small and mundane technologies (sewing machines, typewriters, bicycles, and so on) mingled with the 'everyday life' of ordinary Indians.

Railways, predictably, were the largest crowd-puller of all 19th-century technologies! Ian J. Kerr's *Building the Railways of the Raj, 1850–1900* (New Delhi: Oxford University Press, 1995) has a strong technological focus. Later works explicitly situate the 'railways' in contemporary society and 'everyday life': Ritika Prasad, *Tracks of Change: Railways and Everyday Life in Colonial India* (New Delhi: Cambridge University Press, 2015) and Aparajita Mukhopadhyay, *Imperial Technology and Native Agency: A Social History of Railways in Colonial India 1850–1920* (London and New York: Routledge, 2018). Smritikumar Sarkar's *Technology and Rural Change in Eastern India, 1830–1980* (New Delhi: Oxford University Press, 2014) explores the impact of the railways on the countryside. The growth of engineering (both institutionalization and professionalization) and the technological aspects of emerging industries in the early 20th century are ably discussed in Aparajith Ramnath's *The Birth of an Indian Profession: Engineers, Industry and the State* (New Delhi: Oxford University Press, 2017); Sunila Kale, *Electrifying India: Regional Political Economics of Development* (Stanford: Stanford University Press, 2014); and Suvobrata Sarkar, *Let There Be Light: Engineering, Entrepreneurship and Electricity in Colonial Bengal* (Cambridge: Cambridge University Press, 2020).

Lost in Religion and Translation

The reconstruction and revival of traditional Indian knowledge and its relationship with the Western sciences have begun to attract some significant scholarly attention. This includes Tapan Raychaudhuri, *Europe Reconsidered: Perceptions of the West in Nineteenth Century Bengal* (New Delhi: Oxford University Press, 1988); Amiya P. Sen, *Hindu Revivalism in Bengal, c. 1872–1905: Some Essays in Interpretation* (New Delhi: Oxford University Press, 1993); K. N. Panikkar, *Colonialism, Culture, and Resistance* (New Delhi: Tulika, 2007); Dhruv Raina and S. Irfan Habib, *Domesticating Modern Science: A Social History of Science and Culture in Colonial India* (New Delhi, Tulika, 2004); Subrata Dasgupta, *The Bengal Renaissance* (Ranikhet: Permanent Black, 2007); Mushirul Hasan, *Exploring the West: Three Travel Narratives* (New Delhi: Oxford University Press, 2009); A. R. Venkatachalapathy, *The Province of the Book: Scholars, Scribes, and Scribblers in Colonial Tamilnadu* (Hyderabad: Orient Blackswan, 2015); S. J. Stephen, *A Meeting of the Minds: European and Tamil Encounters in Modern Sciences, 1507–1857* (Delhi: Primus Books, 2016); and Savithri Preetha Nair, *Raja Serfoji II: Science, Medicine and Enlightenment in Tanjore 1798–1832* (New Delhi: Routledge, 2012).

C. A. Bayly's *Empire and Information: Intelligence Gathering and Social Communication in India, 1780–1870* (Cambridge: Cambridge University Press, 1996) offers an important interpretation of orientalism and the early interaction between European and Indian science. So does Kapil Raj's *Relocating Modern Science: Circulation and the Construction of Knowledge in South Asia and Europe, 1650–1900* (Ranikhet: Permanent Black, 2006).V. C. Joshi's *Rammohun Roy and the Process of Modernization in India* (New Delhi: Vikas, 1975); Asok Sen's *Iswar Chandra Vidyasagar and His Elusive Milestones* (Calcutta: Riddhi-India, 1977); Ramatosh Sarkar's *Ramendrasundar Trivedi* (New Delhi: Sahitya Akademi, 1993); Arun Kumar Biswas's *Gleanings of the Past and the Science Movement: In the Diaries of Drs Mahendralal and Amritlal Sircar* (Calcutta: Asiatic Society, 2000); Siddhartha Ghosh's *Rajendralal Mitra* (New Delhi: Sahitya Akademi, 2002); Renny Thomas' *Science and Religion in India: Beyond Disenchantment* (London: Routledge, 2022); Amiya P. Sen's *Bankim Chandra Chattopadhyay: An Intellectual Biography* (New Delhi: Oxford University Press, 2008); and Arun Bandyopadhyay (ed.), *Science and Society in India, 1750–2000* (New Delhi: Manohar, 2010) are some significant contributions.

A New Dawn

Deepak Kumar's *Science and the Raj* (New Delhi: Oxford University Press, 1995; 2nd edn, 2006) draws on much original research and covers both the Company period and the British Raj until independence. Exceptionally useful are Ashis Nandy, *Alternative Sciences: Creativity and Authenticity in Two Indian Scientists* (New Delhi: Allied Publishers, 1980); Gyan Prakash, *Another Reason: Science and the Imagination of Modern India* (New Delhi: Oxford University Press, 2000); and Pratik Chakrabarti, *Western Science in Modern India: Metropolitan Methods, Colonial Practices* (Ranikhet: Permanent Black, 2004). On the 'Triple Helix' of science, the colonial state, and nationalism during the late-19th and early 20th century, there have been a number of interesting works based on meticulous research. Mention may be made of J. Lourdusamy, *Science and National Consciousness in Bengal, 1780–1930* (New Delhi: Orient Longman, 2004); Chittabrata Palit, *Science and Nationalism in Bengal, 1876–1947* (Kolkata: Institute of Historical Studies, 2004); and Jagdish N. Sinha, *Science, War and Imperialism: India in the Second World War* (Leiden: Brill, 2008).

For the history of scientific institutions or individual scientists, see B. V. Subbarayappa, *In Pursuit of Excellence* (New Delhi: Pearson, 1992); Robert Kanigel, *The Man Who Knew Infinity* (New Delhi: Penguin, 1992); Subrata Dasgupta, *Jagadish Chandra Bose and the Indian Response to Western Science* (Ranikhet: Permanent Black, 1999); Kunal Ghosh, *Unsung Genius: A Life of Jagadish Chandra Bose* (New Delhi: Aleph, 2022); Amrita Shah, *Vikram Sarabhai:*

A Life (New Delhi: Penguin, 2007); Uma Parameswaran, *C. V. Raman: A Biography* (New Delhi: Penguin, 2011); Indira Chowdhury, *Growing the Tree of Science: Homi Bhabha and the Tata Institute of Fundamental Research* (New Delhi: Oxford University Press, 2016), and Pramod V. Naik, *Meghnad Saha: His Life in Science and Politics* (Gewerbestrasse: Springer, 2017), among others.

The relationship between women (gender) and science (including medicine) in the colonial and postcolonial period was ignored by social scientists until recently. However, this is no longer the case: Lalita Subrahmanyan, *Women Scientists in the Third World: The Indian Experience* (New Delhi: Sage, 1998); Geraldine Forbes, *Women in Colonial India: Essays on Politics, Medicine and Historiography* (New Delhi: Chronicle Books, 2005); Neelam Kumar (ed.), *Women and Science in India: A Reader* (New Delhi: Oxford University Press, 2009); Abha Sur, *Dispersed Radiance: Caste, Gender, and Modern Science in India* (New Delhi: Navayana, 2012); and Sujata Mukherjee, *Gender, Medicine, and Society in Colonial India: Women's Healthcare in Nineteenth- and Early-Twentieth Century Bengal* (New Delhi: Oxford University Press, 2017), explore the theme significantly. Arguably, the finest biography of a female Indian scientist is, Savithri Preetha Nair, *Chromosome Woman, Nomad Scientist: E. K. Janaki Ammal, A Life 1897–1984* (London, New Delhi: Routledge, 2022.)

Medical Knowledge and Public Health

One area where there has been a remarkable surge of new scholarship is the field of medical history and specifically, public health and epidemic diseases. The early pioneers are David Arnold, *Colonizing the Body: State Medicine and Epidemic Disease in Nineteenth-Century India* (Berkeley: University of California University Press, 1993); Poonam Bala, *Imperialism and Medicine in Bengal: A Socio-historical Perspective* (New Delhi: Sage, 1991); Mark Harrison, *Public Health in British India: Anglo Indian Preventive Medicine, 1859–1914* (Cambridge: Cambridge University Press, 1994); Anil Kumar, *Medicine and the Raj: British Medical Policy in India, 1835–1911* (New Delhi: Sage, 1998); and Kabita Ray, *History of Public Health: Colonial Bengal 1921–1947* (Calcutta: K. P. Bagchi, 1998). Equally important are Roy MacLeod and Milton Lewis (eds), *Disease, Medicine and Empire: Perspectives on Western Medicine and the Experience of European Expansion* (London: Routledge, 1988); David Arnold (ed.), *Warm Climates and Western Medicine: The Emergence of Tropical Medicine, 1500–1900* (Amsterdam: Rodopi, 1996); and Mark Harrison, *Climates and Constitutions: Health, Race, Environment and British Imperialism in India, 1600–1850* (New Delhi: Oxford University Press, 1999).

Later many more came; for example, Sanjay Bhattacharya, *Expunging Variola: The Control and Eradication of Smallpox in India, 1947–1977* (Hyderabad: Orient Longman, 2006); Mridula Ramanna, *Western Medicine and Public Health in*

Colonial Bombay, 1845–1895 (New Delhi: Orient Longman, 2002); Deepak Kumar and Rajsekhar Basu (eds), *Medical Encounters in British India* (New Delhi: Oxford University Press, 2013); M. Harrison and B. Pati (eds), *The Social History of Health and Medicine in Colonial India* (London: Routledge, 2008); and C. Palit, and A. K. Dutta (eds), *History of Medicine in India: The Medical Encounter* (Delhi: Kalpaz Publications, 2005), among others.

Later works enrich the theme to a considerable extent. Mention may be made of Projit Bihari Mukharji, *Nationalizing the Body: The Medical Market, Print and Daktari Medicine* (London: Anthem, 2009); Pratik Chakrabarti, *Medicine and Empire 1600–1960* (Basingstoke: Palgrave Macmillan, 2014), and *Bacteriology in British India: Laboratory Medicine and the Tropics* (Rochester: Boydell and Brewer; University of Rochester Press, 2012); Debjani Das, *Houses of Madness: Insanity and Asylums of Bengal in Nineteenth-Century India* (New Delhi: Oxford University Press, 2015); Srilata Chatterjee, *Western Medicine and Colonial Society: Hospitals of Calcutta, 1757–1860* (Delhi: Primus Books, 2017); Rohan Deb Roy, *Malarial Subjects: Empire, Medicine and Nonhumans in British India, 1820–1909* (Cambridge: Cambridge University Press, 2017); Arabinda Samanta, *Living With Epidemics in Colonial Bengal, 1818–1945* (New Delhi: Manohar, 2017), Projit Bihari Mukharji, *Doctoring Traditions: Ayurveda, Small Technologies, and Braided Sciences* (Chicago: University of Chicago Press, 2016); Srirupa Prasad, *Cultural Politics of Hygiene in India, 1890–1940: Contagions of Feeling* (London: Routledge, 2015); Ambalika Guha, *Colonial Modernities: Midwifery in Bengal, 1860–1947* (London: Routledge, 2018); Shinjini Das, *Vernacular Medicine in Colonial India: Family, Market and Homeopathy* (Cambridge: Cambridge University Press, 2019); and Sheila Zurbrigg, *Malaria in Colonial South Asia: Uncoupling Disease and Destitution* (London: Routledge, 2020).

Science for Development

Shiv Visvanathan's *Organizing for Science* (New Delhi: Oxford University Press, 1985); Robert Anderson's *Nucleus and Nation: Scientists, International Networks and Power in India* (Chicago: University of Chicago Press, 2010); and Jahnavi Phalke's *Atomic State: Big Science in Twentieth-Century India* (Ranikhet: Permanent Black, 2013) provide an authentic account of the assimilation of modern scientific knowledge, and the emergence of an elite scientific community. For the science and development discourse in India, see Benjamin Zachariah's *Developing India: An Intellectual and Social History* (New Delhi: Oxford University Press, 2005). To know more on the Indian National Congress and its resolutions, see A. M. Zaidi and S. Zaidi (eds), *The Encyclopaedia of the Indian National Congress*, 4 vols (New Delhi: S. Chand & Co., 1978).

Post-independence India and the period of reconstruction and rapid institutionalization offer ample research opportunities. Nasir Tyabji, *Forging Capitalism in Nehru's India: Neocolonialism and the State, c. 1940–1970* (New Delhi: Oxford University Press, 2015); Ross Bassett, *The Technological Indian* (Cambridge, MA; Harvard University Press, 2016), Deepak Kumar, *The Trishanku Nation: Memory, Self and Society in Contemporary India* (New Delhi: Oxford University Press, 2016), and Shiju Sam Varughese, *Contested Knowledge: Science, Media and Democracy in Kerala* (New Delhi: Oxford University Press, 2017) throw considerable light on different aspects of science and society in contemporary India.

Returning to general works, A. K. Bagchi, *The Political Economy of Underdevelopment* (Cambridge: Cambridge University Press, 1982); Bipan Chandra, *Nationalism and Colonialism in Modern India* (New Delhi: Orient Longman, 1987); Aditya Mukherjee, *Imperialism, Nationalism and the Making of the Indian Capitalist Class* (New Delhi: Sage, 2002); Medha M. Kudaisya, *Tryst With Prosperity: Indian Business and the Bombay Plan of 1944* (Delhi: Penguin, 2018); Zaheer Baber, *The Science of Empire: Scientific Knowledge, Civilization, and Colonial Rule in India* (New Delhi: Oxford University Press, 1998); David Arnold, *History of Science, Technology and Medicine in Colonial India*, The New Cambridge History of India (Cambridge: Cambridge University Press, 2000); S. Irfan Habib and Dhruv Raina (eds), *Social History of Science in Colonial India* (New Delhi: Oxford University Press, 2007); Jacques Gaillard, V. V. Krishna, and Roland Waast (eds), *Scientific Communities in the Developing World* (New Delhi: Sage, 1997); Thomas Simpson, *The Frontier in British India: Space, Science, and Power in the Nineteenth Century* (Cambridge: Cambridge University Press, 2021); and S. Mohan and Ashok Jain, *India: 50 Years of Independence 1947–97: Science and Technology* (New Delhi: B.R. Publishing, 1999) bring together a vast amount of material and provide useful references to young readers. Two recent publications need to be taken into account: Deepak Kumar, *Culture of Science and Making of Modern India* (Delhi: Primus Books, 2022); and Suvobrata Sarkar (ed.), *History of Science, Technology, Environment and Medicine in India* (London and New York: Routledge, 2022).

Index

Bhore, Joseph, 128
Bhugolsar (Onkar Bhatt), 51, 63
Bhuwah, Mian, 5
Bignan Sar Sangraha, 63
Bihar Scientific Society, 64
Bij-Ganita (Bhaskar), 53
Birla, G. D., 124
Blanford, W. T., 37
Board of Scientific Advice, 118
body, 10, 33, 42, 81, 90, 93, 97,
    99–100, 106–107
Bombay Branch of the Royal Asiatic
    Society, 33, 42
Bombay Durpan, 63
Bombay Plan. *See Plan for Economic
    Development of India* (1944)
Bose, Debendra Mohan, 127
Bose Institute, 127
Bose, Jagdish Chandra, 64, 73, 78–79,
    81, 84, 127, 140
Bose, Pramatha Nath, 39, 75, 78
Bose, Satyendra Nath, 81–82, 131, 140
Bose's theory of magnetism, 127
Bose, Subhas Chandra, 82, 85
botanical gardens, 26
Botanical Survey, 31
botany, science of, 16
Boudier, Claude, 12
Brahamnical *karmakand*, 60
Brahe, Tycho, 4
Brahmachari, Upendranath, 105
Brahmagupta, 3
Brahman (ultimate reality), 60
Brahmana, 6
brahmanda (creation), 54
Brahmanical system, 59
Brahmasphuta Siddhanta
    (Brahmagupta), 3, 51
Brihadeshwara temple, 18
Brihat Samhita (Varahmihira), 1, 3

Britain's 'civilizing mission', 36
British Association for the
    Advancement of Science, 73
British Empire, 104
British exploiters, in India, 121
British India, scientific development
    in, 33
bubonic plague, 101
Buddha, Gautam, 131
    'Middle Path' theory, 6, 124
Buddhist *tantrics*, 7

Calcutta, 26–27, 36
    Asiatic Society, 42
    Botanic Garden, 31
    Dawn Society Magazine, 75
    electric industry in, 41
    Madrasa, 95
    Medical and Physical Society in, 42
    Medical College, 54–55, 91, 94,
        96, 101, 106
    Municipal Corporation, 106
    Presidency College of, 35
    School of Tropical Medicine, 104
    University, 34, 80, 82
cash-crop-oriented agriculture, 32
cash crops, 32
cash raj, 33
caste system, 3
Cautley, Prony, 40
Centre for Development of Telematics
    (C-DoT), 138–139
Chadwick, Edwin, 104
Chandrashekhar, Lalita, 86
Charaka, 7, 8, 15
Charak Samhita (1st century BC), 2–3,
    7
charkha, 123, 126
Charter of 1813, 34
Chatterjee, Ashima, 86